D1265521

ASPECTS OF WORDSWORTH AND WHITEHEAD:
PHILOSOPHY AND CERTAIN
CONTINUING LIFE-PROBLEMS

ASPECTS OF WORDSWORTH
AND WHITEHEAD:

Philosophy and Certain
Continuing Life-Problems

Alexander P. Cappon

Philosophical Library

New York

Library of Congress Cataloging in Publication Data

Cappon, Alexander Patterson, 1900-
    Aspects of Wordsworth and Whitehead.

    1. Wordsworth, William, 1770-1850. 2. Whitehead,
Alfred North, 1861-1947. 3. Poets, English —
19th century — Biography. I. Title.
PR5881.C35 1983   821'.7   82-18904
ISBN 0-8022-2412-1

To my beloved wife
Dorothy Churchill Cappon
and to my daughter
Frances Cappon Geer
who, as in the case of my previous volume,
have read thoughtfully
every sentence of this book
more than once
sharing with me their reflections upon them

Contents

Acknowledgments

In the volume *Aspects of Wordsworth and Whitehead* there are many acknowledgements that must be made to friends and others — some of whom are not now living. The authors who are under discussion in the successive chapters have themselves of course given a great deal, which will be very evident in the book itself. And Wordsworthian scholars are so many that the only possibility is to suggest a very profound indebtedness to these writers. Two of them especially come to mind for specific note: Ernest De Selincourt and Melvin P. Rader. The work of the latter has been philosophically foundational for a great many years.

The help of my wife, Dorothy Churchill Cappon, has been beyond words. The dedication of this volume speaks of this. Nor can I express adequately the help that was given by my daughter Frances Cappon Geer and by my brother, John A. Cappon. In the book I have found it impossible to avoid the use of the word "we" because of what I owe to these three.

Scholars who have written penetratingly on Whitehead are many and their names could fill pages. Among those who come at once to mind are Victor Lowe, A. H. Johnson, Charles Hartshorne, Craig R. Eisendrath, Harold B . Dunkel, John W. Lango, Paul Arthur Schilpp, and Arthur Murphy.

Likewise of great importance to me in my work have been my father and mother, Carl Henry Grabo, Frank K. Kelly, Kenneth Burke, Robert Morss Lovett, William M. Ryan, John

Livingston Lowes, George Herbert Mead, Harold Buschman, David Ray, Raymond Bragg, William L. Crain, Theodore Brameld, Bernard P. Churchill, and personal physicians who were a great benefit to me. For the main part I have omitted mention of titles or honors of those who have helped me.

Publishers have been of value to me, as they are to all mankind: this will be made clear in the volume itself. Cambridge University Press has been an important publisher of Whitehead. Oxford University Press, publisher of the 1805 *Prelude* written by Wordsworth, has been of vital value and also deserves special acknowledgement.

To librarians and to cities I owe a great deal: immediate mention should appear with regard to the Widener and Houghton Libraries at Harvard, the libraries at Yale and the University of Chicago, that of Columbia University in New York, as well as libraries in Milwaukee, Tulsa, and the University of Kansas. I would also express gratitude to the Library of Congress, the British Museum, and to the libraries and librarians in Paris, as well as in Seattle — including the library of the University of Washington, where I taught.

Likewise my appreciation goes to the library of Washington University of St. Louis and that of Montana State University. This list and the list of friends and teachers to whom I owe much cannot be complete. The names of Philip Schuyler Allen, James C. Olson, Vivian Mowry, Deborah D. Feingold, Dorothy Sohm Metz, Robert Willson, Robert Farnsworth, James Weber Linn, and my sister Charlotte Beatrice Blackmun should be added, by no means merely as an afterthought, with my very warm appreciation.

The help of librarians has been extended to me again and again, far beyond the line of duty, to my everlasting gratitude, and likewise the help of the University of Missouri at Kansas City must receive grateful mention, along with its librarian, Kenneth J. La Budde.

10

I must further express my appreciation of the kindnesses of Director Dagobert Runes, Associate Director Rose Morse, and others of Philosophical Library, Publishers.

Alexander P. Cappon
University of Missouri —
Kansas City

Introductory Foreword

Important to everyone is the establishing of an outlook upon life. We are all doing this constantly for better or for worse — usually, however, for the sake of something which we feel might be an improvement in our general life-view. If our experience runs into gross dissatisfactions we stumble about in our thinking and at times happen upon something that seems to help us. But we could do better than stumble about. We could read the philosophers or read about them. Such reading is not as formidable as it sometimes appears. Robert Maynard Hutchins has said that anyone can read the great books. He meant that virtually anyone can. If we have ignored philosophy we can at least make a beginning at one point or another with one of the philosophic volumes that seems to be of interest. In this field it is possible to read little by little, and then talk to someone — anyone who will listen — about what has been read. This was the advice of Hutchins. Everyone has an idea, at least, of what his life-view includes and, if so, is likely to enjoy comparing notes.

The important point is to do this openly and without dread. Sometimes we have a kind of intellectual fear of the outcome of discussion; we are afraid that we may seem foolish or inept. But there are worse things than being inept in this way. We can learn the value of being able to say (as does Teilhard de Chardin) "Maybe I am wrong."[1] This can be constructive. Anyone who can speak this way is likely to be constructively

13

tentative in his philosophical attitudes. The person can be a seeker, concerned not merely with thought but with its relation to living. One thing to be noted here about such thinking is that it tends *toward* the improvement in our mental processes. Our thought gets better with use. It can scarcely do otherwise.

The purpose in the present book is not only to tell about the poet William Wordsworth and the philosopher Alfred North Whitehead, but to offer help to anyone who wishes to build a philosophy of his own. This purpose works not only forward toward the world but backward toward the very individual who reads or, indeed, any person who tries to write such a study as this. He or she characteristically becomes more completely individualized in the process of reading or writing. The writer gains a greater personal identity in the process of writing just as the reader does in reading.

In a preceding volume, *About Wordsworth and Whitehead,* we began dealing with Wordsworth's poem *The Prelude* in relation to the thought of Whitehead, aiming also to bring out, little by little, points that the reader can compare with views of his own. But that earlier volume covered only the first six books of Wordsworth's rather long poem. We intend now to go further. Wordsworth is of special interest because he was a writer who wanted to reach readers and was modestly concerned about philosophy; he was a person who tended to respect his readers and to identify with them: he thought of them as one with himself. Whitehead was similar in this respect. He too had an outgoing quality.

What is presented in our present book can be followed very clearly even without a knowledge of the previous volume. Our intention now is to continue an existential enrichment in the examination of the two figures as their thought is related to *The Prelude.* Existence is the important thing. We shall first re-examine, then, with new insights, the ground that we had presented in the previous work. While making compressions in the earlier material, that is, we shall try to see the content in a somewhat modified existential light. We shall be following the successive books of Wordsworth's first version of *The Prelude*, which is youthful and vigorous. This version, moreover, is readily accessible. The successive chapters of the present book will be in the order in which the various parts of *The Prelude* were first written before 1805. Thus it will be possible to look conveniently from the young Wordsworth to Whitehead or, indeed, from the philosopher back to the poet. Whitehead recommended such a reversible, backward-and-forward approach as it can be applied to much of our thinking about problems or people.

There is a kind of story-approach in what we have to say — an occasional rough chronological quality — since the poet, in this his major work, is telling the story of his spiritual life, that is, his experience mainly in its inward aspects. We have chosen *The Prelude* as a base because Whitehead admired the poem and it seemed to us, early in our study, that he might have been influenced by it in specific ways. He found value, it is true, in other works by Wordsworth, but *The Prelude* seems to stand out especially in his mind. The 1805 Oxford version rather than the 1850 form of the poem suits our purpose because it has a liberal spirit and is close in many respects to certain ideas of our own time. The 1850 edition, in spite of its many merits, is somewhat conventional in its political and religious character.

The life and inner experience of Wordsworth as we have implied appear notably in the 1805 *Prelude;* we plan to examine the interrelation of the thought of the poet and that of Whitehead, moving gradually from simpler aspects toward the broader scope of the philosopher's insight into the world and its meaning. Events in Wordsworth's earlier reflective life will receive rapid reference in our first six chapters, which are in some cases rather short. A more complete coverage of these stages may be read at leisure in our earlier volume. Still, the present book, we repeat, offers a unity in itself and can be read understandingly without a knowledge of any other work. This volume, then, carries with a purpose the title *Aspects of Wordsworth and Whitehead: Philosophy and Certain Continuing Life-Problems.* It will center its main attention (after Chapters I through VI) upon a treatment of the poet's *Prelude,* Books Seven, Eight and on through Book Eleven, using corresponding chapter divisions with numbers the same as the poet used for the divisions in the version of the poem to which we will refer. Such a plan will be a convenience for a reader who wishes to look back at Wordsworth to judge to some degree the validity of what we present. Single words quoted (seemingly unimportant) serve as a guide to a context or to some special aspect of a thought in the original author. Quaint spelling in quotations will be retained. Long quotations are avoided for they would tend to destroy the sequence of the structure in our book.

In the earlier volume, *About Wordsworth and Whitehead,* it was the intention, we have said, to provide a convenient opportunity for a comparison to be made between what we there presented about the two figures and what they say for themselves. This is also true, then, of our intention here. Necessarily there must be some room for individual reader interpretation, and we have aimed to invite such interpretation. The chapters of our book need at times to be compared to the correspondingly numbered books of *The Prelude.* For this our line references to the poem will be helpful.

When it comes to comparing the short quotations from Whitehead with ideas in our text, it will be possible to follow effectively the references to the philosopher's works. Any subsequent quotation from him will be found in the same page as that earlier referred to, unless there is a clear indication of another source. Some of Whitehead's books have different page numbering in editions that appear to be the same, but with care the exact edition we have referred to can be found. Likewise it will be necessary to use the youthful 1805 version of

The Prelude carefully because it contains thirteen books rather than the fourteen found in the old-age 1850 version, and, in addition, the line numbering varies, often considerably from that of the later work because of the poet's revision and rewriting. We shall refer at times to Whitehead as "the philosopher" merely to avoid undue repetition of his name. But we do nevertheless honor him; he has very much to offer us as does Wordsworth. Both figures have special value for our troubled times. But this is a statement which must be judged by reading the volume.

In using the book, it will be helpful to compare one's own thinking or ideas with the conceptions as they are presented step by step. Thus an enlarged personal life-view can be developed by the individual for himself. He need not believe altogether what Whitehead or Wordsworth believed. Indeed he can reject all of it. A concern with philosophy lends itself to a variety of ways of approach. We can see philosophy, that is, as a variable leaving opportunity for an emphasis upon analysis on the one hand or vision on the other hand because these two approaches will appear from time to time. Whitehead affords a splendid example of this method of working. Individuals will differ in the stress that they give to the one or the other tendency, analysis or vision.

Our book, we hope, will provide material for the exercise of analysis as well as for broader speculative reflection, or what Whitehead calls speculative philosophy as exemplified in the latter part of his *Process and Reality* and in his whole volume *Adventures of Ideas*. As he says, innovations in thought come about "from flashes of intuition bringing new material within the scope of scholarly learning."[2] But he does see possible weaknesses in "sheer ventures in rash speculation." He grants that "a certain excessiveness seems a necessary element in all greatness. In some direction or other we must devote ourselves beyond what would be warranted by the analysis of pure reason." Those who read *Aspects of Wordsworth and*

Whitehead, our present volume, may judge whether they agree with this statement. Whether it characterizes effectively Whitehead's own work is another interesting problem.

At a number of points in our volume we refer to Whitehead's theory of the backward and forward reading of history. This theory can apply to the reading of one's personal life or to the reading of any book. It can apply, for example, to the reading of *Aspects of Wordsworth and Whitehead: Philosophy and Certain Continuing Life-Problems;* thus one could begin with Chapter VII, "Wordsworth's Thought in Relation to Whitehead: The Impact of London," and could then tack back to various earlier chapters, after which one could make a leap to Chapter IX, "Wordsworth's Residence in France: Revolutionary Freedom." This skipping about or use of flash-backs might seem like a radical suggestion for this kind of work, but actually it fits into Whitehead's distinctly creative and imaginative mode of thinking. And if one follows this plan (or apparent lack of plan) the integral character of our volume will nevertheless come to light as one tries to put together the materials in a final mental assembling. But for most readers it may be well to begin more conventionally with Chapter I and the question of time as well as of space (they need to be brought together into a space-time unity) which is important in modern philosophy; indeed, it will be shown to be revelatory of the more profound aspects of the thinking of Wordsworth and Whitehead.

Footnotes
1. Pierre Teilhard de Chardin, *Letters to Two Friends: 1926-1952* (New York: New American Library, Perspectives in Humanism Series, 1968), p. 214.
2. *Adventures of Ideas,* (New York: Macmillan, 1933, 1940), p. 138.

Chapter I

Retrospect of Wordsworth's Childhood and School-Time in *The Prelude* as Connected with Whitehead

Any contemporary novelist sets his story in our own immediate time, so far as he can, or he looks forward to a future moment of existence for his characters, or, again, he may look backward until he finds an earlier period within which to work. Likewise, the novelist has before him a *place*, highly imaginative or more or less actualistic; this becomes a part of his temporary consciousness. What has just been said of the novelist and his concern about time can also be said of the poet, or, indeed, of the painter, although the setting used by the painter — in so far as he considers time — seems more vague than that of a novelist or poet; it appears to be more vague because we do not often think of painting in its relation to *time*.

Again, the novelist thinks of manners, often more or less unconsciously; but we soon notice that he is placing before us, for example, the behavior of unusually democratic people who are nevertheless members of the largely privileged classes, or, on the other hand, that he may indicate characteristic gestures and actions of snobs. The problem of time and that of manners will represent philosophical concerns. As to time we find that Wordsworth reveals it through the acts that we can imagine as occurring, for example, in the experience of a Danish king of long ago. But the poet thinks of time, place, and manners as variably exciting or stimulating to his imagination; thus he says in Book One of the 1805 *Prelude*:

Time, place, and manners, these I seek, and these
I find in plenteous store . . . (169 —)

Time, for him, involves action. It is interpenetrating. The poet does not think of time here in a highly abstract way. He does not usually think of it as an essence. It is exemplified in our deeds of promptness or, again, in our pseudo-prudence, or our existential *intentions*, often dragging out spiritlessly in the ineffectiveness which may, even, be a part of a life-view to which we have permitted ourselves to yield. We may show, that is,

A timorous capacity from prudence;
From circumspection, infinite delay. (243 —)

Wordsworth's time of childhood was spent close to a river, the Derwent, which made "steady cadence"; this gave him "a dim earnest" of what he was to experience in wider nature. He refers to the river which "having left his mountains" (the Derwent has a personal self, it will be noticed) came close to the "Terrace" of the house where the young boy lived. It was, indeed "a Playmate," yet a symbol of things he came to appreciate in the experience of life. Sometimes he would spend most of the day, naked, alternately enjoying the sun and plunging in the waters of one of the branches of the river and basking again, or running among trees until the mountainous slopes of the region

and distant Skiddaw's lofty height,   ·
Were bronz'd with a deep radiance . . . (299 —)

This and other events represented the experiential "seed-time" in which he grew up from the age of five to that of nine. But it is not time and the chronology of a story that we must deal with here. Rather we must look back to some of the features covered in the beginning portion of our earlier volume, *About Wordsworth and Whitehead.*

A prospectus of the material presented in a chapter is often of help in a volume dealing with philosophical substance. For the present need, however, we are mainly to provide a retrospectus; that is, we shall have to recapitulate some of the leading points covered in our earlier writing. In doing so we shall refer to the specific chapters in which the concepts were developed, but we will not repeat page references which have been provided for quoted material used in the previous book. Where new sources of material receive discussion (for the purpose of further insight into the problems being reviewed) references will of course be given. The more familiar retrospective material may be read rapidly by anyone acquainted with its substance through his previous reading.

If one looks back at the ground covered in our first volume it may be recalled that in Chapter I we saw that both Words-worth and Whitehead have a tendency to approach life with a decidedly strong psychological or introspective interest. This is part of their philosophy. The inner emphasis tends to represent a valuing of the effort and the drives, and also the power, within the self: in a word, it is a kind of energetics of the self or ego. But it does not involve an overstress on self- importance. Both men are without anything at all like egocentricism. Self-centeredness can be the destruction of any philosophy. Still, the self or the psyche is important.

That Whitehead was interested in psychological ideas is made clear in many places, among them in a comment he made concerning "the great effort required to grasp" the ideas of Freud "in their relationship to larger truths"[1] — a remark that seems to show he had given Freud careful reflection. Here the philosopher's tendency is to have a broad approach to psychology such as that which Ludwig B. Lefebre refers to when he criticizes narrowness: "The 'natural science' type of psychologist, for example, treats with disdain everything that is not tangible and that cannot objectively be shown to exist — but he usually ends up with a psychology without psyche"[2]; Lefebre wishes to contrast such a psychologist with Karl Jaspers who, though a philosopher, was for a decade or more concerned greatly with psychological factors. Jaspers represents in his work a broad type of psychology, as does Whitehead. The latter's feeling about the subject may be seen in his remark: "One difficulty in appealing to modern psychology, for the purpose of a preliminary survey of the nature of experience, is that so much of that science is based upon the presupposition of the sensationalist mythology."[3]

Whitehead's interest in the "Psyche" and the "Eros" have a bearing upon his reaction to Freud. In the philosopher we do not see, however, anything of the death instinct (the thanatos) that has been manifested at times in modern psychology, though a more constructive psychology is now prominent. Nor do we see such a negativistic tendency in Wordsworth. This is not to say that Whitehead and Wordsworth are bald optimists. Both figures, however, show a confidence in life rather than a sense of dejection about it. Both also have a hopefulness of concern for all classes of men, and both reach into history or into the past in trying to understand the world. They equally recognize, for example, that ideals of chivalry are important in

22

our common human background traced to medieval times, and this fact receives strong emphasis in their work.

Later developments in history, such as the advancements of human liberty, are important in the thought of both men. These facts are brought out in our Chapter I of the previous volume. The philosopher's outlook is exceptionally broad, and we get a sense of this from time to time in his appreciation of the breadth of Wordsworth. This appreciation, that is, does not represent a mere surface view. The poet's effect may perhaps also be seen in little evidences of influence which he had upon Whitehead in moments when the philosopher scarcely realized it.

Wordsworth says little about "School-Time" in Book One of *The Prelude*, although he uses the term in his title of this early part of the poem. He thinks at the moment more about hours that are spent away from school between the ages of five and nine, and a little later, and he focusses his attention upon the inwardness of this period of life. He is thinking of that stage of a person's existence as it has a bearing upon philosophic conditions. He is broadly interested in time and its relation to experience.

Whitehead reveals his breadth when he gives recognition to Wordsworth's vital human interest in literature as related to time and society. This perceptiveness receives expression in *Science and the Modern World*. But Whitehead's concern includes more than time and society, and the same is true of Wordsworth. The poet's breadth is disclosed directly in his prose preface to *The Excursion*, a long poem planned as a companion work to *The Prelude*. This preface very definitely interested Whitehead. Quoting from it, he tells how Wordsworth's statement pointed toward a "projected work" which was anticipatorily "described as 'A philosophical poem containing views of Man, Nature, and Society.' "[4]

Wordsworth, as presented by Whitehead, thus indicates the purposes which should guide a philosophical poet. The poet's words referring to philosophy could apply equally to the world-view of Whitehead. Man, nature, and society were prominent features, as we have seen, in the philosophical reflection of both of these men. In the context in *Science and the Modern World* from which we have just drawn the material concerning the poet, Whitehead also makes the penetrating observation that Wordsworth recognizes the importance of "full concrete experience."

Whitehead's philosophy emphasizes the central significance of such full-fleshed existential experience to the understanding of life in the broadest sense. Like Wordsworth he reaches also into experience beyond that of human beings to the interrelation of manifold things (including society and nature) in the universe. Wordsworth's concern for all men, democratically, is prominent, and such a very real concern is in Whitehead also. The poet shows this preoccupation in Book One of *The Prelude* even in his portrayal of children. Degradations or corruptions of democracy do not lead either figure to lose faith in its cause. Neither of them, furthermore, would allow democratic thought to give an excuse for human inertia. Within democratic reflection, ambition has a just place, but it is necessary also to consider the pitfalls that lie within the quality of ambitious or energetic character: that is, the danger, the potential evil, of vainglory.

Whitehead speaks of ambition, or the desire for fame, as an understandable impulse, but he regards it nevertheless as at times having something of the character of an infirmity. Wordsworth also thinks of the problem of ambition and in *The Prelude* uses the term "just ambition" to distinguish the excellence which is possible within ambition. The person who has insufficient ambition is given to irresolution. This, according to Wordsworth, may become a frustrating factor to the mind's proper use; irresolution, that is, may act as "an interdict upon her hopes." It is interesting from the modern point of view to notice that he uses the feminine form in the personification of mind.

The danger of irresolution to which Wordsworth refers appears also in the thought of Whitehead, and may be counteracted in various ways: for example, we can counteract irresolution in ourselves by a study of the long and amazing movement of human history and by an understanding of what Whitehead refers to as generative causal activity. We can become part of the process of history. The philosopher here also considers power beyond that of the human personality. This generative causal activity stands in contrast to an emphasis in philosophy which is limited by a confinement to reflection based directly on sense-data, almost to the exclusion of everything else. Wordsworth and Whitehead were thus both influenced by a tradition that stressed the constructive possibilities within the human personality. In this connection Whitehead recognizes the need of a criticism of intuition, but he does not neglect the importance of being "appreciative of direct intuition." He also stresses the power of "reverence," connecting it, in addition, to one's respect for others.

The problem of fear finds a place in Wordsworth's thought in Book One of The Prelude but he holds that we can learn the judicious use of fears. In such use they may be accepted as gifts, "vouchsaf'd" to the human personality. According to Whitehead's philosophy, if we consider it by way of comparison, fears are connected importantly with a factor in our lives which is "a primitive element."[5] This element, he says a moment later, "is vague, haunting, unmanageable." And he adds, shortly thereafter, it "is heavy with the contact with things gone by, which lay their grip on our immediate selves."[6]

Thinking of these primitive aspects of experience, to which the philosopher refers, we may be inclined to ask ourselves: What are the causes of things? We know that, superficially, one thing — a seeming cause — precedes another. But what ought we to think of more remote causal antecedents? The question is profound, reaching as it does into what is primitive within us. Even beyond our primitive background the effect of the wider universe comes into play. Here, according to Whitehead causative efficacy (he uses alternative phrases for the idea) needs to be considered. Something produces an effect upon us more ultimately.

The most frequently chosen term he uses for this impulse of ultimateness is a deep "Causal Efficacy," and this expression he employs in a section headed "Direct Perception and Causal Efficacy" in his volume *Symbolism, Its Meaning and Effect*. We do have personal power, but the more distant efficacy which Whitehead here has in mind reaches also into regions of the universe beyond our personal efficacy. The conception is connected with his philosophy of time and it may be better understood if we recall Whitehead's later remark (in *Process and Reality*), that "the culminating fact of conscious, rational life refuses to conceive itself as a transient enjoyment, transiently useful."[7] There is something beyond transiency.

There is a power not ourselves, then, which according to Whitehead has importance in our destiny. That he is here also concerned with the forces of causative efficacy is made evident by his remark which immediately follows, having a bearing on "novelty." Thus *Process and Reality* confirms his view that had been expressed in an earlier volume. He adds at once that our "physical feelings are haunted by the vague insistence of causality," but he makes the further point concerning our "higher intellectual feelings" which are mysteriously affected and are "haunted by the vague insistence of another order, where there is no shipwreck"; thus it is that he here also connects his conception of the causal force with something which is larger than self. Time and eternity are involved here.

Near the outset of this chapter we referred to Wordsworth's approach to time, considering it in relation to events. A number of twentieth century philosophers have rejected, or put behind them the notion of time as a special entity or essence, and have focussed, in preference, upon what we *do* in a succession of circumstances. The important thing for them is the activity or the use of moments as they occur. Ludwig Wittgenstein is an example of such a figure, and this is revealed in his comment on the tendency to seek essences: our tendency, "under the illusion that what is peculiar, profound, essential, in our investigation, resides in its trying to grasp the incomparable essence of language."[8] Here he is thinking of the irony of our seeking, which involves a quest for "a *super*-order between — so to speak — *super*-concepts." He is thinking in this book of such a word as "experience" and the fact that the term is understandable through *doing*, "use," and through events.

There are many examples of his concern for actions (cranking something or pulling a lever) as related to philosophical problems. Thus at a later point he thinks of *milking* a rule of some sort out of some intrinsic necessity, and we can see him on a stool with the side of his forehead against the cow he is milking. Thus he thinks of a rule. "It is the only thing which one can milk out of this intrinsic necessity into a proposition."[9] For Wittgenstein the philosophical tendency to think of concepts (and notably of the nature of time) as related to actions and occurrences may be seen perhaps more evidently near the middle of his work *The Blue Book* where he opens a paragraph with the words: "Consider as an example the question 'What is time?' as Saint Augustine and others have asked it." Here and elsewhere Wittgenstein is not seeking a definition or an essence but, rather, he would seek a variety of actions, occasions, happenings. Wordsworth does this. This is not the place, however, to go further into the philosophy of Wittgenstein in its late, fascinating phases.

Whitehead, somewhat differently from Wittgenstein (in the examples we have cited), refers to what he calls an actual entity, but adds that he will at times "use the term 'actual occasion' in the place of the term actual entity."[10] For him "the actual world is built up of actual occasions" and he emphasizes the point that "whatever things there are in any sense of 'existence,' are derived by abstraction from actual occasions." Time is thus implied. The actual here may make us think of Wordsworth and the approach to time referred to at the beginning of our chapter. Whitehead, in explaining his view refers to "the term 'event' in the more general sense" in so far as it can be thought of as a centered combination of "actual occasions"; the occasions have interrelation, he says in one "quantum." Whitehead's "events" may be connected with the problem of time we have referred to in Wordsworth's Book One of *The Prelude*.

But to return to what Whitehead had to say, in our earlier discussion, about causal influences. Human beings are not dominated exclusively by the more primitive element, this power not ourselves, or beyond self, "heavy" with fate. Here it is to be noted that Wordsworth thinks of the elements which make up our life, discordant or otherwise, as dynamic and as constituted in the form of a *society*. Whitehead uses the term society similarly. To understand Wordsworth we need to notice his feeling in regard to

> a dark
> Invisible workmanship that reconciles
> Discordant elements, and makes them move
> In one society. (352 —)

There is a power which is outside us, but we have power also, within, as has been made clear. Still, the more primitive element related to cause is very important. It is a factor showing its effect, Whitehead says, during "periods in our lives — when the perception of the pressure from a world of things with characters in their own right, characters mysteriously moulding our own natures, become strongest" and these are periods which "are the product of a reversion to some primitive state."[11]

We are thus affected according to Whitehead under the influence of "fear, terror, attraction, love" and other "feelings and emotions closely entwined with the primitive functioning of 'retreat from' and of 'expansion towards.' "[12] The idea of retreat suggests escape, a prominent conception in modern psychology, and the concept of expansion can have negativistic connections, as in the effect of the authoritarian personality. But enlargement of self can also have benefits. The whole story of the effect on Whitehead of ideas such as these in relation to time cannot be summarized here, but the concepts we have been dwelling upon are important to it, and they are of special interest in relation to Wordsworth's thinking. They form a part in the effort to achieve an understanding of ourselves and the workings of our minds in relation to the universe. Wordsworth himself addresses the Spirit of the universe as a "Soul" which is "the eternity of thought"; this force "gives to forms and images" an unending motion which in its references to us, whether in childhood or early school days, serves to interconnect in development

> The passions that build up the human Soul,
> Not with the mean and vulgar works of Man,
> But with high objects, with enduring things . . . (434 —)

There is much that can recall Whitehead to our minds in this passage, though all of the material concerning not only passions but feeling in the poet has not been quoted. Causation brings to the philosopher's mind not the dark things of the world only. But for the moment it might seem that the dark predominates.

Aside from presenting Whitehead's theory of what he means by "Causal Efficacy" — a force of importance which is operative in our lives and in the world — we have been summarizing certain of the other leading points in regard to Wordsworth and the philosopher which were presented in *About Wordsworth and Whitehead*. Near the end of Chapter I of our previous volume, then, we explained that Wordsworth in *The Prelude* explicitly says that he wished to "understand" himself causally. He realizes that the human struggle to understand the self is difficult, and he acknowledges that he may not be successful in the effort. It is to be hoped that this aim at achieving a retrospective view of the road we traveled in our previous book will be helpful to a further understanding of the ongoing problem of the Wordsworth-Whitehead relationship.

Footnotes

1. *Dialogues of Alfred North Whitehead*, recorded by Lucien Price (Boston: Atlantic Monthly, Little Brown and Co., second printing, 1954), p. 211.
2. Lefebre, "The Psychology of Karl Jaspers," in *The Philosophy of Karl Jaspers*, ed. Paul Arthur Schilpp (New York: Tudor, 1957), p. 469.
3. *Process and Reality* (New York: The Macmillan Co., 1929, 1960), p. 214.
4. *Science and the Modern World*, p. 118. *The Excursion* was a long poem written by Wordsworth some ten years after *The Prelude*.
5. *Symbolism, Its Meaning and Effect* (New York: Macmillan, 1927, Capricorn Books, G. P. Putnam's Sons, 1959), p. 43.
6. *Ibid.*, p. 44.
7. *Process and Reality*, p. 516. The whole page in Whitehead, following this quotation, is pertinent here.
8. Wittgenstein, *Philosophical Investigations*, trans. by G. E. Anscombe, third edition (New York: The Macmillan Co., 1968), p. 44e.
9. *Ibid.*, p. 116e. The book has also numbered sections; in this case the section is 372.
10. *Process and Reality*, p. 113. Whitehead also says that "an actual entity never moves"; this is somewhat troublesome, but the actual entity should be thought of as being "what it is." Here Whitehead is thinking of it as an existence.
11. *Symbolism: Its Meaning and Effect*, p. 44
12. *Ibid.*, p. 45.

Chapter II

Retrospect of Later School Days as Connected with the Thought of Wordsworth and Whitehead

In *The Prelude*, Book Two, Wordsworth continues to be less concerned with school education than with what he gained in "woods and fields," where he describes week after week, "from month to month" how he and his friends enjoyed the "tumult" of the activities of their early years. These existential delights were carried on far into the night hours, when people had long since ceased to sit on the steps of houses, watching what was going on, when chairs had been all taken indoors. Boyhood activity included a continued "loud uproar" until, at last, rest in bed was sought with "beating mind." Such events or impulses of desire and eagerness the poet would deny to none. Now, looking back, it seems that his sense of event-full identity or of self, represents very largely mere consciousness. A person, indeed, is at times a thing of inner mental "consciousnesses" — a kind of activity; indeed Wordsworth declares of himself

> I seem
> Two consciousnesses, conscious of myself
> And of some other Being. (31 —)

Turning now to an emphasis upon some important material presented in Chapter II in our previous book, we must re-emphasize, necessarily, the aspect of Wordsworth's philosophy in which he rejects any belief in materialism. This does not, however, mean that he is given to the weaknesses of subjectivism, which can also lead to a denial of any sense of the mystery in nature. One's view of nature, that is, can become, in Norman Kemp Smith's words, "a very strange amalgam of subjectivism plus mechanism."[1] Under a subjectivist view, nature may, then, be separated radically from mind. This is a philosophy which Whitehead and his friend Norman Kemp Smith most characteristically oppose, and in their opposition to it they are at one with Wordsworth.

The poet denies that mechanical or external properties can completely explain the world of our experience. Whitehead also, consistently with his immaterialism, is opposed to any belief in relationships which are merely external. This does not mean that he is an "objective idealist" — a position which he definitely opposes when it comes to the analysis of "what the reality of the world involves" and when it holds, as Whitehead declares, that "cognitive mentality is in some way inextricably concerned in every detail."[2] He parts company with the objective idealists at the point that either their position or his position arrives at "the ultimate problem of metaphysics." He does, nevertheless, respect the idealist. He shares something with idealism, but in the end adopts "a position of provisional realism."

The view presented by Wordsworth in *The Prelude* recognizes that knowledge gained from a markedly sensory emphasis (in accordance with the outlook of materialism) represents a power; but this power is a "secondary" factor. We are prone, the poet says, to think of "boundaries" (that really constitute manifestations of the materialistic) as if they were themselves "things"; that is, they tend, in our too hasty thought, to seem ultimate. We need, on the other hand, to see these "things" as relative to a frame of reference. Looking at them not as ultimates, we will recognize their usefulness or the usefulness of science, as a "prop" to other purposes. Here we are really thinking of constructs which man makes to serve his effort to think. The very sense we have of personality is often itself a simple construct. The nature of selfhood is a difficult concept for Wordsworth, and it is difficult also for Whitehead who speaks of "the mystery of personal identity, the mystery of the immanence of the past in the present, the mystery of transience."[3]

For the poet, we have seen, man is a "creator and perceiver both"; our life is characterized by interaction, but our experience is widespread in its character. And it is interwoven with a widely "*active* universe," a point made by Wordsworth which finds a parallel in Whitehead's philosophy. This is connected also with the creativity which characterizes the human being even as a child. Creativity in the child is often needlessly destroyed, as Wordsworth and Whitehead both believe. In this view they are also close to John Dewey, with whom, as we shall see, they share a variety of ideas.

Near the middle of our Chapter II in the previous volume the point is brought out that Wordsworth at a certain developmental stage began to focus his observation on the minuter properties of things. He recognizes the importance of close observation and the fact that "all knowledge" can be a "delight," but he realizes that we can also make a mistake in directing our attention too greatly toward the transitory. This is a matter which Whitehead likewise emphasizes. We know also that a person who is deeply interested in knowledge may as a result turn to solitude very greatly. This Wordsworth stresses, but there is a side of every human being that will never be developed adequately if, working according to the opposite tendency, one turns away from solitude too resolutely. Balance is required. And this is true even in regard to letting oneself be drawn, at least to some degree, toward what we may call the mystical.

As Wordsworth believes, there is an inclination in the human being whereby, largely through solitude, he can sense things when he seems to have no "bodily eyes"; here we have a case of individual viewing, though the active habit of social sharing should never be minimized. Wordsworth refers to the "observation of affinities" between things through a form of close attention which we are inclined to neglect unduly. This may be connected with Whitehead's treatment of a topic which he calls "Importance"; he has a chapter with such a heading in *Modes of Thought* in which he insists that we necessarily, and wisely, exclude many matters from a given focal center. But there is a prevailing disposition to omit ineptly things that need to receive attention (or importance) as we compare one situation with another. Significant affinities need to be perceived. That especially happens in attempting to arrive at a world-view. "Philosophy can exclude nothing."[4] An overstatement, this, but it does provide an emphasis which is vital in the philosopher's thought. He excludes nothing but he emphasizes certain things which are decidedly significant.

Wordsworth and Whitehead both observe affinities which are not present in the ordinary course of events. But some of these affinities in one degree or another can be perceived by a very large number of the members of society. Any of us, however — elite or otherwise — may be overlooking manifold subtleties of affinity. Such affinities are emphatically a part of Whitehead's thought. But according to Wordsworth it should not be assumed that people are to be regarded as stratified in such a way that the extraordinary affinities are, by their very nature, beyond the reach of the common run of people. Effort needs to be made to bring such extraordinary tendencies to the attention and understanding of everyone, provided they wish to come part way in the endeavor to share ideas. Here we are moving toward the problem of the universal in that it is difficult to see accurately the aspects of universalism in mankind.

The problem of the universal is, of course, troublesome in its multiple phases. Wordsworth closely observes "inorganic natures," but whether he is considering inorganic or organic things, all his thoughts are "steep'd in feeling" and his feelings are interpenetrated with thought. The poet stresses the unity of all reality — the oneness of all being — almost as emphatically as Whitehead does; that is, for the poet the essence of this unity is life — the one life — and the inclusion of man and of all selves is implied here. But neither Wordsworth's position nor Whitehead's should be thought of as representing pantheism. The latter part of Chapter II in our previous volume also brings out the fact of Wordsworth's early interest in science. Whitehead's youthful concern was mainly about mathematics, but it soon swung toward an interest in physical science and an effort to relate it more widely to life.

We have thus far been recapitulating some of the important features that were dwelt upon in the first two chapters of our earlier book. But we must not forget *The Prelude* itself, a literary work unfolding its story in successive events which are inward, giving a reader the sense of time involving "Mountains" and the falling of "sounding" waters. These broad occasions of experience he remembers; memories are a part of his philosophy. And among them he tells us, very personally, are the

Mists and Winds
That dwell among the hills where I was born. (441 —)

35

Thus we have been recounting, we will say again, some of the important features in Book Two of *The Prelude* as it is related to philosophy. The intention of our book is to help one in perceiving more clearly the main material of this poem as it is related to the thought of Whitehead. What we have been aiming toward is the larger scope of the philosophy of the two men. In beginning our next discussion our purpose will be to bring together retrospectively some features of the themes that we have developed in part, but that need further emphasis. In our presentation we have been surveying ground which has a bearing upon *The Prelude* as it was first conceived. The initial conception of the poet was to be set forth in a poem of five books. Further material was necessary to the rounding out of Wordsworth's idea, however, and this substance is importantly connected with Whitehead as will become evident in the sequel.

Footnotes

1. Norman Kemp Smith, *Prolegomena to an Idealist Theory of Knowledge* (London: Macmillan and Co., 1924), p. 5. See also our coming comments on this author and his relation to Whitehead.
2. *Science and the Modern World*, p. 132.
3. *Adventures of Ideas*, p. 210.
4. "Importance," *Modes of Thought*, p. 2. Examples of "close analogies" or affinities can be seen in the relation between Buddhism and Christianity referred to in *Religion in the Making*, p. 139.

Chapter III

Retrospect of Wordsworth's First Residence at Cambridge as Related to Whitehead's Thought

We see now the young Wordsworth riding on the top of a coach (like our modern buses) as he is being driven to the town, Cambridge, where he was to enter St. John's college. At a crucial point he suddenly saw for the first time a student "cloth'd in Gown and tassel'd Cap" and we may well wish to know how he felt at that particular moment. Wordsworth was not "master" of his "eyes," he tells us (they were dimmed with tears), till the coach in which he was riding had covered another "hundred yards"; the student on the road in his collegiate dress is a mere incident — what the student represented in the poet's mind is everything.

For the poet, imaginative insight is important, and the same is true of the philosopher. Nevertheless, we have emphasized in the previous volume *About Wordsworth and Whitehead* that both figures are also decidedly down-to-earth, philosophically. There is a danger that we may think of them as being far more abstract and remote from actuality and existence than they were. In Whitehead's case this practicality is brought out in that he is greatly aware of the importance of technology and that he stresses the place of technical training in connection with anyone's education. Yet we pointed out in our previous volume that both men recognized the importance of faith and both held what could be called a common faith. That is, the character of their thought, as related to a common faith, is within reach of virtually all human beings.

The importance of an active imagination, we can say again, likewise receives stress in both men. The possible weakness of a too feverishly imaginative faith will become apparent here. Such a danger is not likely to affect one adversely if he has a goodly measure of saving common sense, and this is true of both figures. They recognize, further, the corrective forces that are found in not assuming too much concerning oneself — in not losing the values which are to be found in humor or even in a degree of fancifulness. But, in seeming contrast to this, it is the deeper elements in life which largely preoccupy them.

The problem of vanity or of an inordinate self-estimate, as we have seen, is also important in any philosophy. Wordsworth recognizes the need of reducing the predisposition toward vanity or individual self-glory: the thing to be desired is sharing with all humanity such values as may be achieved in a true community of persons. Here a reality-principle within the self is important. In this connection we may refer again to Whitehead's book *Symbolism, Its Meaning and Effect* where he speaks of a "sense of vague presences, effective for good or evil over our fate."[1] This, as Whitehead holds, is a form of perception. It is, as he says a few sentences later, a "perception of conformation to realities" which is in the environment and within the individual, operating fundamentally. It is, moreover, a form of perception which has not only connections with our bodies but provides a close link with the outer world. He re-emphasizes its fundamental character, and he indicates finally that this sense of vague presences is difficult to comprehend, or to see with preciseness. Still, we must try to perceive it as well as we can.

Our topic here needs to be given further special mention now. Thinking of the problem of vanity, or of an inordinate self-estimate, it is difficult to see how one could have such a tendency if he became more fully aware of the universe in its relation to the generative causes we have been discussing. The self-estimate likewise is a factor in relation to faith, for faith in Whitehead is not a form of knowledge; that is, the knowledge on which one bases the self, or one's state of mind or action has to be tentatively projected into the future and is only human. But this is not to say that it is mere whim.

The things concerning generative causes previously touched upon receive very special treatment within Whitehead's belief that we live in a world of symbolisms. A symbolic factor in our experience with direct sense-data is minor, or mechanical, as compared with the primitive symbolic element which carries heavily a connection with things of the past that have an importance to "our immediate selves."[2] This primitive element is something which is quietly at work. While being so, it nevertheless has a profound effect on everyone. This kind of profound experience dominates "the primitive living organisms" which, therefore, "have a sense of the fate from which they have emerged"; they have a sense, also, "for the fate towards which they go," though they may at times be scarcely aware of what is occurring or, at any rate, "hardly differentiate" what Whitehead calls "any immediate" emphasis or "display."

Thus Whitehead speaks of the contact with things gone by, and in the very next sentence emphasizes once more its character as a "primitive experience." In contrast to this fateful force there is the factor of sense-experience, or the presentational, which is immediate and which is concerned with the "superficial" — in other words, that which is involved with the external, or with "the show of things." It is to be hoped that what has been said here provides an enrichment or supplement to the matter presented in our Chapter III of the earlier volume which is concerned with the third book of *The Prelude* as it is related to Whitehead. We had referred to the philosopher's statement in *Symbolism, Its Meaning and Effect* concerning "the show of things." But such external things are not Whitehead's main emphasis. He is preoccupied with the more important points in our experience where our perceptions of the outside forces are working upon us and shaping what we become; such times, or periods in our lives, are fundamental to all that is deepest and best (or worst) in our natures.

Our topic concerns the fact that there is a "contrast between the comparative emptiness of Presentational Immediacy and the deep significance disclosed by Causal Efficacy" and that this contrast lies "at the root of the pathos which haunts the world."[3] Whitehead's conception of "Causal Efficacy" stands in contrast with our more usual experience of "the world disclosed in immediate presentation, gay with a thousand tints, passing, and intrinsically meaningless." To bring out his point more strongly he refers to "the haunting lines" at the beginning of the last stanza in the poem by Keats, "The Eve of St. Agnes," where a sense of the passing — or of that which is impermanent — is fused with a sense of the second perceptive mode, "Causal Efficacy," and thus brings to us an eerie feeling about that which is more permanent.

As Whitehead next says, one may at times be even "overstrained" emotionally by an "undivided attention to the causal elements in the nature of things."[4] At such a time the deep significance of underlying forces back of the world gives rise to tenseness and a sense of the appalling. "Then in some tired moment there comes a sudden relaxation, and the mere presentational side of the world overwhelms" us; we are, that is, affected by a sense of the world's "emptiness." Here he has in mind our preoccupation with the sensuous or the sensual. If we give thought to our condition, then, we indeed feel that we are "shades" pursuing "shadows"; our mind has "suddenly lost the sense of causal" factors and it becomes "illuminated" with remembrances of events connected with the deeper forces of life.

It is the ethical side of human beings that Whitehead for the moment is pointing toward, but it is the metaphysical that is his ultimate interest in certain comments which he makes thereafter. We have been considering in summary the general material of our earlier discussion. In Chapter III of our previous book, Wordsworth's feeling concerning mortality is to be discerned in his reference to Newton "with his Prism and silent Face." Shortly thereafter we commented on Whitehead's causal interests. Here we may observe that in one of his still later volumes he has a statement concerning "a vague feeling of causal relationship with the external world, of some intensity, vaguely defined as to quality," to which he adds the point that this is an intensity "with some vague definition as to locality."[5]

What Whitehead says in this later book, and what he had also suggested earlier about "Causal Efficacy" (in *Symbolism, Its Meaning and Effect*) gives the reader a sense of the mysterious forces in life. But the whole development of his approach concerning localization cannot be given here. It is difficult even for Whitehead himself. The problem of localization as it has a bearing on part and totality is of course a vexed one. As Whitehead confesses a number of pages later — in writing further concerning the difficulty in analyzing the causal — "There is no adequate definition of localization" in so far as localization can be thought of as emerging "into analytic consciousness."[6] We could say it concerns space and time and part and totality. He is thinking of relativity. His doctrine of relativity, as involving the profound interrelationship of things, is a factor in any analysis of this kind, including "such local relationships" as leave a "faint impress" upon the consciousness of the individual. "But in general such detailed analysis" as one might desire remains "far beyond the capacity of human consciousness."

Yet it is symbolism which is Whitehead's main problem when he thinks of this vagueness. As he says two pages later concerning the "presences" which have this formidable power, "these controlling presences, these sources of power, these things with an inner life, with their own richness of content, these beings with the destiny of the world hidden in their natures, are what we want to know about."[7] And he gives a humble instance of a possible traffic accident which we do not include because it might be misleading in regard to the depth of the question before us. To understand the depth of the problem, reference could be made to Norman Kemp Smith's view that there are factors beyond sensory details which bring the sensory elements into togetherness through forces which are intuitional. Such forces reach out into enormity, and are suggestive of the vast potentiality of man. Here various categories are of importance, including the category of causality. Like Whitehead, Norman Kemp Smith is concerned with the causal factors in life in relation to symbolism. The causal gives rise to emotion. When Kemp Smith thinks of the symbolic, he refers to "a love of symbolism," and a love of the term "as more than the thought, of language as an instrument of power and not merely of expression"[8]; such language possessing power is "valuable for its emotional suggestiveness as well as for its intellectual content."

We have referred here to Norman Kemp Smith not only because of the value of his thought but because Whitehead himself makes special reference to him both in the "Preface" and in the body of the volume *Symbolism, Its Meaning and Effect*. He makes the reference in connection with the fact that we not only enjoy symbolism but experience factors which are operational as a result of the symbol. Smith may have helped him to his views. The symbols, that is, have the capability of discovering meaning important to us "because, in the long adaptation of living organisms to their environment, nature taught their use."[9] On this point especially Whitehead's thought is related to that of Kemp Smith. They are like two brothers who share innumerable elements of thought, but differ on as many others.

We referred earlier to the problem of an inordinate self-estimate. This problem finds a place in Wordsworth's *Prelude*, and we must return to it now. Whitehead in various places emphasizes a similar point. Vanity leads to exalting one person as against another. Here we may note the evil of a tendency to exalt the allegedly great men where the real need is to recognize them and all men as so many human beings. We dehumanize the so-called great men where the tendency toward exaltation occurs. This Whitehead refers to as a form of "hysteria"[10] in thought, of which we are perhaps all somewhat guilty. We also have to learn not to let people reduce our ego-strength through the unconscious result of their downgrading words or their patronizing actions. This reduction can occur to us through the disservice of people we meet in general experience, or at an early stage even through the action of our friends or of our parents.

The debunking of the contributions which human beings have made in the world is, according to Whitehead, similarly an example of the hysterical. But the rare, creative, the precious potential moments in the lives of all persons deserve emphasis. Such moments can come to one, provided the circumstances are right. The importance of the individual, according to Wordsworth and Whitehead, does not take its form from self-aggrandizement: it stems from his and every person's relation to Deity. This relation is readily available and capable of being shared by all persons. The degree to which it may become potent is dependent, in part, upon supportive circumstances and our own attitudes. Wordsworth makes clear that he feels he has an entire world within himself which, in addition, exists not only for himself and to himself but "to the God who look'd" inwardly upon all persons and individually upon the poet's own "mind."

In our summarizing we would wish to emphasize, then, that the poet's point of view, as seen in Chapter III of our earlier book, contains a complex interaction of things, including immanence and transcendence. This interaction is found also in Whitehead. So it is, likewise, that we personally are within all things, and yet we transcend that which is immediate. The poet, we may say again, had a world within himself which existed not only to himself but "to the God who look'd" inwardly upon the self — that is, upon the individual human mind. Wordsworth, through this, possessed strength; he had "an eye" of power, he tells us, operating in his own "strongest workings" and this eye looked "for the shades of difference" within things. These shades of difference which he observed "lie hid in all exterior forms"; they may be "remote" or they may be "minute," but they are nevertheless perceived with such an eye as he is describing. It is transcendence and immanence that Wordsworth is concerned with. The whole theme is a subject fit for an epic, he tells us, though aspects of it are "far hidden from the reach of words."

Imagination is a factor here. The same quality as that which the poet speaks of is found in Whitehead. We need here only offer an example of it drawn from "Symbolic Reference in Perceptive Experience," a portion of a chapter in the volume with which we have been concerned. In it he speaks of Aesop's dog and the reflection, the appearance, of the meat in a stream. The dog is learning about self-action in relation to reality — indeed, something even of self-perception. "Aesop's dog lost his meat," Whitehead says, "but he gained a step on the road towards a free imagination."[11]

Here we may also add a remark concerning Wordsworth's belief, referred to in Chapter III of our previous book, that each person becomes "a memory to himself." This conception is related to the fact that the human being, as John Dewey has said, "preserves his past experiences. What happened in the past is lived again in memory."[12] To Dewey there are "echoes" which are significant. As in Wordsworth and Whitehead, this conception is important for Dewey in relation to what he calls "a world of signs and symbols." This is a kind of transcending world in which we live our vital lives. His thought is consequential in this connection, reinforcing Wordsworth and Whitehead, as it touches upon a transcending world made symbolically.

Transcendence is felt frequently in Wordsworth and we ourselves can feel it when we think of those human beings who were not only memories to themselves but who come echoing to us throughout our memories. We think, that is, of those human beings who have done great things, and who, in their character as immanent, nevertheless form small parts of a vast whole. Wordsworth, as he thought of the great ones who had long ago walked the paths of Cambridge University, found that they could appear not only in their greatness but also in the guise of being "humbled" in these places, surrounded as they are in thought with a vast universe of profound associations.

Both Wordsworth and Whitehead see the danger of being ruled by an impulse toward fame. Stress on this is important, though it was discussed more completely in the volume *About Wordsworth and Whitehead*. That discussion was presented in connection with educational motivation. It is necessary, that is, that an ideal be present for the best achievement whereby all human beings are together to be benefited. An ideal, though high, may be recognized as an ideal *aim*. Even though

45

one may throughout life fall short of the ideal's purpose of lofty excellence, it nevertheless is functional in the on-going life of the self and of humanity.

We come back then, once more, to the importance of the transcending, as well as to imagination, in the thought of Wordsworth and Whitehead. As they consider education both at times tend to be extreme in their critical statements. But it is the motivation toward ideal things that is influencing them. Necessarily there may at times have to be an as-if in our thought if we are to function in relation to any ideality, or with an aiming-goal. In this connection we may recall such expressions in Wordsworth as "high-attempt" where the word *attempt* might well have been underlined. We may note also the educational application of the word "religious" and Wordsworth's reference to "holy joy" as applied to learning. The religious aspirational aim in Wordsworth, as in Whitehead, is a marked one.

Religion for both figures needs to be held as a very high ideal even for the sake of what such an ideal has in its effect on one's accomplishments in all areas, including science in its loftiest reaches. The creative not merely as an action, but as an ideal, is prominent in both Wordsworth and Whitehead . Yet the poet checks himself from time to time, even as does Whitehead, in order to keep far from the mere dreaming, or in the word of *The Prelude* the "phantasying" of an ideal.

Near the end of Chapter III of the earlier book we pointed out that Wordsworth expresses a belief that probably he would have been better off at Cambridge if he could have enjoyed a "freer pace" for his studies, and likewise Whitehead recognizes the educational advantages to be gained in a free pace in one's pursuit of the values that are to be desired. Still, both men, though they are critical, feel deeply what they owe to the university and to the world for what had been fortunately granted to them in the way of an education.

The substance of our first few chapters has been retrospectively touched upon and further amplified for the purpose of new insights because certain points with reference to it will have a special bearing upon what is to follow. But we must return for a moment to our thought about Wordsworth, Whitehead, and John Dewey and the fact that each person is within himself a memory. Surprisingly enough, Dewey has a sympathetic attitude toward Whitehead rather than an antagonistic one, as many people have thought. What was quoted from Dewey contained the idea that the manifold substance of our past is alive for us "again in memory."[13] There is, indeed, Dewey says, "a cloud of thoughts concerning similar things undergone in bygone days." This is part of our world of today, and it is what makes us human. For an animal, Dewey goes on, "each new doing or suffering stands alone." For a human being there are "reminiscences of what has gone before," which are reminders "of other things." Thus, Dewey stresses the fact that we live "in a world of signs and symbols."

One may wonder why Wordsworth and Whitehead are here brought into close contact with the reflections of John Dewey, often held to be almost a mechanist. But the point is that we are all closer to each other than we think. Dewey's phrases concerning our "reminiscences of what has gone before," along with his other remarks that we have quoted, remind us, then, of Wordsworth's view that the individual is a memory to himself. In the uses of memory, imagination has supreme importance. With imagination, art as symbol comes to mind, and religion has its place. "A flame," Dewey remarks, near the passage from which we have quoted, "is not merely something which warms or burns, but is a symbol"; it reminds one of "the household" and of manifold emotions. But more: aside from its other features, "it is the hearth at which one worships," and with the latter phrase in Dewey our thoughts are brought back to Whitehead.

The quoted remarks are drawn from the beginning of Dewey's volume, but in the end of the work he returns to the theme of memory or what we store up from the world, or through our "way of envisaging life."[14] Our stored ideas and beliefs, colored by the imagination, finally "take on religious value." Continuing, he refers to a "religious spirit" which thus becomes "revivified," and some five sentences thereafter he has the further remark that philosophy has had for several centuries "the problem of adjusting the dry, thin and meagre scientific standpoint with the obstinately persisting body of warm and abounding imaginative beliefs."[15]

The transcending or idealizing factors in life appear in his references to what in experience is ever-changing in "possibility, progress, free movement and infinitely diversified opportunity," and this element in the new, more completely open-ended kind of life has been especially notable in "science." It may unfortunately at times have the tendency of a "once-for-all ordered and systematized" view which is paralyzing to man; as long as this crystallized type of thought is ruling one dogmatically, Dewey adds, "the ideas of mechanism and matter will lie like a dead weight upon the emotions, paralyzing religion and distorting art." These words of Dewey have the ring of the very expressions of Whitehead; but they are of course completely original in their author. Later, on the same page, Dewey refers to "the emotional force, the mystic force, one might say, of communication of the miracle of shared life and shared experience" which needs to be "felt," and he suggests that when it is felt "the hardness and crudeness of contemporary life will be bathed in the light that never was on land or sea."

Dewey in this volume clearly has an aspiring, a decidedly religious impulse, it would seem. The words referring to "the light which never was on land or sea" are drawn from "Elegiac Stanzas" by Wordsworth, which the poet wrote in the year in which he finished the 1805 *Prelude*. Dewey's use of the words "mystic" and "miracle" in our last quoted passage is especially notable for the atmosphere that he is attempting to create.

And we may note that Dewey elsewhere speaks approvingly of the breadth of Whitehead's conception of nature which "authorizes us to carry over the main conclusions of physical science into explanation and description of mysterious and inexplicable traits of experience marked by 'consciousness.' "[16] He comments, further, in criticism of "dogmatic mechanistic materialism" and shows admiration for Whitehead. Dewey admires the way Whitehead "opens the road to free observation" of all kinds — "free, that is, from a rigid frame of preconceptions." Dewey, in some of his writings is, then, a helpful commentator on Whitehead and he aids us toward insights into Wordsworth also.

But we must go beyond Dewey at this point and refer once more to Norman Kemp Smith, who suggests his view that nature in the end reveals herself "as Super Nature"[17] — he does not hesitate to use this word, though he does use it somewhat questioningly. A few sentences later in the same work (the volume to which Whitehead expressed indebtedness), Kemp Smith speaks of "Nature" as a force "engaged in bringing about the knowing mind"; not only does nature bring into existence the mind of humanity, but she herself is further engaged "in responding to the faculties with which she endows it." The personification in the use of "she" as applied to "Nature" is Norman Kemp Smith's.

We have spoken earlier of Wordsworth's rejection of any belief in materialism: the idea that nature is non-mysterious. In Kemp Smith's use of the Whiteheadian philosophy (and he does use it), this very conception of anti-materialism finds an important place. He draws an idea, for example, from Whitehead in regard to time: a notion which includes a criticism of "a trimness" about time and the sense of a "vanished past" and a "non-existent future" along with "inert matter."[18] Whitehead, as quoted by Kemp Smith, says, "This trimness" takes us back to the medieval: it "ill accords with brute fact." Whitehead urges a theory which "admits a greater

49

ultimate mystery"; what he has in mind may not be altogether clear, but it is helpful to see a correlated idea expressed by him: "The passage of nature which is only another name for the creative force of existence has no narrow ledge of definite instantaneous present within which to operate."[19] Time plays its part here. It is a great ultimate mystery that Whitehead is concerned with, a profundity which transcends any insight that materialistic theory could possibly provide.

At the end of our "Introductory Foreword" we noticed Whitehead's thought concerning the fact that "a certain excessiveness seems a necessary element in all greatness." We as thinkers need to "devote ourselves," at times, "beyond what would be warranted by the analysis of pure reason." Was this true of Wordsworth? It seems true as he presents to us what was happening to him in existent time, when he was gazing at his university world

> roving as through a Cabinet
> Or wide Museum (throng'd with fishes, gems,
> Birds, crocodiles, shells) where little can be seen
> Well understood, or naturally endear'd,
> Yet still does every step bring something forth
> That quickens, pleases, stings; and here and there
> A casual rarity is singled out . . . (652—)

All this "gaudy Congress" brought to the poet a state in which one's "head turns round and cannot right itself"; so it is that events in time often represent a problem involving a "gay confusion" yet little in the way of "wise longings and but little love" — this last being most important of all. For Wordsworth and for Whitehead, love is of great moment in the development of a philosophy, as we shall see in our following chapters.

Footnotes

1. *Symbolism, Its Meaning and Effect*, p. 43.
2. *Ibid.*, p. 44.

3. *Ibid.*, p. 47.
4. *Ibid.*, p. 48.
5. *Process and Reality*, p. 268.
6. *Symbolism, Its Meaning and Effect*, p. 55.
7. *Ibid.*, p. 57.
8. Norman Kemp Smith, *The Credibility of Divine Existence*, ed. A. J. Porteus, R. D. Maclennan, and G. E. Davie (London: Macmillan, 1967), p. 196. See also Smith, *Prolegomena to an Idealist Theory of Knowledge.*
9. *Symbolism, Its Meaning and Effect*, p. 57. Here Whitehead refers to Norman Kemp Smith.
10. *Ibid.*, p. 77.
11. *Ibid.*, p. 19.
12. Dewey, *Reconstruction in Philosophy*, Enlarged Edition (Boston: Beacon Press, 1948), p. 1. See also the edition of 1920; probably Whitehead was influenced by Dewey, and Dewey was influenced by Whitehead.
13. *Ibid.*, p. 1.
14. *Ibid.*, p. 210.
15. *Ibid.*, p. 211. Dewey's remarks here serve almost to clarify the ideas of Whitehead.
16. Dewey in *The Philosophy of Alfred North Whitehead*, ed. Paul Arthur Schilpp, p. 648.
17. Norman Kemp Smith, *Prolegomena to an Idealist Theory of Knowledge*, p. 232.
18. *Ibid.*, p. 157. The words are Whitehead's as quoted by Smith.
19. *The Concept of Nature*, p. 73. Norman Kemp Smith does not quote this sentence, but he is working from the passage in which it appears, and he has it in mind.

Chapter IV

Retrospect of Summer Vacation after Wordsworth's First Cambridge Year as Related to Philosophy

Time is connected with the existential and can be understood philosophically, in one way, in relation to that which is existent, as we have seen thus far in *The Prelude*. We can observe this fact once again in Book Four of the poem where we see Wordsworth on his first summer vacation after his initial year in college. When he returned to the "Heights of Kendal" — the beautiful region which anyone who visits northwestern England can still view appreciatively — he crossed the "Moor" and found himself overlooking "Windermere." Thereupon he "bounded down the hill" and shouted loudly to "the old Ferryman" who, in turn, gave the young Wordsworth "a cordial welcome." After leaving the boat the excited St. John's collegiate proceeded in "a short hour's walk" until, having made a final turn, he came directly upon "the snow-white Church" of his boyhood region. Entering the house where he had lived he greeted his loving foster-mother who perused him, perhaps holding him out at arm's length, "with a Parent's pride." He thinks of her directly and of an existent time within her experience, her gradual changes in "little daily growth," and her contentment with her lot, a person

> by the strangers to thy blood
> Honour'd with little less than filial love. (27 –)

Moving now in our retrospectus toward a consideration of some things that appeared in Chapter IV of our previous volume, we may remark that Wordsworth, who had discussed education earlier in connection with his first Cambridge University study, returns again to the subject more broadly. He thinks of an ideal in self-growth which, as we found, is paralleled in Whitehead. Matter concerning education is presented in this part of *The Prelude* undoubtedly because of the poet's feeling of its extreme importance. It might be imagined that one could penetrate to the most vital substance of the world-views of Wordsworth and Whitehead without considering education as related to philosophy. But this would be wrong. We need not go so far as to suggest that education is central in every person's philosophical outlook, but we can surely say that it is very important in both of our figures. In their works, certainly, there is a very pervasive concern about education.

As to Whitehead we may note that symbolism itself can be connected with learning and can be brought to bear upon philosophy in its relation to education. Our Chapter IV in *About Wordsworth and Whitehead*, however, moved into a variety of things other than the problems of education. Wordsworth's interest in symbolism appears in the reference to the poet's self as a "brook" as well as in the breadth of his vision when he refers to the "faces" that he remembered (on his return home from Cambridge) including the face of a dog, formerly a "rough terrier" but now changed because of his life in a new service. A dog, like a human being, can perform service and is indeed part of what we call society or community. The dog is not a faceless being. Whitehead has views somewhat similar to this in his broad imaginative visions of the world of human beings and the world of animals, though again like Wordsworth he also possesses a reach into the universe of organic forms including rock and hill. The poet, as we know, was a figure in a highly imaginative creative period which Whitehead refers to as an important "triumph" in the history of humanity.

Somewhat before the mid-stage of Chapter IV in our previous book the point is made that Wordsworth and Whitehead are both interested in the process of self- origination. Imagination and existential time are involved in this. The poet speaks of a transmutation of self; that is, he became "self-transmuted" and his soul, he says, seemed as if "in the presence of her God." Wordsworth at this time felt that he had attained an awareness of self-perception which led to a sense of peace. Here the question of self-perception connected with peace becomes significant in its relation to the needs of all human beings and the necessity of giving them justice. An important problem related to education and peace is that of the essential rights of human beings, and this matter is referred to near the middle of our earlier Chapter IV. It is a question of vital significance to both Wordsworth and Whitehead. The conception of such rights for humanity developed in the world gradually, and the poet relatively early in his career was wrestling with the problem.

The period in which Wordsworth lived contributed to his concern for human rights. And here we may naturally think of

Whitehead, and his remark that during "the last quarter of the eighteenth century, Democracy was born" — this birth occurring in the very formative period of Wordsworth's life. Whitehead, of course, does not maintain that democracy came fully into existence during the closing years of the eighteenth century. A long development obviously lay ahead. Refinements in the process of democratic growth still are before us. But in Wordsworth's thought the incipient spirit of a full democratic brotherhood is apparent. Along with this spirit of brotherhood there is also in Wordsworth, as in Whitehead, the aspiration to work toward some grand end. This recognition of the height to which one may strive under a variety of circumstances needs, of course, to be reconciled somehow with a strong, almost paradoxical democratic belief in human leveling.

Some persons would say that aspiration and leveling are irreconcilable. Here we have a problem to which the philosopher Newton Stallknecht has devoted attention. There is a danger, he believes, that the democratic philosophy may produce a harmful effect. There is a hazard that through a conviction of the importance of human leveling one may "come to suspect even his own strength."[1] But the essential Wordsworth, in the period of the 1805 *Prelude*, does not make this mistake. There is no tendency in the poet — or in Whitehead — toward a leveling into mediocrity. A related theme, dealt with in Chapter IV of our previous book, appears in Wordsworth's interest in the philosophy of change. Later in the chapter, reference is made to Whitehead's perspectivism which involves an active realization of the importance of past, present, and future, in their interrelationships. For both figures a live sense of change, time, and the future must be reckoned with. It has to be accepted not stoically but with broad perceptiveness and insight into what is happening.

For Whitehead our evanescent perceptions reveal so much data that difficulties in conceptualizing arise in the seeming chaos of evanescence connected with past, present, and future. As we consider change, there may be a danger that the fluid character of all experience will be destroyed and that there may arise in our thought a separateness of things which can result in a relatively crude philosophy. The word "crude" is Whitehead's term. Such a crude, crystallized kind of world-view is being criticized by Norman Kemp Smith when he speaks of a certain form of naturalism. He has in mind those naturalists who refuse "to accept, as compatible with naturalistic categories, any mode or form of transcendence"[2]; indeed, transcendence itself, as he believes, may well be regarded as "a process which in general type is co-extensive" with natural physical reality. We have used the words of Kemp Smith as lending themselves to the purpose of our present context. The union of mind and nature is important in his philosophy, as it is in the thought of both Wordsworth and Whitehead. On this point of such a union of mind and nature John Dewey himself quotes Whitehead appreciatively: "It is a false dichotomy to think of Nature *and* Man. Mankind is that factor *in* Nature which exhibits in its most intense form the plasticity of Nature."[3] A philosophy which assumes the existence of a fragmented or atomistic world tends to reject the kind of togetherness which is characteristic of Whitehead's thought.

Near the close of Chapter IV in our earlier book, *About Wordsworth and Whitehead,* we referred to the importance of the existent human being as a person, and to the fact that in this tendency toward a kind of personalism the individual deserves to be valued in and for himself. In a sense we are thinking here of an event-full time (not, so much, a "timeless truth"); "we can still find a growing human truth," as the philosopher John Wild says, "in the changing human world of man."[4] Cox's expression for time, "an arrow in uncertain flight" — which we have quoted in our footnote — is a strikingly effective one. In his book *Turning East* the view of the creative self, as related to a philosophy of time, is traced to the Hebrews; many passages in the Old Testament reveal the working of the philosophy of time, and this active viewing of time comes down of course to later religious and philosophical thought.

The importance of the human being as a person, valued in and for himself, valued not merely as a duty but as a manifestation of love, represents a theme which has a place of significance in Wordsworth and Whitehead. This theme involves a doctrine of togetherness, to use an expression reminiscent of part of our own modern thought. A philosophy which assumes the existence of a fragmented or atomistic world tends to reject or feel uncomfortable with the doctrine of togetherness which is prominent in the conceptions of both men. But valuing a person in and for himself does not negate a large or cosmic philosophy. In the development of Wordsworth's highly personalized point of view presented throughout *The Prelude* we observe that a steady tendency toward broadening or expansiveness is characteristic of him. It is also characteristic of the personalism in Whitehead.

The dangers of a world-view centered upon separate private selves (in dubious self-realizations) receive emphatic emphasis in the philosophy of John Wild, as a form of dominant rationalism in the Western world. "In fact," he declares, "every influential ethics that has been formulated in our intellectual history is some version of self-realization."[5] Here he stresses the point that such an ethics is reduced to "objective analysis and calculation." Love is not apparent. In the ethics of Wordsworth and Whitehead this markedly calculating factor is by no measure of means a principle. Warmth of human relationships is dominant in their ethical thought. Sociality is the requirement, but not a sociality based on a self-serving self-orientation which is forgetful of our fellows in their human need. An example of such human need appears near the end

58

of Book Four in *The Prelude* where Wordsworth tells of encountering late at night a worn-out person, who

> in his very dress appear'd
> A desolation, a simplicity
> That seem'd akin to solitude. (417 —)

Let us imagine such a person exemplifying the human being unattached to any other — representing, indeed, a kind of ultimacy of "solitude" or desolateness, as Wordsworth has it. We could imagine ourselves, also, about to pass by on the other side, figuratively speaking. This is so often the case in our human frailty that it seems almost universal; we at first do not want to do anything about the situation. We feel within ourselves a mingling of "fear and sorrow." We are often even afraid of the person who is in distress. Such was the "specious cowardice" which Wordsworth describes. Nevertheless, let us imagine that we overcome this specious cowardice. We address the person and perceive that he is a worn-out soldier when he responds to our word with a more or less automatic salute; that is, "with a lean and wasted arm" he raises his hand to his cap. This is the situation that Wordsworth would have us imagine. Here we see personalism in his point of view. Thus we hear that the soldier had served "in the Tropic Islands" and was now trying to make his way home. Nearby it was not possible to gain help for

> all were gone to rest; the fires all out;
> And every silent window to the Moon
> Shone with a yellow glitter. (451 —)

What was to be done? The upshot of it all was that together (and here we can imagine ourselves as part of the experience) they measure back their way to the home of a laborer, a "Friend," as it happens, of the poet. The exhausted soldier was thus given a place to stay, as well as food. So it develops at the

59

end of Book Four, the poet's "Comrade" — for this is the way Wordsworth now thinks of him — was given "comfort" and the poet made the long way back toward his own home. A personalistic human solidarity is emphasized, but there are other forms of human solidarity in the effect upon us of the reading which we do, and this reading can be — or in part always becomes — social in its effect. To this theme we shall turn in the next chapter.

Footnotes

1. Stallknecht, *Strange Seas of Thought* (Durham: Duke University Press, 1945), p. 227. His other works also are important.

2. *Prolegomena to an Idealist Theory of Knowledge*, p. 6.

3. Dewey quoting in *The Philosophy of Alfred North Whitehead*, ed. Paul Arthur Schilpp, p. 647; Dewey is quoting from Whitehead's *Adventures of Ideas*, p. 99.

4. Wild, *Human Freedom and Social Order* (Durham: Duke University Press, 1959), p. 151. Note also time as "an arrow in uncertain flight" with a self which cannot be crystallized because, for it, "no archetypal pattern exists." Here we quote from Harvey Cox, *Turning East* (New York: Simon and Schuster, 1977), p. 83.

5. *Ibid.*, p. 155. Perhaps this is an overstatement; we read a measure of love in Kant's writings and in his influence.

Chapter V

Retrospect Concerning Stored Learning as Related to Wordsworth and Whitehead

What can we think concerning the state of the world (with its Vietnam veterans and Indo-Chinese refugees); how are the feelings of an individual affected by existent national and wider political conditions? Near the close of the last chapter we were dealing with full-fleshed human reality; that is, through Wordsworth, we had been "turning to the world of lived experience," to use John Wild's expression, in *Human Freedom and Social Order*, and this is a kind of experience that our own "modern art and modern psychiatry are approaching each in its own way."[1] Should we now think of starving people in India as, in some sense, a responsibility, or is this human misery a matter of unimportance to us? The twentieth century has responded strongly to such questions and that response (perhaps not so strong a response as need be) is one of the factors giving rise to a new, a modern, existential approach. To some thinkers of our time the state of humanity now, or indeed in long past ages, has excited bewilderment, nausea, or despair. Wordsworth at the outset in Book Five of *The Prelude* speaks of the fact that even in his steadiest moods, when "reason" is foremost and when he tries to put "sorrow" in its proper perspective, in view of the "transitory" nature of "pain," he nevertheless "grieves" over the human condition. He is not thinking of a self-directed self-orientation here. Though the human being is, he says, a "paramount creature" — that is, in a very high state in one sense — the poet, looking even at the long and magnificent history of the race, nevertheless suffers grief. Why does he feel this strong emotion? It is, strangely enough, for the "palms" that have been positively gained by the person that he grieves; he says for these things actually achieved by the human being — by you —

> Through length of time by study and hard thought,
> The honours of thy high endowments, there
> My sadness finds its fuel. (7 —)

It is for the ultimate loss of everything that humanity creates — its literature, its science, its philosophy and its inward achievements of all kinds — that Wordsworth now feels distress. It seems that he believes our creations should themselves be immortal, and, if he accepts this, here he is close to Plato. He is close also to Whitehead. It is the problem of books and stored learning — what they mean to us — that he is facing. They contribute to us and to the long development of the race, a problem that Chardin in our time often pondered, for example, in *The Future of Man*, where, writing in 1949, he speaks of "a thinking envelope" which is now, and ever, being shaped round us or "being shaped round our planet"[2]; he holds that one should not think of this shaping as being merely plausible.

In a later essay he speaks of the "extension of this thinking network over the surface of the globe" and the fact that "Humanity might be wholly unique in its destiny and structural potentialities."[3] Wordsworth also thinks of that which is destined, though more broadly, and he is aware of the immensity of this thinking envelope, or stored learning, but for the moment he is struck by the fact of its ultimate fading into nothingness, a point which *should* impress twentieth-century thinkers as much as it does Wordsworth. But, while he stresses the question in its ultimacy, he is also concerned about the problem of extending upon earth and putting to use what has been referred to as the thinking network. This will be evident in our Chapter IX concerning his experience during the French Revolution. But for the moment we have before us the problem of mortality, as it is related to books and to human culture generally.

Can anything be said about the question, or ought we to ignore completely this aspect of mortality? Does philosophy itself or does religion in a measure help when we are confronted with the fact of such an ultimate and inclusive loss? We cannot attempt to give a complete answer to this philosophic question for the moment. Perhaps the answer, such as we can make, will be implied as we proceed. But we can ask now whether a partial answer has been given in John Wild's view concerning the self: that of "a *new self* barely born."[4] This is a point of view, he says, very different "from traditional theories of self-realization." In his philosophy the stress is placed upon an appreciation of the "sacrifice that is found in all human creation." A glorious view this — as he deems it — but it involves tragedy "for there is no human creation that can last, and in which we can find final rest." The parallel here to Wordsworth in the fifth book of *The Prelude* is striking.

Our present retrospectus has amplified in various ways

material in *About Wordsworth and Whitehead*. In the fifth book of the poet's *Prelude* he showed some embarrassment because he had presented so extended an account of the development of his mind and his attitude toward life. Before bringing the five-book form of *The Prelude* to a close, however, he felt the need to trace more carefully the importance of reading to his individual growth. At this point in our Chapter V of the volume *About Wordsworth and Whitehead* we made some reference to Whitehead's life-long interest in the work of Plato, and in doing so we turned to certain reflections on the self, or the "Psyche" concept in ancient Greece and in later times, particularly as it is referred to by Whitehead. The view of the philosopher and that of Wordsworth stresses self-giving rather than self-realization in the sense of a dominant and private self-concern. This self-giving is a point that John Wild emphasizes as a kind of clarion-call in the page to which we have referred, and thereafter, in *Human Freedom and Social Order*.

We have capitalized the word "Psyche" in making comments on Whitehead's conception of it because this is the usage that he most frequently follows. In modern thought the idea of the psychological self and the psyche appears importantly in such books as Erich Fromm's *Escape from Freedom*, and it is used in the very title of certain works, an example of which is Jung's *The Structure and Dynamics of the Psyche*. In a long section of the latter volume, the crucial point of the world is seen within the psychological self, for "not only is it the one great condition for the existence of the world at all," it is, indeed, "an intervention in the existing natural order, and no one can say with certainty where this intervention will finally end."[5] In taking this point of view one would not necessarily have to maintain a theory of absolute idealism. A philosophy of realism could be compatible with it.

In what sense could the psychological self, as here contemplated, be an intervention of importance in the natural order? One respect in which it has intervened appears in the suggestion by Jung in another context that psychology, more than any other non-material force, "demonstrates the spiritual transition from the classical age to the modern."[6] The ideas presented in parts of this volume may seem slightly extravagant when thought of in relation to Wordsworth and Whitehead, but some of them may serve to suggest the relationship of the philosopher's views (along with a number of differences) which are to be found occasionally in psychological conceptions today.

But a further Jungian example, provocative to thought, should be cited. In it reference is made to attempts "during the last three hundred years, to grasp the psyche" as "part and parcel of that tremendous expansion of knowledge which has brought the universe nearer to us in a way that staggers the imagination."[7] A later passage from the same writer stresses the fact that "all knowledge is the result of imposing some kind of order upon the reactions of the psychic system as they flow into our consciousness"; and he goes on even further to bring out the point that this "order" is one "which reflects" the action "of a *metapsychic* reality, of that which is in itself real."[8] These statements appear in a chapter entitled "On the Nature of the Psyche." The word which the author has italicized (*metapsychic*) may be troublesome, but it expresses the conception of broad and basically profound relations between psychology and philosophy. And it is such relations that also concern Whitehead.

Other modern psychologists could be quoted to provide a different emphasis; as one example, Erich Fromm stresses the "awareness" of individual separateness which "remained very dim over long periods of history."[9] There is a close relationship between the individual and "the natural and social world from which he emerged"; that is, though the human being was "partly aware of himself as a separate entity," he sensed, nevertheless, that he was "also part of the world around him." The

65

complexity of the relation between the individual and the many millions of other individuals (as well as between other forces) in the universe constitutes a story of importance in Buber. Erich Fromm has touched upon it in a variety of volumes. Something of the spirit of Fromm, when finally understood, may be suggested by two sentences from a quotation on the self, or the psyche, which he places at the head of a volume. The quotation addresses the psyche: "To thee alone we gave growth and development depending on thy own free will. Thou bearest in thee the germs of a universal life."[10]

Connections between Whitehead and modern psychology appear in the stress that the philosopher gives to the personalized self as it is related to a wider universe and to religious love. But we need only for the present mention Erich Fromm's conception of love (essentially *agape*) as related to the psychological self and a constructive spontaneity. For Fromm this love is to be conceived not as "the dissolution of the self in another person," nor is it "love as the possession of another person, but love as a spontaneous affirmation of others, as the union of the individual with others on the basis of the preservation of the individual self."[11]

We come thus to a world of "oneness," but "individuality is not eliminated." Here Buber again comes to mind. The "Psyche" conception in Whitehead can be related to self-integration in modern psychology in that one's most deeply-realized individuation can be thought of as in some respects coming from beyond that which is most *personal* in the selfhood. Every single person has the quality of a deeply-reaching selfhood. In the writing of Wordsworth this conception appears in the extended, the far-reaching relationship of the individual person to all things and, ultimately, to God. The recent modern psychological conception of the archetypal generally, or that hidden in the unconscious, has a connection with the thought of Whitehead, and it fits in also with that of Wordsworth.

Near the middle of Chapter V of our previous book we referred to the poet's continuing preoccupation with education.
There is a relationship, we suggested, between that subject and
philosophy, and this may be seen basically in the long process
and the potency of education in human development in the example of the individual or in the case of society most widely
viewed. Once again, as we move on in our reflection upon the
last part of the five-book *Prelude*, we can raise more extensive-
ly the question of the connection between education and
philosophy. And we will here call upon Dewey's thought in
regard to the ideas we have been developing. Not only does
Dewey say that the subject of education is important to
philosophy: in his view education is a matter of producing very
fundamental changes or establishing basic philosophic states
within the person.

In the generality of his educational theory, Dewey feels that
philosophy itself can be best brought to a definition through its
bearing upon education. He emphasizes his point by using
italics for certain concepts related to a world-view. Dewey indeed feels that philosophy of education can well become the
most central factor to be considered when attempting to attain
a total philosophical outlook. As he puts the matter,
"philosophy may even be defined *as the general theory*" that
one has with regard to "education."[12] And some three pages
later he emphasizes his point again: "The most penetrating
definition of philosophy which can be given is, then, that it is
the theory of education in its most general phases."[13] Some
twenty-five years later in commenting on the book in which
this statement appeared he did not change his emphasis.
Without going as far as Dewey goes, we can at any rate stress
strongly the basic conception of education (such as Wordsworth and Whitehead are both deeply concerned with) in its
fundamental relation to a world-view.

In the latter part of the five-book *Prelude* Wordsworth is
dealing, we have said, with the importance that books may

have in the growth of the individual. Here we may think of the question of self-identity, with its crises and depths. The *identity* is the deeper self. The conscious part of the self copes or learns to cope with actualities. We may clearly see the danger of attempting to crystallize the self, or to manipulate and form the individual from the outside. Manipulation deals with surface things. Recognition of this danger of manipulation appears in both the poet and Whitehead. The importance of the internalization of self, the deeper self, is given stress in Whitehead. "Life is an internal fact for its own sake, before it is an external fact relating itself to others."[14] Is the self something we are born with? His point is sometimes misunderstood in that it has been supposed that he denies the social significance of the self and the sociality of religion. But in his view the internalization of self can contribute to that which is social, and it is this that actually makes the social aspect of religion itself possible.

Our present summarizing remarks have sketched a few of the main points concerning the relationship between Wordsworth and Whitehead. A sense of the individual and his powerlessness, or his lost character, has often in our times received great stress. In opposition to this, in Wordsworth and Whitehead we find that emphasis is given to the ideas of self-power of a social kind, a point which appeared in the middle of Chapter III in our previous book and which is implied at certain stages in the discussion we presented in Chapter V of the volume. Whitehead, in thinking of education, mentions the importance of the attainment of power (without loss of constructive sociality) during one's childhood and in the period of youth.

Personal inner strength may be achieved under certain circumstances through the process of thinking and living. Such thought and life include for Whitehead, as we have said earlier, an appreciation not only of external things but also of "fully clothed feeling"; this is attainable through moving into the heart of whatever thing is experienced, or through what he calls ingression. The point has a relation to Buber and also to modern psychology which we have referred to earlier in the conception of the tremendously wide integration of the self through its many sources of personal value-experience. The bond with twentieth-century psychology is present not only in such experience, however, but also through certain values (bringing the "universe nearer to us") as it has been represented in *The Structure and Dynamics of the Psyche*.[15]

This can form a part of the extreme significance of process in our lives. "A gracious Spirit" is at work, according to Wordsworth, or it may be brought to operate, within human beings. But it is also a functioning force in the world outside ourselves. Something of this conception is developed by Whitehead in connection with the vision of religion which, as he says, may be recognized in the fact that the "reaction of human nature to the religious vision is worship."[16] For him, religion in history "fades and then recurs." He implies the importance of experience and the existential in this respect, in that when religion "renews its force, it occurs with an added richness and purity of content." Such is its evolution. It is clear that he is not thinking of mere religiosity as he presents his idea. During the year in which he expressed these thoughts and in the following years leading toward the writing of *Process and Reality* in 1929, he was increasingly concerned with thought of this kind. There is a parallel here to Jung.

Wordsworth's reference to the "gracious Spirit" which is at work in the world, and which is of assistance to human beings, is united with the question of what we should do to assist in the process of human development. And here again the matter of education arises in that only some favored few, it might be assumed, can make use of educational possibilities for such a purpose. To what extent ought we to make obeisance to elitism? Can society in a deterministic manner judge the individuals for whom paths should remain open toward what

69

Shakespeare has called "the wide world dreaming on things to come" — this is surely important. Whitehead quotes these words from Shakespeare in connection with "an analysis" he has given which he feels is "more concrete than that of the scientific scheme of thought," but which starts "from our own psychological field, as it stands for our cognition."[17]

But to return to the subject of the education which is needed for a modern world. As to this, both Wordsworth and Whitehead embrace the cause of humanity and recognize that human condition as being full of promise, provided only that the self is not exaggeratedly magnified and that the tendency toward mechanized results is not glorified in a way leading to stultification or to the unsocial. Whitehead, like Wordsworth, considers the mortal side of man, and consideration of mortality leads to his writing of an essay on "Immortality" which he produced at a late stage in his career. But in *Process and Reality* he cites the word "mortal" as giving rise to difficulties, and he says that before we could arrive at adequate results in dealing with the word, we would need much "metaphysical knowledge."[18] All of his thoughts in this respect are associated with creativity and the needs of *humanity* for its creative development. As we may say in moving toward the conclusion of our retrospective view of Chapter V in our previous book, he would have the human being gain access to the heavens, and this surely means that a whole vast area, in his perspective, lies before us.

Much in this way, Wordsworth speaks of the creativity in literature using reference to a vast, strange space like that of the "Heavens filled up with Northern lights"; the rarity of the lights, in that they are not to be seen from every point of vision on the globe, adds to the suggestiveness of the comparison. Dealing with such problems, or in trying to perceive them clearly, may entail something which at times may be about to escape us, or may seem in the poet's terms to be "nowhere, there, and everywhere"; this very perceiving could well include our seeing or trying to understand things that are, as Words-worth says, in multiple places. What he points out is that they need to be seen "everywhere at once." Thus he is thinking in terms of a split-second in time and also of the ultimate grandeur and vast extent of space.

It will be recalled that in Book Five of *The Prelude* the poet was thinking mainly of the profit to be derived from reading. But what we can gain from books springs from a wider reference to the world. In our total experience, if it is reflected upon, there is something deeper than that which is ordinarily sensed. This deeper quality referred to in *The Prelude* is sensed, Wordsworth says, in the "motions of the winds," and in this it is the divine that he has in mind. He is thinking of presences which, as he believes, at times seem to speak to us. Here we have in the poet's work a theme concerning clair-voyant factors in human experience. Similar factors having a somewhat eerie quality may be found in Whitehead in many places — for example, in his very large vistas and even in his conceptions about the method of extensive abstraction as it may work downward, in respect to a moment. It does this by what he calls "the law of convergence to simplicity by diminu-tion of extent."[19] Such a conception would involve moving downward through smaller and smaller fractional portions. Whitehead's mathematical background is a factor in his con-ception here. John Dewey felt that the mathematical had prob-ably an unfortunate effect in Whitehead's philosophy. But the validity of Dewey's view here is exceedingly doubtful.

The method of moving downward through smaller and smaller fractions (one phase of Whitehead's "extensive abstrac-tion") will appear more understandable, philosophically, through a wider reading of Whitehead. But now, as we look back, we may recall again Wordsworth's suggestion that a per-son is "a memory to himself" and we may assuredly rest our thought upon Whitehead's view concerning the idealizing tendency and its relation to internal "experiences" as "closely

71

connected with our imaginative reproduction of the actual experiences of other people, and also with our almost inevitable conception of ourselves as receiving our impressions from an external complex reality beyond ourselves."[20] There is an element of "good chance"[21] in the life of the theorist, according to Whitehead, and when he thinks of the theorist in this respect he does not mean "a man who is up in the clouds" (the philosopher's words) but rather a person who is concerned with events as they happen. "A successful theorist should be excessively interested in immediate events"; if he is not, "he is not at all likely to formulate correctly anything about them." In this way Whitehead emphasizes the importance of theory and the close and attentive utilization of actuality. And he adds, "Of course, both sources of science exist in all men."

In the fifth book of *The Prelude* Wordsworth had been thinking of the importance of books, but for the poet as for the philosopher the vitality of inner life as related to action and aspiration is the main objective. They might hesitate to refer to this in relation to "the kingdom of God,"[22] as Dewey surprisingly does in a somewhat similar context, but they would both stand with him in emphasizing the spirit of spontaneity in relation to the creativeness of any vital and profound individual and social living.

Footnotes

1. *Ibid.*, p. 238. The expression is John Wild's, but it is very applicable to Wordsworth. Wild uses the expression in a very different context, however, from that which we have here.
2. Pierre Teilhard de Chardin, *The Future of Man*, trans. by Norman Denny (New York: Harper and Row, 1964), p. 244. See also p. 176.
3. *Ibid.*, p. 246.
4. Wild, *Human Freedom and Social Order*, p. 174.
5. Carl G. Jung, *Collected Works*, second edition (Princeton: Princeton University Press, 1969), p. 217.
6. *Ibid.*, p. 159.
7. *Ibid.*, p. 168.
8. *Ibid.*, p. 171.

9. Fromm, *Escape from Freedom* (New York: Holt, Rinehart and Winston, 1941, 1964), p. 24.

10. Quoted by Fromm from Pico della Mirandola, *Ibid.*, p.v.

11. *Ibid.*, 261.

12. Dewey, *Democracy and Education* (New York: Macmillan, 1944, 1964), p. 328. The italics are his.

13. *Ibid.*, p. 331.

14. *Religion in the Making* (New York: Macmillan, 1926, 1930), pp. 15-16. Compare, in some modern psychologists, the notion that the self is something we are born with. See, for example, Jung.

15. See earlier references to Jung, *The Collected Works*, VIII, particularly referring to p. 168. Note also p. 32.

16. *Science and the Modern World*, p. 275.

17. *Ibid.*, p. 107. But note his objection in *Religion in the Making*, p. 123, to "the subconscious." He objects to "advocates of the uniqueness of religious experience." The words here quoted are from E. S. Ames, on whom Whitehead comments.

18. *Process and Reality*, p. 18. But in *Religion in the Making*, p. 123, he stresses the importance to religion of a situation involving "knowledge acquired when our ordinary senses and intellectual operations are at their highest pitch of discipline."

19. *The Concept of Nature*, p. 79.

20. Here Whitehead is dealing with the organization of our thought, *The Aims of Education*, pp. 160-161.

21. *Ibid.*, p. 155.

22. *Reconstruction in Philosophy*, p. 212.

Chapter VI

Retrospect: *The Prelude* Expanded — Cambridge, the Alps, and Philosophy

Late in Chapter IV we saw Wordsworth, at the end of his vacation, assisting a returned veteran soldier who appeared like a symbol of desolation. Now in the new section of *The Prelude*, at the beginning of Book Six, we find that the poet, having put behind him his home region in northwestern England, with its yellowed autumnal leaves, has returned to St. John's college at Cambridge University. The young man is not so "eager" as he had been when he left college for his trip home, but he definitely is "undepressed"; he is, indeed, in a state of anticipation as he looks forward in time. He thinks of the things ahead with something like happiness. The poet now entered his own university "Cell" (suggestive of St. John and religious devotion) intent upon "pleasant thoughts." In the new school year he "read more, reflected more," and, at the same time, developed a more complete sense of the spiritual importance of society and feeling.

Wordsworth recognized the value of skimming certain books and devoting to others very serious and deliberate attention. Here, in the poet's skimming of volumes, we may think of Whitehead's experience with the works of Hegel which he did not read with care but which might, he says, have somehow influenced him indirectly. How do you want such surface reading to benefit you? The problem of intention thus arises here. Wordsworth confesses his failure in following up in the work he felt he ought, according to his intention, to have covered. This tendency to let one's intentions move around in meaningless circles is a weakness which was recognized even in the period of medieval philosophy and later, for example, in Husserl. Intention can be a spiritual quality which leads to very vital action. But as a dead, unspirited, vacillating thing it becomes a fault. Though the poet was guilty of this fault in intention amounting even, he says, to "cowardice," he nevertheless continued (in his aspiration) to think of the career of the thoughtful, reflective poet.

Book Six contains a striking picture of an ash tree symbolically representative of creativeness. It is overgrown with ivy in the summer and made resplendent with frost in the winter. Looking at this tree, the young poet felt the call of a very daring imagination drawing him toward natural and also toward "human Forms"; he perceived in the tree a suggestion of the special powers of which humanity is capable. Wordsworth thinks even of the symbolic which is far from the practice of the creative writer — that is, he thinks of the nonpoetic in symbolism. Many levels of the symbolic are of moment. Whitehead, too, stresses the symbolic and the wide importance of the sign (or semiotic) factor as well as the dangers in it. Our very evolution is dependent upon its many complex aspects and also upon the artistic or the aesthetic. It is related also to the daring, the adventurous.

Wordsworth sees a lack in himself as a poet in that when he was a student, and also somewhat later, he was a better judge of thoughts than of the language of poetry. We may at first doubt this. But if he is right in this view of himself it would seem that his basic talent in his youthful stage is drawing him toward philosophy. He sees a danger in the slavish classical education he has known (in its concentration on the isolated word rather than upon broad meanings), a weakness in the training of the classicist which Whitehead also observes. And here we may recall Wordsworth's famous remark about those who "murder to dissect"; despite this statement about the murderousness of dissection he recognized the value of a study that involves very close scrutiny of things. A view of totality (including dissection) is important.

Education as he thinks of it is, for all practical purposes, philosophy and unity. Our intellectual and spiritual growth, including the early or late self-education which occurs, is vital to a person's philosophy. The importance, moreover, of the background of scientific appreciation (in Wordsworth and Whitehead) should never be minimized, even while we see their approach toward the universal. The universal should, however, be thought of as something which we can work toward as a limit rather than as an intellectually attainable actuality. The word which stresses universality could here be placed in quotation marks except that such marks could lead one to slight the real value and significance of the universal; language is imperfect and has need of flexibility in use, as the poet and the philosopher well see. Still, in the thought of both, the divine itself can be approached as a limit when we cannot reach it as anything like an arithmetical fact given in performing an action in multiplication — for example, the multiplication of fractions whether small or of considerable size, including those that could help us reach to the moon and place human beings upon it.

Here we may be reminded of the thought of both Wordsworth and Whitehead concerning the transcendent which was touched upon shortly after the middle of Chapter VI in our previous volume, *About Wordsworth and Whitehead*. In this connection of the transcendent the philosopher is concerned with the "fluent," or with those things that flow. With respect to this neither he nor Wordsworth would minimize the particular. Both would, of course, eagerly move toward the larger aspects of matters; they would not be distressed by the flow, or the seeming perishing, the transiency of things in time. But they would not magnify unduly an absolutistic perspective. The importance of the personal as applied to this is never lost in the poet or in Whitehead. Neither would wish to lose sight of that intimate aspect of life. We may note, however, Wordsworth's appreciation of the "Schoolmen" — that is, the Scholastics — and the fact that Whitehead, also, does not lose sight of their contribution.

Is there a connection of the personal and the universal when Wordsworth at the end of his third Cambridge year thought of the Alps? He and a friend decided at this time to take a summer's walking tour across France and Switzerland and on into Italy. In the sequel, or perhaps even before, the Alps become significant to Wordsworth in their suggestion of aspiration. He found at a certain moment, when he wished to experience the feeling of reaching the topmost point in the divide, he had actually already crossed over that stage *without realizing it*. He uses italics with reference to this. There is no doubt that the aspect of aspiration which he has in mind is here being presented symbolically.

Sometimes when we have the good chance to reach a thing with which we are working, or about which we are experiencing something significant, we proceed fortunately, as the poet suggests, without "a struggle to break through." So it was

78

in the Alps. In Wordsworth's case it is imagination which is taking over, so he tells us, but that moment of imagination had, of course, a background of conscious and unconscious preparation. He had attained, at a fortunate moment in the mountains, a perception of an "invisible world," and he related the idea of imagination to hope and to approaches toward infinitude, along with effort. Peace thereupon also comes to him although this does not mean that tumult will not continue to be a part of the ongoing process in which he must live. He has a sense of moving forward (and here he takes recourse to the symbolic) as if he were a "sunbeam" or a breath of air.

There is something perhaps of Whitehead's feeling for the symbolic that appears in Wordsworth. So at least we can come to understand it as we read their works in conjunction. Neither Wordsworth nor Whitehead accepts a frozen view of things; they are wary of the crystallization of thought. Both, like Hegel, are possessed of an activity-principle and a multifariousness that can lead at times almost violently to new thoughts and new things.

We have spoken earlier about time in experiential terms as related to events; so Wittgenstein thought of it. And in Wordsworth, too, time is exemplified in event-full happenings again and again in The Prelude. But the existent happenings of the poet's experience were both outward and inward. He was not "a mean pensioner" on what is purely external, or on what is a matter of mere materialism, during his experience in the Alps. It was not simply the "outward forms" that dominated him when he was confronted with that "magnificent region." In the end, as he says, whatever else he "saw, or heard, or felt" acted upon him as "a stream" flowing "into a kindred stream," or like an energizing "gale" moving him forward; thus the things he saw and heard and felt

> did administer
> To grandeur and to tenderness, to the one

Directly, but to tender thoughts by means
Less often instantaneous . . . (675 —)

The factor of tenderness is suggestive of an important aspect of Whitehead's philosophy just as it finds its place in the poet. But there is, on the other hand, a contrasting matter connected with war, in the passing of European troops that Wordsworth now sees from time to time round about him. There was a sense that a new "glorious time" had come, in that the evidences of French and other revolutionary action were now visibly under way. A feeling of triumph was in the air, which could be seen in the faces of people, who expressed without words or in "common language" of the eyes, their exultant hopes. Wordsworth's pure joy in the face of these circumstances was, he says, like that which is felt when we hear the "Blackbird's whistle in a vernal grove."

All this, as he makes clear, showed that he really as yet knew little of "social life" and its complex and painful aspects. Time is unfolding for him, however, and people, in relation to time and its developments, will be seen more fully when he is flung into the midst of myriad complexities, which we shall observe in the next chapter, in London, and thereafter in renewed and vital experience in France during later aspects of the Revolution.

Chapter VII

Wordsworth's Thought in Relation to Whitehead: the Impact of London

Wordsworth's feeling in regard to the variousness of the world — its kaleidoscopic character — parallels Whitehead's nonstatic sense of things, we have seen, but it is in our thought of the period of the poet's residence in London that this variousness comes most prominently before us. We often tend wrongly to think of him as a person who was concerned almost exclusively with external nature, but the excitement of being in a great city also moves him deeply. It is true that in his earlier stages nature in the country wins his almost complete love. But he was to become later, perhaps somewhat ambivalently, a lover of the multifarious city, a lover of crowds.

This fact grew out of his increasingly warm affection for his fellow human beings. But there are other possible reasons for his preoccupation with the city. To see this we must go beyond what Morris Janowitz calls the "romantic aspirations of city dwellers,"[1] and the best approach to the poet's new feeling will be to confront our problem with a generally questioning attitude, not with hasty preconceptions as to romanticism: for example, the view that the essence of romanticism is escape into the country.

Why, then, was Wordsworth attracted to the city? More broadly, we may ask, why are people drawn to cities? It is not enough to say that the poet was drawn to the largest metropolis of his nation because he wanted to go where the action is, any more than to say that Whitehead was drawn from Cambridge to London for such a reason. But life in the great city affected both men markedly. It is true that, once in a city, there is a tendency of social psychology where people move toward those places where others are crowding. As a poet, however, Wordsworth was seeking new insight into life — he needed an understanding of a more nearly total world. London could help in this. He was attracted to the great city undoubtedly by other factors, but for the present it will be enough for us to see him in the city, and to observe the things which receive his response. His writing in Book Seven of The Prelude is a type of the "expansive literature" to which we have referred in some previous chapters.

Wordsworth suggests something of the contrast or antithesis between country and city as he opens his "Residence in London" portion of The Prelude in a relaxed or indulgent mood, drawing upon the pleasure that he takes in a complex associationism. He thinks first of an earlier time, five years in the past, when he was on the outskirts of Bristol — then one of England's two greatest cities — and he describes the "animating breeze" which he felt outside the walls of the town. He associates his feeling of freedom at that time with the freedom that he feels at the present moment of writing. Now, living in the northwest part of England, his sense of untrammeled joy in the country presages a renewal of imagination and of confidence in the poetry he is hoping to produce. This joy that he savors stands in contrast to his former uncertainty. Heretofore he had a feeling that he was proceeding somewhat inadequately in his *Prelude* task of personal psychological analysis. It is evident that he felt the need to get on toward the experience of his growth after having "bade" good-bye "for ever" to the private life of "gownèd Students"; he has now, indeed, to have a far different life in the city — thus in *The Prelude* he recaptures in memory the feeling he had at the point of leaving Cambridge. For his new venture in experience he uses, somewhat strangely, the image of living in a "vagrant tent" as

A casual Reveller and at large, among
The unfenc'd regions of society. (61 —)

The private, or perhaps introspective nature of the vocation of a student is in this portion of *The Prelude* contrasted with a life that takes one out into the vagrant, casual, and unprotected existence in a wider world. The unexpected "tent" image that he uses is of interest, suggesting as it does something of a free frontier of experience, as compared to consciously organized civil life in a metropolis. At the same time it prepares us, perhaps, for the disorganization of the city and of the self that he was to encounter. Under these circumstances he made his way to London. It was a time when he felt in no way fenced in or restricted by the requirements of earning a living or by the necessity of attaining status. He was, rather, released "from all ambition personal"; this was a state that suited his aim, which was to become a serious, reflective poet.

As Wordsworth proceeds in the development of his subject it is evident that he has no special theory of the city. Nevertheless, he is not completely ingenuous: he presents in his somewhat analytical portrayal of the things that are before

83

him, dual, three-fold, or at times multifarious modes of observation. If we reflect on the situation at the beginning of our
own century, recalling large-city tenements and the cubicles
where many people spent their sleeping hours, we may recap-
ture in our minds something comparable to the situation that
Wordsworth, with very little money, was moving into. People
in American tenements (we are thinking of a time a century
later than Wordsworth's period of writing) did not by any
stretch of imagination have a home. They had an "abode"
which they accepted at the close of the day in sufferance. Their
real life, like the poet's earlier in London, was spent elsewhere.
The "abode" was regarded for the moment as a place where
they could hang hats or a few rudimentary garments. They
spent their waking hours within the external city itself.
Sociologists in our time have thought of this dormitory existence[2] of the masses in a city and have often like Wordsworth
so described it. In London he was a "transient," being
satisfied, as he says

> my abode to fix
> Single in the wide waste, to have a house
> It was enough (what matter for a home?)
> That own'd me; living chearfully abroad,
> With fancy on the stir from day to day,
> And all my young affections out of doors. (75 —)

All this reveals the aspect of the sociology of the city that
Wordsworth learns to understand. London was a place where
he had a mere "abode," as he emphasizes. His dwelling place
was housing and no more. His whole life was wrapped up in his
psychological affect-experiences beyond his mere dwelling.
What living he was doing occurred "out of doors." We would
not say that he was a forerunner of modern social and
psychological thinkers, but it is evident that he was perceptive:
his social and psychological insight here and elsewhere provides a useful ballast for his broad philosophical *tendency*.

In considering London Wordsworth proceeds to his some-what analytical portrayal of the things that are before him, in-cluding at times a shock technique in which contrasting ideas are implicit. Sometimes triads of confusion rather than dual effects of contrast occur in his presentation of what he has observed. More often, however, we see a kind of multi-farious-ness in his thought, comparable to that with which a social thinker in our own time is faced, for example, in considering the modern population expansion and the collisions of various races or kinds of people — or the competition of cities, or of those who are within them, for glory or gain. We now even contrast cities themselves; the study of them becomes for the modern sociologist a great part of his thought and indeed of his vocation. Wordsworth, however, in thinking of cities at times uses an allusive method where a sociologist would be ex-plicit.

In our last chapter we saw that symbolic reference plays an important part in Wordsworth, and that in Whitehead all thought is connected with it. Allusion is part of this, and it can operate backward as well as forward; for example, the various phenomena associated with a vast aggregation of houses and people in close association serve to symbolize for us a number of things, among them the word "city" itself. And in turn the word "city" can be used to call forth the phenomena we have just cited. Whitehead gives as an example of backward and forward symbolic reference the phenomena of a forest and the word "forest" itself.[3]

In The Prelude we can also cite the symbolic allusiveness of the mention Wordsworth makes of Alcairo, Babylon, London, Persepolis, and "Cities ten month's journey deep" within the wildernesses of a continent beyond our first-hand experiences. The palace-city of Persian Persepolis, more than five thousand feet high among the clouds, may call to our mind the "veritable forest of hundreds of pillars, each one 66 feet high," carrying by repute "the ceiling of the king's throne room, which was lavishly decorated with gold."⁴ Indeed the throne itself was "arched over by a golden canopy." If the reader does not know of ancient Persepolis, his imagination will carry allusions of various kinds connected with one or another of the places Wordsworth mentions as "golden Cities": Babylon might well serve as an example of symbolism to those who know the literature of Judaism or of Christianity.

There is the problem also in this part of *The Prelude* of appearance, or "some beams of glory," as against reality. Before Wordsworth had traveled to London, the city had seemed to him a fairy place filled with anticipatory visions some of which — for example, that concerning the Lord Mayor, whom he mentions — may well symbolize hopes he had for his own future

> Dreams hardly less intense than those which wrought
> A change of purpose in young Whittington,
> When he in friendlessness, a drooping Boy,
> Sate on a Stone, and heard the Bells speak out
> Articulate music. (113 —)

The sense of wonder is a prominent feature of Wordsworth's poetry, and this appears strikingly in his feeling with regard to Whittington and the city, though the solid achievement of Whittington as mayor is also in his mind. This latter is a part of Wordsworth's realistic practicality. The ambivalence of his affection for London can be noted, however, in his horror — or perhaps bafflement — when he thinks of the actual city as a place where people live as "next-door neighbors" but being perpetually separate "and knowing not each other's names." Wordsworth had been in London on a visit two years earlier, but his expectation was still alive with impressions — the "proud" bridging of the river, the endless streets, the "Churches numberless," sculptures, the "flowery gardens," all these impressions followed by throngs of other things to which he makes allusion. London was immense, a city of almost a

86

million crowded and teeming people in the period of his visits there, when he was perusing it like a book, or studying it closely "day by day," as a familiar embodiment expressive of man's hopes, dreams, and follies. Ethical considerations are in the background here we shall see.

The city's motleyness does not escape him. But there is "keen and lively pleasure" in the view he has, even of those things that he in part regrets or that arouse in him strong "disappointment"; the city, regardless of its state, somehow had to be accepted. It ruled for the moment as king over his mind. Certain things were (one could not gainsay them), and in some sense when we think of the long story of man's development they had to be. Indeed, one could here consider the use of the "ought," and Wordsworth does not hesitate to reflect upon the choice of this word and finally to accept it. These things *ought* to be. The whole problem can also be connected with Whitehead's conception of the immanence of "the present" and his doctrine of "the necessities to which the future must conform."[5] Our creativity is of course connected with and hampered by the things of the past that are as they "ought" to be — that is, within the necessities under which we operate.

Do we, out of necessity, create useful fictions in our experience? What part of our experience is played by our expectations; can we accurately copy Hume's "impressions" that come to us, as Whitehead with some adaptation would have us seek to do? This kind of thinking is incipient in Wordsworth and something like it he on his own part would attempt, though things that are unnumbered "half seem" to be the works of "fancy." We have by implication the problem of the dreamer — which is the dream and who is the dreamer? Often Wordsworth's expectation is surpassed by the actuality with its

> quick dance
> Of colours, lights and forms, the Babel din
> The endless stream of men, and moving things,
> From hour to hour the illimitable walk

Still among streets with clouds and sky above,
The wealth, the bustle and the eagerness . . . (156 —)

Wordsworth is concerned about things which are inexorable. He was almost overwhelmed by the "colours, lights and forms" as well as by sense impressions of various sorts. There was much more in London: the "pamper'd Steeds," the din (there are recurring references to roaring sounds), the kaleidoscopic character of events, the constant movement. In his earlier years, living in the country, he had been much out of doors; now, in the city, it would seem that he spent scarcely any waking moment in closed rooms. We observe his love of the city's manifold activities (comparable to Whitman's enthrallment with his Manhattan) including, as Wordsworth pictures it

the sturdy Drayman's team
Ascending from some Alley of the Thames
And striking right across the crowded Strand
Till the fore Horse veer round with punctual skill . . .
(167 —)

In a sense everything is solid, tangible. But viewed in another way all that the poet sees is appearance, now seen now gone. Transiency rules. The energy of the city on the one hand and the weariness of the people on the other, the "Comers and the Goers," face turned toward face — or turned away, "face after face" — and the "dazzling" objects observed in the windows of "shop after shop" — these are things that he sees. Always there is implied the question of meaning. We may well wonder as he wonders, What *is* the city? Before we are finished we may feel that we are interpreters.

External "Symbols" are here — Wordsworth refers to them. There are various "allegoric shapes," but there are figures of "real men" who are emblematic, and among them it is notable that Wordsworth remembers Boyle and Newton. Other contrasting things — the "raree-show" which he sees, the "children gather'd round," the "dancing dogs," the group of Savoyards, the "unsightly Lanes" emitting from time to time a harrowing scream — these also have significant symbolic reference. This is true, too, of the inviolate squares where the fortunate classes dwell, the "privileged Regions" that cannot suffer violation by the intrusion of an ordinary person. These are the squares

> Where from their airy lodges studious Lawyers
> Look out on waters, walks, and gardens green. (203 –)

The polarized aspects of the city, the conflicting forces, the oppositions that greet one's eyes — whether, in perambulations, one leaves the thronging crowds to traverse "wider Streets" and breathe "suburban air" (or sees "Advertisements of giant-size") — these things do not for a moment escape the observing poet. There are other passages revealing the printed sheets or "files of ballads" hanging from dull walls of buildings or the "travelling Cripple, by the trunk cut short," who stumps along "with his arms"; the poet wanders everywhere in the city, from the center to the outskirts, dominantly viewing with friendly eyes all conditions, kinds, and races of people, from the "military Idler," lolling away his day, to classes of people in the suburban areas, including

> the Dame,
> That field-ward takes her way in decency. (225 –)

We have spoken earlier of the emphasis Wordsworth places on the variousness of the world, and we have connected this with a similar tendency in Whitehead who contrasts the desire for a static, reified "One" with a frank realization that the world as we experience it is "more Hegelian," full of oppositions, seeming inconsistencies, discords, paradoxes, collisions, polarizations. Wordsworth's view of life, we have suggested, like Whitehead's, recognizes and even values such contrasts, oppositions, and paradoxes. For Whitehead, as we saw, there is the contradictoriness of the Hegelian-like elements in this sense of the variousness of the world: the world of conflicting forces. In his philosophy there are not merely dual oppositions of different kinds. There is an appreciation of the doctrine that life is made up of series after series of experiences, each involving thesis, antithesis, and synthesis. The third term, synthesis, may start a new triadic series: it never represents a stable, a fixed conclusion of the pattern. Every seemingly new so-called synthesis is no more than a new thesis which has to be followed by a further antithesis.

Something of this kind of understanding of life appears in Whitehead, though in other respects he disavows being Hegelian in his philosophy. At any rate, one who reads Whitehead will be struck by the multifarious complexity of his view of life. And this is true, though to a less extent, of Wordsworth. Both Wordsworth and Whitehead have a strong bent toward the social (the word "sociological" crops up in many pages of certain books written by Whitehead), and in Wordsworth's case an active concern with regard to life in the city is part of his larger grasp of things. Faced with the living reality of a great metropolis, he has the problem of trying to work his way through the maze that confronts him. He must find his way among these paths of almost irreconcilable social oppositions and conflicts. This is the expansiveness to which we have referred.

In our own day the sociologist, observing the intermixture of peoples strives to clarify in his mind a social theory; Wordsworth, though he does not develop a social theory, feels the need to have a similarly broad encounter with his fellow men. As in the case of Whitman or Whitehead, nothing human, nothing experiential is alien to his vision. His thought moves from contemplation of the "Italian with his frame of Images" (which he carries above his head) to reflection upon the "stately and slow-moving Turk" carrying his merchandise, to the picture of all races and conditions of people. He is interested in "all specimens of Man," as he says — the Swede, the Russian, the Frenchman, the Spaniard, as well as

> The Hunter-Indian; Moors,
> Malays, Lascars, the Tartar and Chinese,
> And Negro Ladies in white muslin gowns. (241 —)

The impressions Wordsworth presents of his "specimens" of humanity, and the catalogues of things such as he here lists, are by no means naively placed before us. The time in which he is writing — the early part of the nineteenth century — represented the beginning of findings pertinent to the life sciences, a period in which particularities are being noticed with interest; at such a point in the development of these sciences it is observation that is mainly being carried on. In any new development we have to become gradually aware of aspects of importance that are emerging. As Whitehead says, in the period to which we have been referring certain of these life sciences were as yet not even born or "were still in an elementary observational stage"[6]; they were only incipient. Paralleling, as observational, the state of these sciences is the presence of things Wordsworth observed in the city: animals, "wild Beasts, birds," the creatures of "all climes," and we will not be amiss in adding the representations of "the absolute presence of reality" by people of literal minds. The poet's attitude is kindly, even warm toward these things which express "as in a mirror, sea and land," the characteristics of "earth" and "what she has to shew"; he does

> not here allude to subtlest craft
> By means refin'd attaining purest ends,
> But imitations fondly made in plain
> Confession of Man's weakness, and his loves. (252 —)

To the very human observations we have cited, Wordsworth relates the productions of naive artists who, working "with greedy pencil," attempt something grand, or the efforts of those who, utilizing even more "mechanic means," reduce things being presented to "scale exact," whether in "miniature" or in larger aspiration. The imitative, the semiotic, the signifying aspect of man — so important to mental and moral development — is here in evidence. Then, as Wordsworth observed London, he attended shows, even those that were "lowest," which he responded to at that period of his life apparently with some misgiving. The problem which is in the background of the poet's thought is whether one should give such exhibitions a seemingly tacit approval. Should a person have patience with them? Before the end of the passage, however, it is evident that Wordsworth's attitude toward the humblest and crudest "shows" is, like Shakespeare's, a generous one. Ultimately the question, of course is: How generous should one be in his catholicity?

Tolerance, which is evident in the passage we have referred to, is also one of the marked characteristics of the philosophy of Whitehead, as it is revealed in many passages of his works. How shall we evaluate toleration; what is the place of tolerance in a philosophy? Has it a place in ethics? "It is the greatest thing of all," a certain philosopher said in effect, when answering questions concerning what he regarded as an admirable view of life. That philosopher, a close associate of Whitehead's who had shared with him the writing of a volume requiring long co-operation, was Bertrand Russell. Certainly both men desired to attain the quality of tolerance, though in Whitehead it is more consistently manifested than in his friend and collaborator. Speaking of tolerance, Whitehead remarks in one passage, "The duty of tolerance is our finite homage to the abundance of inexhaustible novelty which is awaiting the future, and to the complexity of accomplished fact which exceeds our stretch of insight."[7]

In Wordsworth tolerance represents a consummation clearly to be desired; his work points toward it in many of his portrayals of character and in the human warmth shown in his amassing of his observations of people. His sympathy for the frailties of humanity appears in the feeling he reveals toward "shows" — those which as we have said were "lowest"; he apologizes for any immature snobbery he may have displayed at any time, and his very apology makes explicit that he would not wish to be

> Intolerant, as in the way of Youth
> Unless itself be pleased . . . (289 —)

The alert awareness of Wordsworth's consciousness, and his sense of sharing at all times, is evident in this book of *The Prelude*. There was "recompense" for him in the activities of "Rope-dancers" and "Clowns, Conjurers, Posture-masters" and in the uproar of nondescript people. He tried to understand what induced in them the acceptance of something false which, with a more delayed response or deliberate appraisal, could have been rejected. The stubborn maintenance of received opinion, or the rationalization persistently practiced by human beings, he found fascinating. The naivete of the populace was of the utmost attraction to him. In ethics he seems to be aware of the principle of importance: the relative weights which we should give to things and to people. But he does not hastily assume a principle of *unimportance* and weigh persons and matters, finding them wanting.

For Wordsworth there was pure "delight" in watching "crude nature work in untaught minds"; these people to whom he refers are not looked upon as inferior — rather, they are "untaught," untrained. The poet is concerned about credulity. He is interested in trying to perceive "the laws and progress of belief"; people tend to be "obstinate" (he includes himself in this), but these very people nevertheless "willingly" proceed in their "travel" in other self-directed ways to their narrowly- conceived advantage. The credulity of the London rabble seemed to be almost without limit. Wordsworth has himself at times been charged with naivete, and he does seem willingly to par-

93

ticipate in the response of the throng who delighted in the antics of an "invisible" Jack the Giant Killer on an impromptu stage, who walked and achieved

> his wonders from the eye
> Of living mortal safe as is the moon
> 'Hid in her vacant interlunar cave'.
> Delusion bold! And faith must needs be coy;
> How is it wrought? His garb is black, the word
> INVISIBLE flames forth upon his chest. (304—)

In contrast to such an enactment there was a kind of dramatic reporting of actual events — of real life incidents — got up shortly after they took place. Ballads of current happenings were promptly published for the enthrallment of a gaping populace. Wordsworth was interested in all forms of the literature or drama of the affections, or emotions — the representation, for instance, of "some domestic incident" of notoriety throughout the land. An example of this is a story from the life of a girl whom he and Coleridge came later to know in the Lake District. The presentation of a painful part of her life provided for Londoners the equivalent of an event recounted in a modern sensational newspaper. Here was a kind of raw material of the feelings which an author like Wordsworth — or one like Dreiser or others in our century — might try to use with value through treating it with insight. Such matters at first could seem trivial; this is true

> Ere yet by use we have learn'd to slight the crimes
> And sorrows of the world. (362—)

Reality and the appearance of reality, life and the mirroring of it — these are problems before Wordsworth constantly. One example he gives concerns a prostitute's child, seated upon a "Board" where refreshments were being served, while "oaths, indecent speech" filled the air, where springtime "songs of birds" would have been suitable. Again through the associa-

94

tionism with which Wordsworth is fascinated, we see the attractive child in the poet's memories "a thousand times," an appearance merely, but for him it is, though a memory, like life itself.

The theater, that mirroring place, that demi-reality, had been Wordsworth's delight, even when he was a boy in the Lake District where he sometimes had the opportunity of attendance in a "Country Playhouse." Seeing actuality — a beam from the sun, through a "fractured wall" — he was awakened to the real, but he turned from the world of actuality back to the phantasmal world with enhanced delight. It is the contrast between appearance and reality that he notices now, on later reflection. Is Wordsworth in this "Country Playhouse" turning away from reality, or seeking escape? In the Prelude passage he is recalling real experience that he had. Sitting in a theater and giving attention to the works of human imagination can itself be a reality. The experience, which Wordsworth had, became in actuality a part of himself, and therefore in The Prelude it has its reason for being. We find, also, that once more he is making use of the principle of double recollection, including the past of his boyhood and the past of his London experience. He is trying to represent truth which can never be seen except in part. For truth is always necessarily an incomplete thing. The boyhood happening he presents is, as he says,

> Romantic almost, looked at through a space,
> How small of intervening years! (474 —)

This material in the poem is slight, seemingly casual. It is not "dignified," he says, but it is a representation of value, particularly to those who realize how "the perishable hours" fit into "each other" — how they sustain "the world of thought" and provide its very existence. Do some of the poet's terms remind us, at times, of Whitehead's language? Increasingly, it seems evident, they do. Here we may think again of the variousness of the world which we referred to at the beginning of the chapter, including allusions to Hegel which were earlier given. For Wordsworth "the world of thought" which he refers to appeared momentarily, in *passage*. At the time in London of which he speaks that world of thought was only within "the suburbs of the mind"; the contrast between this and the active *city* of his mind, as we might say, is striking. Whitehead's emphasis upon the perishing hours, or perishing moments (though more subtle than Wordsworth's emphasis), nevertheless fits well with the poet's conception. The place of concreteness or of the particular in Whitehead and Wordsworth might also be cited here, in opposition to change or passage.

A philosophy in Whitehead's view (this is true of Wordsworth's thought also) should be "at once general and concrete"; it should be, the philosopher says further, both "critical and appreciative of direct intuition."[8] In connection with the "concrete" character of a philosophy we may cite the fact that he regards the term "particulars" as "somewhat misleading."[9] The term "particulars" corresponds to a degree with his expression, "actual entities." One objection that he has to the term *particular* is that "subjective forms are also 'particulars.' " For Whitehead there is an important connection between so-called gross actualities and profundities. This connection works both ways, backward and forward. In Wordsworth too, even in his references to profundities there is a conscious realization of the function of the particulars, or of "gross realities"; if there was anything of "real grandeur here" in his London experience it could be truly seen through the "gross realities" which actually become, he says,

> The incarnation of the Spirits that mov'd
> Amid the Poet's beauteous world, call'd forth,
> With that distinctness which a contrast gives
> Or opposition, made me recognize
> And by a glimpse, the things which I had shap'd

And yet not shaped, had seen, and scarcely seen . . .
(509 —)

Moving beyond this point, Wordsworth returns again to particularities: he tells how he observed "the brawls of Lawyers in the Courts," and the "great Stage" honored by England's "Senators, tongue-favour'd Men," the envy of all. Of no less interest, he now sees in his mind's eye — in remembrance — the preacher, after having devoted much time to the creation of his self-image as a preacher, "ascend" to the place from which he is to deliver his speech. He assumes a "seraphic glance" as he gazes aloft. Then "in a tone elaborately low" he begins, leading

> his voice through many a maze,
> A minuet course, and winding up his mouth,
> From time to time into an orifice
> Most delicate, a lurking eyelet, small
> And only not invisible, again
> Open it out, diffusing thence a smile
> Of rapt irradiation exquisite. (550 —)

As Wordsworth criticizes the frailties of man — he gives "few" examples, he says, where he might have cited "ten thousand" — one might feel that his strictures on man are bitterly pessimistic. He does criticize "extravagance" in many things, including "dress," the folly of man's tendency toward "singularity" which involves a kind of "strife" between human beings. All these are "lies" and, indeed, companions to "lies" having virtually no end. Ethics is involved here. Of mankind he might have said, I read you (he uses the word "reading" in his context), and I find you wanting. But he is not unkind. He is "pleased" with the items he accumulates, much as Aristotle finds the accumulating of the particularities of knowledge a pleasure. Often he includes himself and all mankind in what he presents. But he never is hopeless in his attitude. He is simply taking "note" of things, he says, just as a collector of natural objects — for example a collector of "shells" — might do. It is not in the city only, but everywhere that one can catch sight of "foolishness, and madness on parade." What is lacking so often in man is a sense of genuine importance, or an appreciation of priorities — the sense which Whitehead emphasizes.

Wordsworth's purpose is not exclusively observational. Far from presenting an exhibition merely, he is wondering about the meaning back of the things which the city dramatically illustrates. What impresses him particularly again and again — whether within the city's center, among its "overflowing Streets," or in the suburban regions — is the inscrutability of all things, the fact that, as he says, "the face of everyone" who is seen presents "a mystery." But mystery or not, what Wordsworth sees needs to be dealt with, pondered. Of the multifarious things before him, he must ask: To what are they directed — can we explain their relation to time, penetrate into their cause, and tell how they operate? All these questions are explicitly in Wordsworth's mind. The relation between present, past, and the future (in its connection with hope) troubles him. It is also, indeed, a problem in Whitehead, where the idea of importance, ethically applied or otherwise touches upon infinity as a limit. Clearly the ethical act includes loyalty, or being loyal, to importance, or to that which is important. But it has larger reaches in the direction of transcendence.

The philosopher has a whole chapter in *Modes of Thought* entitled "Importance." In it he indicates that, for him, "mere fact" is no light thing; it is, indeed, a "triumph of the abstract intellect."[10] The "single fact in isolation is the primary myth required for finite thought, that is to say, for thought unable to embrace totality." As Whitehead says on the very next page, we need perspective, or "gradation of importance."[11] This we obtain through feeling. "Apart from gradations of feeling, the infinitude of detail produces an infinitude of effect in the constitution of each fact." A sense of perspective helps to give one an understanding of the importance of things. In the last seven pages of Chapter Two of *The Function of Reason*, after making a jibe at the University of Cambridge and its dividing of knowledge into "natural science and moral science" keeping them forever separate, Whitehead introduces his thought that we cannot justifiably polarize descriptive knowledge and "moral science"; we cannot in all justice divide natural science and ethics. Things in knowledge attain importance by virtue of their relationship to moral insights.

Whitehead connects ethics with importance, then, and importance, for him, is something like a Platonic idea enveloping, as we shall see later in the volume *Modes of Thought*, even logic and aesthetics which "are at the two extremes of the dilemma of the finite mentality in its partial penetration of the infinite."[12] And still later he explains this idea, which we have related to Plato, as arising from "fusion of the finite and the infinite."[13] It is no vacuous infinite that he has in mind. This he clearly explains. For Whitehead ethics necessarily reaches beyond the present. Moral science — the term may seem somewhat distasteful here — involves a consideration of consequences to reflection. It recognizes the importance of consequences for theory that lies ahead. It leads to creative thinking in the future, both as it concerns us and as it concerns other human beings and the world of existence beyond persons.

But to return to Wordsworth. The laws of man's dynamism, whatever they may be — the laws, that is, of man as what the poet calls an "acting" and a "speaking" force, he is trying to ponder "amid the moving pageant" of the city. He is interested in the important, amid much that seems on the face of it unimportant. Discrimination of values is important in determining what is good or right, as viewed in a long-range consideration. This is essential in Whitehead's ethics as it is in the poet's reflection. As the philosopher says after speaking of reverence at the close of his first chapter in *Aims of Education*: "Duty arises from our potential control over the course of events." Ethics, as we know, is essential to duty. If it is possible for us to attain knowledge we have a duty to possess it. If knowledge is within our reach (but ignored) it must be remembered that "knowledge could have changed the issue, ignorance has the guilt of vice." Duty has a relation, Whitehead holds, to "reverence" and to "eternity." This is his climactic thought at the terminal point in the chapter which is entitled "The Aims of Education." And we have referred to it because of its relation to the poet, in London, seeking education beyond that of his college days.

Wordsworth is seeking education in a spirit of ethics, reverence, and importance of emphasis, but constantly thinking of it in relation to eternity. The last word we have used here, "eternity," recalls to mind Whitehead. But it must also be remembered that the philosopher is interested in an ethics which, considered from the point of view of an as-if, or an ideal, strives constantly in the direction of a loyalty that *aims* to be loyal forever. What Wordsworth in *The Prelude* sees before him takes on a kind of structuralism or functionalism involving an interdependence of force with force — that is, of the shapes that society seems to be assuming. There is an interaction that is taking place certainly. But often what that interaction is would present difficulties for anyone who would perceive it. This is true of Whitehead's thought also, even though his philosophy involves a greater perfection of conscious functionalism with the institutions and the persons somehow bringing about a measure, although almost a blind measure, of cultural and social unity.

It would be difficult to imagine Whitehead reading the London portion of *The Prelude* without perceiving that something of the fellow feeling in his own thought, and something of the very functionalism of it, was incipiently present in the thought of the poet. Wordsworth sees a label indicating a fact or so about a seated blind man, and it seems to the poet a summa-

100

tion of his own life, or, as we might say, it was a kind of capsule-statement symbolizing your life or mine. In the "label," so Wordsworth indicates, there is an "emblem," a "type" of the life of every person: blind, planning things, proposing but not *disposing* — never knowing what is to come. Thus it is that he thinks constantly of outward manifestations and inward aspects of matters which are bewildering and puzzling — including not only events but even, as he says, the very silences. He is troubled, also, by the noise (there are many references to this, as we have said) and by the outbreaks arising from what we would call mob psychology: the

> times, when half the City shall break out
> Full of one passion, vengeance, rage, or fear,
> To executions, to a Street on fire,
> Mobs, riots . . . (645 —)

All of the foregoing circumstances lead up to a climactic portion of Book Seven, concerning an event which is held, ironically, in a place where martyrs of past days underwent suffering. The event is St. Bartholomew's Fair, and it is a kind of "hell" which the "eyes and ears" of human beings undergo, an "anarchy" fit for the barbaric side of people, indeed, quite hellish,

> a dream
> Monstrous in colour, motion, shape, sight, sound.
> Below, the open space, through every nook
> Of the wide area, twinkles, is alive
> With heads . . . (660 —)

The region is "throng'd with staring pictures, and huge scrolls" serving as "proclamations of the prodigies" being served up for the delectation of the people. Wordsworth sees "chattering monkeys dangling from their poles," while close at hand children are "whirling in their roundabouts"; people "crack the voice in rivalship," and "buffoons against buffoons" grimace, "writhing, screaming" — all these things pass before the poet's eyes. He beholds

> him who grinds
> The hurdy-gurdy, at the fiddle weaves;
> Rattles the salt-box, thumps the kettle-drum,
> And him who at the trumpet puffs his cheeks,
> The silver-collar'd Negro with his timbrel,
> Equestrians, Tumblers, Women, Girls, and Boys,
> Blue-breech'd, pink-vested, and with towering plumes.
>
> (672—)

There is much more — including Indians in war paint, "the learned Pig," the man who eats stones, and other far-sought "perverted things." But the picture we receive of the Bartholomew Fair occasion does not represent Wordsworth's feeling with regard to London as a whole. Historically there have been, according to Carl Schorske, three views of the city generally. These "three broad evaluations" of it, which we will consider in relation to the thought of Wordsworth, are "the city as virtue, the city as vice, and the city beyond good and evil."[14] In eighteenth century thought — for example, in Voltaire and in Adam Smith — the city was considered as deserving special commendation. In the view of the former, a major virtue of the city lay in its great respect for "talent"; this is Voltaire's word, for whom the origin of the city was the fortunate work of monarchs. The city was admirable also in that it prepared an underpinning for both industrial and cultural progress. Adam Smith was in agreement on these points.

How does this view of what goes on in a city compare with Wordsworth's conception? We shall see later. But to return to Carl Schorske's analysis, for the later eighteenth century there arose an antithetical conception: "the city as vice." The view was reflected in the early nineteenth century. Here the influence of crowded tenement life and growing industrialism,

102

with its attendant evils, was a factor in the changing current of thought. "Finally there emerged, in the context of the new subjectivist culture born in the mid-nineteenth century, an intellectual attitude which placed the city beyond good and evil."[15] More could be said here about these three views of the city. But what is important for present purposes is the fact that Wordsworth was far from viewing the city as admirable, especially in its relation to the efforts of monarchs or in connection with industrial or cultural progress. On the other hand, he was also far from regarding the city of his day as unmitigated evil, though like historians and sociologists of our own time he condemned many of its aspects.

Wordsworth's view of the city is more nearly a detached one than either of the first two historical conceptions that have been mentioned, though he leans, of course, somewhat toward the view of the city as evil. The third view — that of the city as "beyond good and evil" — had not developed in Wordsworth's time. It can be associated with ideas in Nietzsche. Or, apart from Nietzsche, it may be connected with a crude mechanistic conception of life. It is a conception, however, by no means as understanding or even objective as that represented by the poet's story of his own experience in the city. Wordsworth's view in Book Seven is closer than any of these views to an approach characteristic of the twentieth century, and this seems clearly a further indication of his forward-looking breadth. He is distinctly moral in his emphasis. He would by no means consider himself as a person who is beyond good and evil.

Today we often think of the multitudes of people who, because of our automative existence — whether in the city or elsewhere — have lost all color of selfhood or of personality. They have permitted themselves, in an expression Wordsworth uses in *The Prelude*, to be "reduced to one identity"; in other words, the problem that the poet emphasized exists also in our day. Our seeming "differences" in personality, as Wordsworth suggests, are variations having all too often "no meaning" or goal. If this is true for many of us, there is something oppressing man — apparently something from which, as Wordsworth explains, "the strongest are not free."

Much of the time there is confusion within us, and this would seem to mean that we lack a philosophy in any adequate sense of the term. Indeed, our whole view of things — not only of those features which are internal, but also of those things which are outside ourselves — is so distorted that it represents "an unmanageable sight," a fact which seems to be an inevitable condition of the processes whereby we make use of our initial impressions and our subsequent more complex perceptions. Wordsworth is making an acute comment here. This is a criticism to which Whitehead, it seems, would give firm assent. The situation is not entirely hopeless, however, for "modes" of thought — or of "education" — can help us in our processes of attention, comprehension, and memory, as Wordsworth says. There is a kind of empathy by which we become, in a sense, a part of the things around us, or they become a part of us; in this sense

> By influence habitual to the mind
> The mountain's outline and its steady form
> Gives a pure grandeur, and its presence shapes
> The measure and the prospect of the soul
> To majesty . . . (721 —)

We have said that, for Wordsworth, "modes" of "education" or of thought can help us in our processes of attention, comprehension, and memory. Through such a means a greater measure of power and insight may be ours. We need an orientation toward a larger view such as we see in a "mountain's outline"; this broader perspective must be added to our use of our sensations and perceptiveness, the poet believes, if we are to have an enhanced sense of "order and relation." A certain number of those who live in London or indeed elsewhere grasp such principles, though this is rare. Such was Wordsworth's view when he dwelt "in that vast receptacle." In the receptacle "appearance" was rife.

The word "receptacle" is interesting as applied to the city, for it seems to comprise what the poet has experienced personally in London, including on the one hand appearance and on the other hand reality — as well as the difficulty of sorting out what is the essence of either one. The term "receptacle," if used in this way, involves a reflective action whereby after one first notices what *seems* to be reality one stops to consider in what sense it is lacking something deserving to be regarded as real within perception. This is based on experience in process, and it takes place in time. The consideration of appearance always brings in the factor of time. And for Wordsworth the experience within London includes, moreover, the factor of space, in so far as he is in constant movement from one thing to another. The manifold character of life, spatially, is here.

The "receptacle" is, then, the city as dynamically contemplated, both in space and time, and the conception of it may very naturally be extended so that the city may serve as a symbol of life. The "receptacle" is not merely external, and it is of no narrow scope. It can include the very countryside itself. It involves a relationship between a larger sense of "nature" than is given us when we are merely in the country observing things externally. It also includes beauty. For Wordsworth in the city — in the "receptacle" — an appreciation of the depth, or the

> Soul of Beauty and enduring life
Was present as a habit, and diffused
Through meagre lines and colours, and the press
Of self-destroying, transitory things . . . (736 —)

The "lines" and "colors" are impressions, in what we have called earlier a sense similar to that of Hume's impressions. These, like sense data, are "transitory," if considered psychologically, and they are combined with the more general

105

aspects of perception, one of which appears in the experience of beauty. Thus the spirit or the soul of beauty becomes "diffused," as is indicated in *The Prelude*, throughout the wider series of occasions or events which came to Wordsworth in the metropolis. What, then, is the *meaning* of the city? This was a problem posed for consideration near the middle of the chapter, and it now assumes a new form: What is the meaning of life? The word "receptacle" used by Wordsworth is a term also employed by Plato as applied to life. It is something comparable to what Wordsworth has been presenting as a thing within which we are to a certain extent enclosed. His references to countless individual human beings within London suggests something of the vast range of personality within the universe. For Whitehead in a 1948 volume personality is an outstanding example of value as realized. In personality in the world — that is, in personal identity — we have to consider the tremendous range of "more or less; there are grades of dominance and grades of recessiveness."[16]

We ourselves might be inclined to say there are grades of almost infinite merit and grades of relative worthlessness. But worthlessness as applied to persons seems not to be in Whitehead's vocabulary. He sees in the passage from which we have quoted "patterns" in people, and the patterns have had at times great opportunity to develop and on occasions minimal opportunity, but within the persons, and their structures, may always be found "ideal entities which they involve": the patterns and the ideal elements within them "constitute the character of that persistent fact of personal existence in the World of Activity." Personality has a place, also, in Wordsworth's receptacle. Can we doubt that it has a place in Whitehead's receptacle concept which was developed somewhat parallel to that of Plato?

The notion of the receptacle in Wordsworth is not uncomplex. And in Plato it is a difficult one, as Whitehead indicates. Speaking of the receptacle, he declares, "we may safely put aside easy explanations of it."[17] In another context, referring to appearance and reality, Whitehead uses the term "receptacle" in connection with his own philosophy and explains: "On a moonless night, the faintly luminous stretch of the sky which is the Milky Way is an Appearance of the contemporary world, namely, it is a great region within the 'Receptacle' of that world as it appears."[18] More could be said about the concept but further discussion of it would not be appropriate here. Later we shall make additional references to the receptacle. The value of Wordsworth's experience in London which we have just discussed is placed in a further view when we find him in the next book of *The Prelude* proceeding once more to a retrospective pondering of his situation. He wishes to bring more closely together what he has known of nature and what he is to learn increasingly of man. This recapitulative view then, to which Wordsworth turns, will be the subject of our following chapter. We shall also be continuing there our study of the relation between Wordsworth's thought and that of Whitehead.

Footnotes

1. Morris Janowitz, "Introduction" to *The City*, by Robert E. Park and others (Chicago, 1967), p. ix. Fifth impression, 1968.

2. The sociologist Robert E. Park, for example, refers to the city dwellings as "dormitories" in *ibid.*, p. 114 and elsewhere. The title of his article — "Community Organization and the Romantic Temper" — is of interest in connection with our present subject. Most of the material in the volume was reprinted from an earlier edition.

3. *Process and Reality*, p. 277.

4. Wolf Schneider, *Babylon Is Everywhere* (London: Hodder and Stoughton, 1963), p. 97.

5. *Adventures of Ideas*, p. 250. See also those things that are "inexorable," *Process and Reality*, p. 373 and p. 132 for the "impressions" of Hume.

6. Whitehead refers to the background of the life sciences in the latter part of the eighteenth century, *Science and the Modern World*, p. 92.

7. *Adventures of Ideas*, p. 65.

8. *Ibid.*, p. 125. The "concrete" character of a philosophy may, of course, connect it with science as in Whitehead.

9. *Process and Reality*, p. 76. "Actual entities" are also referred to as ac-

tual occasions. We have been somewhat technical in referring to "actual entities," but our reference may be helpful to readers who wish to follow up Whitehead's ideas in his own works.

10. *Modes of Thought*, p. 12. See also p. 84 concerning "the infinite."

11. *Ibid.*, p. 13. See also "Whitehead's Moral Philosophy" by Paul Arthur Schilpp, p. 572, in *The Philosophy of Alfred North Whitehead*, ed. Schilpp (New York: Tudor, 1951).

12. *Ibid.*, p. 84.

13. *Ibid.*, p. 108.

14. Carl E. Schorske, "The Idea of the City in European Thought," *The Historian and the City*, ed. Oscar Handlin and John Buchard (Cambridge, Mass., 1963), p. 96. See also p. 97.

15. *Ibid.*, p. 96.

16. "Immortality," *Essays in Science and Philosophy*, p. 67.

17. *Adventures of Ideas*, p. 354.

18. *Ibid.*, p. 317.

Chapter VIII

Wordsworth's Retrospect: Nature and Mankind as Connected with Whitehead

Wordsworth had been dealing with the teeming multitudes of the city, as we have just seen, but he next turns back (in Book Eight of *The Prelude*) to reminisce upon his early life experience when he lived close to nature. He proceeds thoughtfully in this backward reconsideration, or analysis of the value to him of the region from which he came. As he reminisces he holds in mind also the experiences that he had lately undergone in London. Our previous chapter has made clear that even when he was living amidst the great masses of people of the city, nature was still a continuing theme of interest for him. He talks from time to time about nature, whether he is picturing cities or making allusions to them. His theme of nature becomes, for the moment, more prominent now in Book Eight as he deals with the problem of nature and mankind, and whether or not love of nature comes first and ultimately leads to love of human beings.

Our love of nature comes, we today usually suppose, largely from our culture. In our own time we often think of the basic biological human person who, in the process of growing up — or of absorbing a culture — feels that it oppressively surrounds him. The youth of our day often expresses this sense of oppression: he feels in almost fundamental conflict with the culture, though he usually is not aware that it is natural to feel this way. The prevailing cultural force is to a certain extent in seeming enmity with him as he is undergoing biological development and needing freedom.

This, very often, is the state of mind of youth, and it is to some extent, then, biologically based. The biological organism needs to grow. The ways of society — its regulations and conventions — take on the form of an Establishment against which the growing physical individual finds himself, from moment to moment, in rebellion. The natural condition of the person in his state of youth seems to be not one in which love of mankind in a broad sense arises readily. Wordsworth would say love of nature comes first — love of nature leads later to love of mankind. Nature, rather — if we think of it as the surrounding condition of man in his early developmental stage — is the force which causes biological man to seek freedom of self-activity, or what Whitehead calls individual absoluteness.

But the human being, particularly in growing from childhood into young maturity, is not merely a biological being. He (we think here of Wordsworth) is also a social creature, though his growing social nature takes form under many physiological difficulties. This is the problem with which Wordsworth is faced in *The Prelude*. Love of nature is, for the poet, a personal and aesthetic, indeed almost a private thing.

110

It is at first narrowly self-oriented, but it is also a refining force. Wordsworth feels that somehow this love of nature *leads* to love of man. Perhaps this is so; certainly love of nature engenders increased fineness of response. We have been thinking here mainly of external nature, but Wordsworth does not use the concept of nature exclusively in this external sense. It is a heterogeneous or expansive conception that he often employs, and it is functional in its effect upon the individual — and upon the person, Wordsworth. The forces *within* external nature and the forces within the human being are taken together and for him become a part of nature in the larger view. Heterogeneous or *wide* thought about nature, as we shall see, is presented in Whitehead's later works.

Even when Wordsworth was in London he still looked back, as he now says in Book Eight, to the nature he had known as a boy; in the bustle and din and the pressing of the crowd about him, he did not forget the beauty of natural forms. He had not weaned himself from a preoccupation with these forms. Now he glances back at his life and his development, pondering the relationship between love of nature and a large view of the totality of things: considering how such love may, through this larger process, lead toward a love of mankind, as he believes. The revolution in Wordsworth whereby his overabsorption in external nature gives way to a major concern for his fellow human beings is not, however, made complete even at this stage. And here the problem will be somewhat involved. The transformation in the poet must wait upon experiences carrying him out into a still wider world than he had yet known successively in his home region, in Cambridge, in Europe, in Bristol, and in London. But his experiences in contact with nature in Westmorland and elsewhere had prepared the way for a deeper insight into the problems of human beings. We begin, perhaps, with the psychological experience of the world, which we sense, in nature, and we move toward wider and wider perceptiveness. A consideration of the relation between Wordsworth and Whitehead beyond any that we have yet given may be helpful here.

A conscious realization of what is involved in the psychological experience of the world of sense-data, and its further reaches beyond sense, appears in Wordsworth and Whitehead. It forms, indeed, an important part of the latter's philosophy. In *The Concept of Nature,* a work written in the middle-period of Whitehead's career (originally published in 1922), we find him struggling with the problem of sense-data and its relation to nature. At the beginning of the volume he is concerned, he says, with the "Relations or Want of Relations between the Different Departments of Knowledge." And he very shortly points out the importance of the study of philosophy as connected with the ideal which is working toward unification. Philosophy would "set in assigned relationships within itself all that there is for knowledge, for feeling, and for emotion."[1] In the first chapter of *The Concept of Nature* which is entitled "Nature and Thought," he makes clear that he is mainly for the present "thinking 'homogeneously' about nature."[2] That is, he is thinking limitedly about nature.

Here it is important to know that Whitehead has a very strong impulse in this volume to avoid the dangers of subjectivism. We must keep in mind, furthermore, that the center of his attention in the work is directed toward science. Thus he points out that, from his present perspective in the book, "sense-perception is an awareness of something which is not thought." He also maintains emphatically in the next sentence that "nature is not thought." To the reader this statement gives rise to a question: What is the *relation* between thought and nature? Whitehead in his writing of the time seems to be working toward a wider and wider perspective. All along he is speaking of nature, however, mainly in its bearings upon the natural sciences.

Somewhat later in the volume he declares that nature is a

"complex of related entities" and that this " 'complex' is fact as an entity for thought"[3]; here, again, he is trying to think of nature in its relation to the natural sciences. His point of view is complicated, but had he presented ideas concerning nature in its wider or heterogeneous aspect, his approach would have been still more complex. All this has a bearing on our thought concerning Wordsworth, for the poet's view of nature is heterogeneous. Two sentences beyond the passage from which we last quoted, Whitehead, speaking of nature, says that "the structure of the natural complex can never be completed in thought, just as the factors of fact can never be exhausted in sense-awareness."[4]

What shall we say of that which can "never be completed in thought," and what shall we say of fact that "can never be exhausted" under certain conditions — is there a problem in the question of such inexhaustibility? It is clear that philosophy in the end would need to think of nature more widely than would science as Whitehead centers upon the latter in his volume. More will appear concerning this later. In *The Concept of Nature* Whitehead seems to be wrestling with problems which he has not entirely clarified for himself. "Unexhaustiveness is an essential character of our knowledge of nature."[5] It would seem from this quotation that even while Whitehead is thinking mainly from the restricted point of view as to science his thought moves toward the concept of an approach to infinity as a limit. Here we must keep in mind his view that "there are thoughts which would not occur in any homogeneous thinking about nature." The world is wide. It is wider than any homogeneous (that is to say, scientific) thinking about nature could possibly be. In other words, if we move beyond the homogeneous perspective (the natural science approach) to nature, a far greater complexity would confront us. This we find in Wordsworth. Why have we been commenting on this book by Whitehead? It has been considered by some thinkers the most important volume on nature written in the twentieth century. This and the fact that Wordsworth has a pre-eminent place in regard to nature as it is reflected in the nineteenth century presents a kind of challenge. Whether we can meet the challenge remains to be seen.

An example of moving beyond the homogeneous limits that Whitehead is for the present mainly setting himself would appear in our entering the realm of poetic perception or the perception of other art forms. But he is himself being drawn toward art. Still later, in thinking of the unfortunate divisions (the bifurcations) of nature that have at times been made, Whitehead refers to the fact that he desires to make a criticism of "the concept of matter as the substance whose attributes we perceive."[6] We should here emphasize the word *attributes*. He is opposing, as we see in the very next page, what he feels has been "disastrous both to science and philosophy, but chiefly to philosophy."[7] That is, he is concerned about the neglect of "the grand question of the relations between nature and mind"; he feels that this question has been lost in the modern preoccupation with "the petty form of the interaction between the human body and mind." This latter would appear to be a sort of behaviorism.

The title of Whitehead's chapter here is "Theories of the Bifurcation of Nature," and it refers to the theories he attacks. What he is controverting is, essentially, materialism, and this materialism may be understood best in a context of eighteenth and nineteenth century thought. In such a context materialism, he says, is "the belief that what is real in nature is matter, in time and in space and with inertia."[8] For Whitehead's main purpose in *The Concept of Nature* it is not necessary that we should "make any pronouncement" about "the psychological relations of subjects to objects"; nor need we assert anything "as to the status of either in the realm of reality."[9] Such further discussion as this sort of "pronouncement" would require is exemplified by Whitehead in a quotation from Lossky, an author who "considered the subject-object

114

called nature in its activity of self-constructing. In order to understand it," we are told by Lossky, "we must rise to an intellectual intuition of nature."[10] Wordsworth's view involves an intuition of nature. In the Lossky quotation given in Whitehead's volume a criticism of materialism is implied. Intuition is emphasized. "The empiricist does not rise thereto, and for this reason in all his explanations it is always *he himself* that proves to be constructing nature." The italics are in Whitehead's volume.

To emphasize Lossky's point further (about a possible wider field of reference) Whitehead quotes an additional passage which concerns the Platonic doctrine of immortality. He cites this passage because, although he wishes to restrict his point of view, he would have the reader aware of the wider possibilities of reference to nature or to other things. There can be a wider purview carrying one beyond the scientific consideration of nature. But Whitehead's main purpose is to present a criticism of materialism. Later he carries forward his attack in a chapter dealing with "Time"; there he speaks of materialism which, as he says, is based on "a certain circle of concepts" that are "rigid and definite as those of the philosophy of the middle ages" — concepts "accepted with as little critical research."[11] He explains that this materialism is "the philosophy" which he had been examining in the first two chapters of the book, and he continues his attack against materialism for three or more pages. Wordsworth would delight in this.

Whitehead's volume that we have been discussing has at times been misunderstood because of its main focus upon science. But it is plain that in it he refuses adherence to a world-view based on materialism. The same is true of Wordsworth. Both men conceive the reality behind nature as something other than material particles, or bodies, acting in time and space inertly. The problem of *acting* is the key to the fallacy concerning the seemingly inert. In Whitehead's work which we have been discussing we have said that he had been thinking mainly about science. His attitude on nature and the world becomes more clear in his next important volume, *Science and the Modern World*, where he is concerned again with the scientific scope of perception and its importance to the world of the twentieth century. What is really needed, he says, is "a wider field of abstraction, a more concrete analysis, which shall stand nearer to the complete concreteness of our intuitive experience."[12] Nature is involved here in its complexity.

But we must return to Wordsworth and nature. In the opening circumstances of Book Eight of *The Prelude* we find the poet viewing a group of human beings. This group stands out in one's perception in very strong contrast with the crowd in the St. Bartholomew Fair presentation, referred to near the end of our last chapter; that earlier Fair scene was in London. Now, on the other hand, in the country, we find before us a gathering of some forty men and their families at a "festival," as Wordsworth calls it, a country fair. As in the city scenes of our last chapter we find that the crowd is variegated: here "a lame man" who has come to beg, there a blind person who has joined the group "to make music," or finally an "aged woman," come to hawk things of various sorts which she is carrying. But they are close to nature. This panoramic presentation we see in the subjectivity of Wordsworth. Though we are within the mind of the poet we are also in the district where Wordsworth grew up as a boy among rural people. As he says,

> How little They, they and their doings seem,
> Their herds and flocks about them, they themselves,
> And all that they can further or obstruct!
> Through utter weakness pitiably dear . . . (50 —)

But little as they are, these country people have a place in the larger cosmos, despite the fact that they are, Wordsworth says, like "tender Infants" and can further few purposes, or even rarely stop *anything* from occurring. In a sense they are

116

hemmed in by a universe that might to some persons seem an enemy. And yet their connectedness with the larger world is emphasized in the hyperbole concerning the sensitive, the animated stones — even in the personifying of "light" in the expression of the idea that they are loved by "the Morning light" which "glistens on the silent rocks" and by the very stones, high above them.

The nature that seems external is alive: the rocks watch or observe the people that are below, as do the small "Brooks from their invisible haunts" upon the heights. The nature scene itself, however, is overshadowed by a mountain. The vantage point that the poet has taken is a reducing one — above the small crowd. Nevertheless, his purpose is to enlarge the people we see; there is greatness in the minuscule human beings, observed in a fashion as from the height of the overlooking mountain, "conscious" Helvellyn. There is furthermore a love which is extended not alone from the light, from the rocks, and from the "lurking Brooks," but indeed from the mountain itself.

A principle of love, or what we might call an "Eros," is implied here: the love is within the universe and it is also a kind of creative force. Here we recall Whitehead. Of this creativity Wordsworth would wish to be a part, even if a minor one. He would himself wish to have a love which is extended to anyone he may encounter, though the person might be a complete "stranger" in his path. Love is related to congruence. Earlier in the present chapter we referred to a passage from *The Concept of Nature* in which Whitehead indicated his view that the conception of nature involves a variety of complexities. The conception of nature involves "a complex of related entities" and this " 'complex' is fact as an entity for thought"; we must add the point that to the "bare individuality" of this fact, "is ascribed the property of embracing in its complexity the natural entities."[13] Here he is stressing nature. Whitehead would analyze this conception in its relation to space and time.

117

This he does in two later chapters. After presenting a body of material, then, touching on space and time, he proceeds to a discussion of what he calls "Congruence" and explains that the question has been raised concerning "the factor in nature which might lead any particular congruence relation" to play a part pre-eminently "among the factors posited in sense-awareness."[14] He adds immediately that he "cannot see the answer" to this question and certain other matters if one goes along with "the materialist theory of nature."

Whitehead's conception in regard to this "congruence relation" brings out an important abstract aspect of his philosophy. We see the abstract factor in his thought, for example, in his conception of *objects* which are at times not physical things. "Thus objects for our knowledge may be merely logical abstractions."[15] This point is brought out in his chapter entitled "Congruence." But he has a more complete discussion of objects and abstraction in the chapter that follows. As to sense-recognition, Whitehead says that he is "quite willing to believe that recognition," as he understands it, should be regarded only as "an ideal limit"; in addition, he points out that "there is in fact no recognition without intellectual accompaniments of comparison and judgment."[16]

The problem here is that of the relation between sense-data and the activity of mind. But, for Whitehead, the important thing is the event. And his theory of the event requires a consideration of passage or the flowing which occurs in all experience. The vital thing is continuity. "The discrimination of nature is the recognition of objects amid passing events."[17] This discrimination would imply thought or consciousness. Near the end of his book *The Concept of Nature*, he admits that the view he has presented is "not a simple one. Nature appears as a complex system whose factors are dimly discerned by us."[18] But he goes on to ask, "Is not this the very truth?" Things are not clearly discerned, that is, in anybody's experience. Nor would this be denied by Wordsworth.

Here we may also cite the point that "the philosophy of organism" — that is, Whitehead's later philosophy to which Wordsworth's thought is connected — "attributes 'feeling' throughout the actual world."[19] We find that in one of Whitehead's still later books he mentions with regard to "animal life," in contrast to the inorganic which precedes it, that there is "no reason to believe that in any important way the mental activities depart from functionings which are strictly conformal to those inherent in the objective datum of the first phase."[20] That is, the first phase, having to do with so-called inorganic nature, is tied in, through feeling, with the second phase involving more obviously conscious beings. Whitehead's philosophy is thus related to Wordsworth and to earlier historical developments in the poetry of the English romantic movement. Romanticism is perhaps most profoundly understood as growing out of this kind of relationship and development.

We have referred to the principle of love in speaking of the poet's passage on "the morning light," and this love is somewhat comparable to the Eros in Plato, which Whitehead describes as "the soul stirring itself to life and motion,"[21] and which Whitehead connects with excitability. It involves, also, freedom "directly derived from the source of all harmony."[22] The quality of love in Whitehead's own philosophy is clearly related to "Plato's Eros, which he sublimates into the notion of the soul in the enjoyment of its creative function, arising from its entertainment of ideas."[23] And "Eros means 'Love' "; Whitehead goes on to add that "in The Symposium Plato elicits his final conception of the urge towards ideal perfection." This conception as urged is love.

The quality of love in Whitehead's philosophy is related, then, to Plato's Eros, but this does not mean it is identical with it. How much of what we have just quoted can we connect directly with Whitehead's own philosophy, or, indeed, with Wordsworth's views? The question is not an easy one to answer.

Whitehead has certain reservations concerning Plato, which we have already mentioned, but, applicable to the present problem he has a further stricture: "Plato in the earlier period of his thought, deceived by the beauty of mathematics intelligible in unchanging perfection, conceived of a super-world of ideas, forever perfect and forever interwoven. In his latest phase he sometimes repudiates the notion, though he never consistently banishes it from his thought."[24] Whitehead goes on to indicate (we shall refer to this again later) seven basic features of Plato's philosophy and adds, "I hold that all philosophy is in fact an endeavor to obtain a coherent system out of some modifications of these notions." His dependence on Plato is clear.

Continuing, he stresses on the next page the importance in Plato of love in relation to the Psyche, or the soul, and he adds, "The 'life and motion' " — and these are important — "are derived from the operation of these two factors."[25] The two factors are Love and the Psyche. Here, though we are referring to Plato, we are close to Whitehead's own conceptions. The words "life and motion," which Whitehead puts into quotation marks, moreover, echo Wordsworth's language in *The Prelude* and in "Tintern Abbey." So likewise on the same page the philosopher parallels Wordsworth's reflection on "appearance" in relation to reality. He favors a "modern development" of Plato's basic principles, that would include a stress upon process (we have seen this also in Wordsworth) which, as Whitehead insists, "involves a mental side which is the soul entertaining ideas." A "synthesis" is produced "which is the Appearance woven out of the old and the new," and which includes in some fashion a future. "The final synthesis of these three complexes is the end to which its indwelling Eros urges the soul." This is brought out in the page to which we have referred. Whitehead does not hesitate to use such a concept as that of the soul with reference to his own philosophy. Nor does he hesitate to think of a force such as the soul having a relationship to the larger universe, apart from the human being and his force as personally applied.

In Wordsworth's references to the light, the animated rocks and brooks, which we have earlier mentioned in this chapter, there is something more than hyperbole. This must be granted also concerning the mention of the animated clouds and his statement about the mountain, "conscious" Helvellyn; he is doubtless using, in a certain measure, a figure of speech, and we can see that he does such things as this in various other places in his work. Clearly such a passage should not be read in a literal-minded way. Nevertheless as we have indicated earlier, Wordsworth is attempting to present a view of wide scope and this large grasp includes not only the externality of light, or of an objective brook or mountain, like Helvellyn, but its relation to our subjective feelings. He is thinking of nature broadly. The author is attempting to suggest a relationship between man — even the humblest of men — and the larger cosmos.

Hyperbole or not, the passage expresses something of his feelings in regard to the "inner" and "outer" worlds. In our own century, in Whitehead, there is a parallel to Wordsworth's view and this appears in the philosopher's statement that "the difference between a living organism and the inorganic environment is only a question of degree," involving importantly, however, "a difference of quality."[26] To this latter point Wordsworth could give full agreement. The "joy and love" which Wordsworth feels with reference to nature and man is illustrated in a *Prelude* passage concerning "a day of exhalations," the latter having symbolic reference to the "process" of the forms of external nature and the figure of a man on

> a day of exhalations, spread
> Upon the mountains, mists and steam-like fogs
> Redounding everywhere, not vehement
> But calm and mild, gentle and beautiful,

With gleams of sunshine on the eyelet spots
And loop-holes of the hills, wherever seen,
Hidden by quiet process . . . (84—)

The figure of a man then appears, almost as an exhalation
among exhalations. The picture also, it is to be observed, is
one of retrospect. Wordsworth, looking back, tells how he had
been wandering in the hills as a boy. During this wandering he
came upon the spot heavily enshrouded in shifting mists. The
scene as we have noted is almost etherealized. On the occasion
he saw a little way off — above his line of vision — what appeared to be a small "aerial island" among rocks, a single spot
where a shepherd was standing with his dog. Could anything
on the face of it be in essence more homely? And yet the clair-
voyance of the imagination is stirred by the scene. In the midst
of the encircling clouds, the vision of the shepherd and the dog
seemed to the boy's eyes to be itself moving along, though of
course only the clouds were in motion. A feeling of both
wonder and of simplicity is given by the floating picture in
which both animal and human life are blended. Love of
nature leads to love of man.

The theme as the poem continues consists in what the poet
owes both to external nature and a "nature" which is within.
God is a part of nature for Wordsworth — is immanent in
nature, but transcendent also. It is not a God characterized
by what Whitehead calls "individual absoluteness."[27] The
philosopher uses this term in connection with heightened personal power of the individual, but he connects it also with what
he regards as an unfortunate conception of the deity. We can
see his idea in a somewhat different form when elsewhere he
refers to a God who represents "Law as imposed" dogmatically.[28] There is a tendency to reject "imposition," and to reject
the grounding of philosophic thought upon will, both in
Wordsworth and Whitehead. What Wordsworth requires is
something akin to the notion of Whitehead — a solution of the

122

problem "exhibiting the plurality of individuals as consistent with the unity of the Universe, and a solution which exhibits the World as requiring its union with God, and God as requiring his union with the World."[29]

Associations of experiences — and the bringing together of ideas and feelings — play a part in the creation of consciousness which Wordsworth presents. Recalling at the moment of writing still another experience, he pictures a man who, waving his hand to and fro, "gave signal to his dog" — in order to teach him to drive a flock of sheep through "the mazes of steep crags." In a fashion somewhat similar to that of the previous almost etherealized scene Wordsworth reveals how the sun gilds the surroundings where the shepherd trains a loved creature, his dog. The sun on this occasion, gives notice of love; he — in Wordsworth's personification — makes known or publishes abroad, or indeed actually

> proclaims the love he bears
> To mountain regions. (118 —)

In these pictures concerning shepherds, as in the scene of the country fair, nature appears to Wordsworth not as a threatening force but in her guise as enveloping man and also contributing to man. Again, Wordsworth is thinking of nature broadly. It is a total view. The "domain" where the young Wordsworth grew up (the word "domain" is suggestive of the boy's spiritual possession of all the land) has Biblical connotations because of the shepherding done by man in the environment. The region with its accompaniment of human beings going about their symbolic tasks was for the boy a

> tract more exquisitely fair
> Than is that Paradise of ten thousand Trees
> Or Gehol's famous Gardens . . . (121 —)

Again Wordsworth is resorting with intentional artistic purpose to hyperbole. He is telling us how he felt about his home region, rather than stating mere actual fact. And the problem of appearance and reality is implicitly once more in his mind. Obviously he could not personally know all of the fabled regions that he refers to in continuing the passage — including palaces and domes of pleasure which recall the gardens of Kubla Khan, or haunts — containing the associations of religion — where inanimate objects are taught to take on the form of beauty, where mountains *embrace* all, and waters are at times, as he says, "asleep." The animation Wordsworth imposes on nature in earlier passages is again evident here. The hyperbole of the comparison he is making receives further stress in the remark —

> But lovelier far than this the Paradise
> Where I was rear'd . . . (144—)

It is necessary to speak with strong emphasis, he feels, for the beauties of his modest home region are of a kind that people usually fail to observe closely or to absorb spiritually within themselves. Such beauties, that is, often pass unnoticed. The use of overstatement, then, is with purpose. Wordsworth would like us to see the great beauty of the world, much of which, being in a sense "familiar," is often overlooked. Things of simplicity can be beautiful. This is a truism but at times it needs restatement. In Wordsworth's Lake District "nature's gifts" were as generously bestowed as any to which the imagination could give form, but there was, in addition, the human being living a life of independent simplicity as an actual fact

> working for himself, with choice
> Of time, and place, and object . . . (152—)

Thus in such circumstances one may make choices, man can choose his own time for activities of movement or of relaxation. A theory of leisure or of peace in contemplation has a place in Wordsworth's philosophy, as it has, also, in

124

Whitehead's thought. The poet makes much of the value in constructive "idleness" — a value which was not only enjoyable for the person possessing it, but contemplative. The district he describes lent itself to the virtue of contemplation. The leisure that could be enjoyed there added to the beauty of the place as seen. For beauty, to the poet, has its subjective side; it is not exclusively an external thing. Like Whitman, Wordsworth enjoys the possibility of choosing idleness which recalls the joy of childhood. But he includes also the pursuit of group needs. It is evident that he wishes a reconciliation or balance of ends with the satisfaction of human purposes including both "individual ends" and "social"; such group purposes can, indeed, become at times a part of us, though we may be almost unaware of their influence. Thus Wordsworth feels we may all be affected by

> the common haunts of the green earth,
> With the ordinary human interests
> Which they embosom . . . (166 —)

So it is that we gradually undergo development, and we learn to love things of beauty "not knowing that we love"; indeed, we "feel, not knowing whence our feeling comes." Joy can be made to fill our lives — joy made up of the two principles which the poet has set before us concentratedly: love and feeling of various kinds. Wordsworth's first human affections, apart from those of a child directed toward his mother and immediate family, were inclined, we learn, towards human beings whose work brought them close to nature and nature's laws, those whose attention was centered on "little but substantial needs"; and yet there was beauty for him in their lives, even in the distresses and dangers that they suffered. The awe-inspiring character of natural forces and the powers within the universe which may lead to pain for the human being — as to these things, he says

> I heard and saw enough to make

125

The imagination restless; nor was free
Myself from . . . perils; nor were tales
Wanting, the tragedies of former times,
Or hazards and escapes . . . (213 –)

Of these stories he chooses to recount the tale of a shepherd's son who, seeking a lost sheep, the "Straggler" of the flock, is himself almost lost. The creature is referred to as an "Adventurer, hunger-press'd," seeking a "green plot of pasture"; allusions to the Bible give the story something of prophetic character. When the strayed sheep was almost saved, it "sprang forward," but failed to make its way to safety, being carried "headlong by the roaring flood." The sheep is lost. And the boy's own personal condition parallels that of the lost sheep in that he is left, a "Prisoner on the Island," surrounded by the raging stream. Later he is saved by the aid of the shepherd, his father, who through the use of his outstretched staff brings the boy to safe land. The theme of danger and distress which seems to have a philosophic meaning for Wordsworth may be connected with chance and adventure as related to human life.

In Whitehead's view there is a repetitious mechanism in the universe with which we must struggle, as well as a creative side with which we may co-operate. As he well says, "life is an offensive, directed against the repetitious mechanism of the Universe."[30] There is, then, discordance and capriciousness with which we must struggle, as the shepherd's son and the shepherd (like Wordsworth) well realize. Such problems as these are pervasive in Whitehead's philosophy. A merely defensive approach to them is not sufficient. Creation is needed. Process contains danger, but it is a constant factor in a life that is fully human. For Whitehead one should be steady in his feeling or in his reliance upon the fact "that fine action is treasured in the nature of things."[31] And here we must think also about aspiration which brings peace: a feeling arising "from aim beyond personality."[32]

The experience, the adventure, of Wordsworth's shepherd illustrates the point. The shepherd's experiences may be compared to experiences referred to in Whitehead which involve a "closeness of status, such as the relation of parent to child or the relation of marriage"; such a closeness can also "produce the love of self-devotion where the potentialities of the loved object are felt passionately as a claim that it find itself in a friendly Universe."[33] Here discord is destroyed within the mind, according to Whitehead, and his doctrine fits well the context in Wordsworth. Presenting a contrast to the real shepherds who have potential tragedy always lying in wait, Wordsworth next makes allusion to those legendary men watching their flocks on the shores of "delicate Galesus," reminiscent of Virgil and Latin pastoral literature, with its comfortable "herdsman and his Herd," or of the mount above Horace's farm,

> cool Lucretilis, where the Pipe was heard
> Of Pan, the invisible God, thrilling the rocks . . . (320—)

Wordsworth confesses that his own "Fancy might run wild" at thought of imaginary things of this kind or at remembrances of real places where he has known the shepherd to live. Such a real person was protected by the sheltering geography of the land, "a rolling hut his home," living in not overlabored "pleasure," at times having no duty more "toilsome than to carve a beechen bowl"; the idling shepherd lives many of his spring-time and summer hours in what seems a world of daydreams. But he leaves his "beechen bowl" behind, where someone else, a "Traveller" may find it for his use, at "Spring or Fountain." This "traveller" is also portrayed as a figure parallel to that of the idling shepherd. He too is an idler in the land who pursues his course, seemingly in accordance with his own willfulness. And there is room, we feel, for such idling in the world, an actual need for it. As Whitehead also says there is great need for freedom, or independence — need for

127

"elbow-room within the Universe."[34] Such freedom, or elbow-room, "provides each actuality with a welcome environment for irresponsibility." In some sense one should not always be serving as his brother's keeper. Whitehead makes a point of this. But it is not that he would deny that in certain cases we have a responsibility for another person. I *should* ordinarily be my brother's keeper. There are times, however, within the life of each individual when that person's own individuality is of importance to him.

For Wordsworth the need of elbow-room is evident, but, thinking about the shepherd, he takes pains to indicate (we again emphasize the idea) that when the shepherd leaves behind him his "beechen-bowl" it may well be found by another wayfarer in the world. This is the "reality" which is intermingled with the world of seeming, the world of apparent daydreaming "idleness." But it is reality in a more painful sense that repeatedly calls Wordsworth back. What we refer to is the reality which takes hold of his mind, he says, "with firmer grasp" — the reality with its uncontrollable "snows and streams," its "terrifying winds"; this it is which makes the human being feel how alone he is in the universe. But it is a reality which is not negative: it is not envisaged in abandonment from all thought of a hope, an ideal.

The shepherd, as a symbol of the human being, must "wait upon the storms" and guide his flocks in accordance with them. Later, in a more pleasant season, at a time when "all the mountains dance with lambs," he follows them "through the lower Heights," making his "rounds," and thereafter mounting ever "higher"; daily he leaves his moving home at the dawning of the morning light. The kinship of man and animal with each other — and indeed with the total creation — is manifest here, and is signalized most especially later when we picture in our minds the shepherd as he "breakfasts with his dog"; he lingers, characteristically, more than he should, but finally

> springs up with a bound, and then away!
> Ascending fast with his long Pole in hand,
> Or winding in and out among the crags. (380 —)

There is no need to follow the shepherd in his "day's march," Wordsworth says. The important thing is the man's state of mind, as he enjoys his freedom "wedded to his life of hope" which includes "hazard, and hard labour" alongside "that majestic indolence" which is indeed welcome to all. Wordsworth, then, like Whitman feels that in human life there should be abundant room for loafing and inviting one's soul. Like Whitman, too, he has a feeling of closeness to the lower creation. The animal creation is magnified in the symbolic reference of the expression "Sheep like Greenland Bears," referring to creatures in the fog seen in his childhood. On the other hand, Wordsworth emphasizes his conception of the grandeur of man in presenting in his poem the sudden figure of a shepherd following his tasks in mist, "in size a giant," or

> described in distant sky,
> A solitary object and sublime,
> Above all height! like an aerial Cross,
> As it is stationed on some spiry Rock
> Of the Chartreuse, for worship. (405 —)

So Wordsworth felt in his boyhood. The symbol of the cross serves to glorify the conception that he held of the human being he had observed. Unconsciously the author, during the later stages of his close contact with external nature, was moving toward an ever-increasing respect for the human element and appreciation of that quality of nature which too is deserving of reverence. It is a heterogeneous nature that he has in mind. Thinking of the figures created by authors such as Shakespeare he suggests that humanity, on the side of its unsubstantiality, spirituality, or immaterialism, may be compared to them. Humanity properly should have closely inter-twined relationships with nature and is, in this very fact, like the figures in literature. Wordsworth has a high respect for literature. His words here speak eloquently of the close associa-tion of various intangible things, such as human ideas, with the physical being of the living individual person. Any person, though a simple artisan, may have his own learning and be quite capable of teaching things of value to others at the same time that he is capable of acts of folly and fear. Such a person was, for Wordsworth, a *token* which discloses or expresses something — a veritable "index" (he uses this word, with its voluminous connotations), a being

>spiritual almost
>As those of Books . . . (416 —)

There is a somewhat Platonic reality here — in the notion of humanity which Wordsworth is proposing. A person, in the abstract, has connections with the Platonic forms, the Platonic ideas. He is "more exalted" in this sense than are fanciful replicas or creations that we find in books; he is "an im-aginative form," possessing potentialities suggestive of the commonness but also of the complexities of family life: teacher, sufferer, admonisher, given to his own wretchedness and tragic condition. This latter, darker side, which Words-worth mentions, he did not clearly perceive in his young days, but he tells us he did *feel* something of it.

Such conceptions as these Wordsworth holds in a spirit of in-dividual relatedness, not that of "Individual Absoluteness"[35] (to use again the term employed for the most part negatively by Whitehead). Nor is the poet in the least dogmatic or coer-cive concerning these ideas; rather, they are held by him ten-tatively. He realizes that his complex conceptions of shepherds, or of men generally, may be regarded as examples of "ap-pearances" merely — a "shadow, a delusion"; we must not, however, miss "the spirit of things" concerning the person, or

Wordsworth's view that truth involves motion — indeed, that it is "a motion or a shape" filled "with vital functions" pointing toward other growths. It is not, as some suppose,

> a Block
> Or waxen Image which yourselves have made,
> And ye adore. (433 —)

Wordsworth is bringing his attack in this important passage actually against a view of life which is nondynamic, a philosophy which is nonoperational, or one based on a conception of mere inert matter. Related to this is his criticism, in the more extended context of *The Prelude*, of those whose conception would reduce a human being to a status of practical helplessness in the universe — a pawn having virtually no power to produce effects, among them those of social change. The poet's larger view of the universe, including his conception of God, is advanced not dogmatically, but tentatively. And in this spirit of tolerant reflectiveness his view is paralleled by tendencies in Whitehead and paralleled "by Plato's publication of his final conviction, towards the end of his life, that the divine element in the world is to be conceived as a persuasive agency and not as a coercive agency."[36] We can co-operate with it.

In the reflective passage by Wordsworth from which we have previously quoted, the poet is presenting (though tentatively and critically as we have said) the static view of human life made up of blocks of matter or images of wax. The negative terms "Block" and "waxen" are in the context as we saw. The criticism the poet is making parallels to some degree Whitehead's criticism of certain tendencies in philosophy through a period of several centuries. Wordsworth's criticism of blocks and constructions made of wax may be closely paralleled in the philosopher's criticism directed against what he calls simple editions of more complex things which we should be in fact more profoundly observing as we try to

131

understand life and the world about us. These "simplified editions" (we use Whitehead's expression) are what he calls "constructions"[37]; they themselves are *not* the *actuality* which we may suppose exists in the world that we experience. We ourselves make them artificially as supposed concrete entities.

We, if we blunder, have separated out such "simplified editions" from the wider experience we have in contact with the world, or we have in other words separated or abstracted them in our minds. We then, according to Whitehead, proceed to make these constructions (which are comparable to what Wordsworth calls blocks or waxen images) appear as if they were concrete entities and hence we think of them as real; but it is not so — we have been guilty of what the philosopher calls the fallacy of misplaced concreteness. This "error" can still have usefulness for some purposes. It can at times be a valuable as-if when one is dealing with delimited problems.

In Wordsworth's conceptualizing of man there is, as in Plato, an intermingling of the "purified" ideal (which should not, he feels, be suppressed); there are also the ethical values related to the good — values which need to be considered, as connected with the transcendent. So comparably, in regard to knowledge, Whitehead stresses a transcending factor: that which we know is "an actual occasion of experience, as diversified by reference to a realm of entities which transcend that immediate occasion"[38] of experience. The transcending entities are transcendent "in that they have analogous or different connections with other occasions of experience." The view of cognition explained here includes something akin to the Platonic ideas, or the eternal objects of Whitehead's terminology. And on the next page he comments: "It is the foundation of the metaphysical position which I am maintaining that the understanding of actuality requires a reference to ideality."[39] Cognition in any high sense is related to the good.

Thus it is in Wordsworth also: the attaining of knowledge is related to good. For Whitehead the consciousness of ideas itself requires a conciliation of the actual and the ideal. For him consciousness is, in addition, closely connected with art. In another volume he explains that consciousness "raises the importance of the final Appearance relatively to that of the initial Reality."[40] Or, as the philosopher says in a context about a page later, "it results from the influx of ideality into its contrast with reality, with the purpose of re-shaping the latter into a finite, select appearance."[41] Thus consciousness emerges from art and "at once produces the new specialized art of the conscious animals — in particular human art." Consciousness with its ideality passes on into art which most broadly viewed is civilization. And a few sentences later he says, "Civilization is nothing other than the unremitting aim at the major perfections of harmony."

In a later book, *Modes of Thought*, Whitehead comes back to a conception of *aim*, which it seems evident is very important to him. Aim can, of course, be related to limitation and system, and he emphasizes the view that "system is essential for rational thought."[42] The danger, however, lies in the fact that any "closed system is the death of living understanding." What we need is "insight" which will involve "a mixture of clarity and vagueness." At a subsequent point in the same volume, Whitehead speaks of "aim" as "the exclusion of the boundless wealth of alternative potentiality, and the inclusion of that definite factor of novelty" by which we can bring about a kind of "unification."[43] This is a characteristic of life. In every respect it involves creativity. A similar combination of aim and creativity is also essential to Wordsworth's view of things. For the poet there is the question: Are the appearances of human beings that he tries to recall merely shadows or delusions? Would it have been better if he had never conceived such idealized figures? On the contrary, he feels blessed that through the divine in "Nature" and in "Man" he was brought to perceptions "at a distance that was fit." The problem of prepossessions arises here. The "distance" enables him to have

133

presuppositions or idealized conceptions which are basic, in one fashion or another, to all thought. Indeed

> so we all of us in some degree
> Are led to knowledge, whencesoever led,
> And howsoever . . . (440 —)

As we think of the adequacy or inadequacy of our knowledge and its relation to the good, the problem of prejudices (so important in our day) naturally arises. We live on a globe that is bringing us closer and closer to many different kinds of peoples. And with this fact come attendant evils. Are we hemmed in almost completely by the world's prejudging and its many erroneous prepossessions or presuppositions; are we helpless in the face of such evils? We are all of us *led* to our knowledge, which is definitely limited in character as Wordsworth suggests in the passage previously quoted, and we may paraphrase a further statement he makes by substituting for his word "evil" the word "prejudice"; we are, that is, led actually toward goodness or knowledge, pitiful though it may be. For "were it otherwise," if we found prejudice — "evil" — as

> fast as we found good
> In our first years, or think that it is found,
> How could the innocent heart bear up and live! (443 —)

Here we have the problem of the ideal. The word "evil" (Wordsworth's word here) presents a broader conception than that of prejudice, but the latter conception, considering prejudice as a form of evil, is of more immediate application, and it has its connection with the generous side of the thought of Wordsworth and Whitehead. We have seen this in our earlier comments on the evils of intolerance, and we observe it in the tentativeness, the thoughtfulness, with which hypotheses are considered in the works of both men. Whitehead's philosophy is one long attack on irreflective presuppositions — that is, prejudices. He sums up the arrogance of the dogmatic attitude in many contexts, one of which contains a rhyme about an unenlightened administrator of a college who holds that what he knows not is "not knowledge."[44]

But Whitehead is also similar to Wordsworth in another way which is somewhat unexpected. Whitehead recognizes the fact that prepossessions or presuppositions can have a function; they may at times have their merits. Again and again he says that we *must* have various perspectives, and these are at times prepossessions. "All systematic thought must start from presuppositions."[45] Frequently Whitehead thinks of the use of "assigned patterns"[46] in relation to one's thoughts. We assign these patterns, and as we do so we limit our "choice of details." We thus escape the infinite, as is necessary, but we may delimit things to our loss. On the page following these references he speaks of the fact that "advance is partly the gathering of details into assigned patterns."

But there is the danger that "dogmatic spirits" may let themselves be ruled by patterns. We must give careful thought to a "type of progress, namely the introduction of novelty of pattern into conceptual experience." Whitehead's view as to the use of patterns is, broadly speaking, to be noted in "an ideal of human liberty"[47] and activity whereby people co-operate. This ideal has one of its manifestations in the American government. We are thinking here of the ideal present in the document on which our federal government is based. "It has never been realized in its perfection"; in its absence of "characterization of the variety of possibilities open for humanity, it is limited and imperfect." Nevertheless, "such as it is, the Constitution vaguely discloses the immanence in this epoch of that one energy of idealization, whereby bare process is transformed into glowing history."

In every respect thought involves, or is within, frames, and this means limitations. For "there are no clear divisions anywhere."[48] We have to remember, that is, that "there are no clear divisions when you push your observations beyond the

135

presuppositions on which they rest." Everywhere in the process of thought we have to make a decision or a cutting-off of one kind or another in working within a given frame of thought. There are fruitful givens and unfruitful ones. Wordsworth realizes this also, but he would have us scrutinize with care the complex prepossession, for example, which would assume that a person is corrupt basically and that he can bring forth nothing that is good. The important constructive point is to be "furnished with a prepossession without which the soul" is completely at a loss, or attains "no knowledge that can bring forth good" or at least some "insight" of value. Wordsworth also comments on the danger of "laughters and contempts" which cause one to think with little "respect" of fellow human beings, but he soon adds that he was himself still "unripe" and had much to learn concerning a full appreciation of humanity. External nature most often still held the place of eminence in his thought.

The poet's continued effort in *The Prelude* is to raise the mass of his fellow human beings to a higher status. It is part and parcel of an idea of social dynamics. He directs his attack against self-oriented, self-aggrandizing egoism which would act as an element in opposition to social change. From his point of view we can admire humanity taken in the large. The tendency to lose respect for our fellow human beings is at the center of much conventionalized philosophy. This is self-oriented ego. Why not lose respect for ourselves? We tend to negate ourselves inadvertently when we lose respect for others. The poet in this part of *The Prelude* is summing up the value of his experiences; he is giving us his reflections upon them.

The wide love for one's fellow man, or even an adequate *respect* broadly considered, does not come early. In Wordsworth it came as a process working its way forward through a number of years. We have some unconscious sense of what is happening to us in the growth of a widespread love, even when in our "unripe time" our dominant concern is our emotional relation to our personal desires or to our external sensibilities.

Our "animal activities" come first, Wordsworth says, and this was very true of his early personal self-orientation. But even when he had passed beyond these more "trivial" tendencies, he tells us, and actually "long afterwards," when nature had become more profoundly felt

> until not less
> Than three and twenty summers had been told
> Was man in my affections and regards
> Subordinate to her . . . (481 —)

The actual point in Wordsworth's life when this change took place cannot be stated with certainty (some scholars feel that he was twenty-two, not twenty-three), but it is clear that, as he says, it was beyond the time of his awareness of nature's "viewless agencies" — the time of his "rapture" in the external beauty of the world. Thus Book Eight is an extension of Book Seven. His full appreciation even of the life of animals and birds seems, nevertheless, to have come to him later than his love for his fellow man. Before this development had occurred, however, there was for Wordsworth a time of something like fantasy, which stood in the way of accurate and profound perceptiveness — a kind of "wilful" play-activity of the mind wherein the youth drew upon nature to adorn an object in a fashion which was alien to it; that is, he took recourse at times to some spurious gilding to lend extravagant and unneeded color to nature herself. Such "fictions" (Wordsworth uses this word) are to be expected in normal existence. The "wilfulness of fancy" may even make a contribution to one's life. But there is the danger that hurtful distortions may occur — that the tragic, for example, as he says, may be made "super-tragic" and that other disadvantages may come. This weakness which affected the young Wordsworth is common among younger people. Such are the "wild obliquities" which carry one away from the vital realities available to us through direct and honest observation of things like

slender blades of grass
Tipp'd with a bead of rain or dew . . . (548—)

The faculty of "wilful fancy" (Wordsworth uses the term, in effect, twice) he regards nevertheless as a "Power" which can rise in importance. It rises in the proportion with which it may unite itself with the higher imagination that pierces or enters more deeply than fantasy, or the "fancy," can penetrate into the reality of things. What saved him from the *dangers* of fancy more than anything else, however, was the fact that he constitutionally had about him and habitually took recourse to "a real solid world" of valid imagery. Wordsworth is here recapitulating the substance of his experiences related in previous books of *The Prelude*, and, among them, he turns to those connected with his life at the university. There he was guilty of an "abstraction" or a cutting away of essentials from a sound conception of the essence of humanity. But still the sense of history, or an appreciation of the workings of centuries, somehow helped his vision or at least "solemnized" it; thus he tells us his scope widened and he

thought of human life at times
With an indefinite terror and dismay
Such as the storms and angry elements
Had bred . . . (658—)

This seriousness of view saved him, and led him, at least for the moment, away from the tendency toward idle fantasy. It led him, that is, toward a conscious recognition of the importance of a life of action, with due deliberation and understanding of what fruitful acting might consist in and of what its implications might be. His recapitulation of what life had to offer him and what he had learned from it brings him, near the close of this part of *The Prelude*, to a further consideration of London; this city served as a disciplinarian instructor, in his continued education. Here he was seeking "inner meanings"; he was not ignorant of the fact that "high things" were to be found in the huge complex of forces making up the city in its age-long growth. There indeed he felt the eternal, the cosmic force of a great metropolis, including "weight and power" — he reiterates the point with regard to power and combines it again with "weight," and he relates it finally to the "divine."

To explain in Book Eight what the experience in the city meant to him he makes use next of cave imagery — the figure of a cave, seen by a "Traveller," presented in an elaborate account of some twenty-five lines. Within it, as the sojourner's eyes become accustomed to the sights around him, he envisions the space as it "spreads and grows"; at length he imagines "the roof above his head" or, it may be, the actuality of it is there. At once, however, the seeming actuality of it "unsettles and recedes," and he has no sense of whether he has observed something which is substantial or a mere "shadow" form. This elaborate figure which Wordsworth employs will be reminiscent of Plato's cave for certain readers; the poet presents the cave with its intermingling of "light and darkness" and

> Shapes and Forms and Tendencies to Shape
> That shift and vanish, change and interchange
> Like Spectres . . . (720—)

After a certain time, what the traveller (on this earth, as we may say) has seen begins to work "less and less," and finally what is before his eyes is hard and firm, "lifeless" and yet complete. Still, as he pauses for a moment and attempts to "look again," things appear to be different as a result of "a new quickening," which begins mildly but creeps rapidly until "all which he beholds," whether by means of "projections" and "cavities" or through the streaming of hues, works upon him with force comparable to that of a magician. Thus it is that the "pageant" he presents "parts" and

> Unites, embodying everywhere some pressure
> Or image, recognis'd or new, some type
> Or picture of the world . . . (734—)

The references to forms, with "mass," "projections," and "cavities" may remind one of the projections of geometry. The thing before the eyes of the mathematician or the sojourner on earth is, coupled with Wordsworth's imagination, a "Spectacle to which there is no end." It may be thought of as the receptacle to which reference was made near the close of the last chapter, with its relations to the thought of Plato and of Whitehead. It refers to the experience of life, evidently, as well as to that "Fountain" London and our general destiny. Thus Book Eight re-emphasizes the ideas of Book Seven. For Wordsworth there was greatness in the city, he tells us, something imperial. In that period of his life, if he understood rightly his main drive, he was not seeking knowledge but "craved for power," and this he found manifest in the operations, past and present, in the great city.

London, as we have seen in the previous chapter, was for Wordsworth (he now re-emphasizes this) a place of overwhelming sensations — mostly physical — but these features of the external world had also an inner aspect, as he came finally to recognize, partly because many things in the city suggested not only the living present but certain intangibles. This was mainly brought about through the glorious memorials to the past in London standing eloquently before the young Wordsworth's eyes. It became more and more characteristic of him in that period, he says, to crave for not mere knowledge, but for deeper understanding, as well as for the perception of the relation of a thing to that which is efficacious — or, in a word, that which contains power. While striving to understand the power that was everywhere so visible in the city of London he at the same time sought those things which had a dynamism for himself — conceptions, as we may interpret his thought, which could have usefulness in the future production of a literature characterized by vitality.

Nothing had a "circumscribed" effect upon him, he reminds us in Book Eight; rather, "objects" were "capacious" — they

140

expanded outwardly as his mind did with them. We can think here again of the imagination of the geometer, as we do at times when we read Whitehead, but as in the case of the philosopher the projections are not merely mathematical; they are much more. Wordsworth himself was not a presence limited in existence to a single mathematical point, "punctual," as he says; rather he was a soul (a portion of the Psyche, as we may think of it in Platonic and Whiteheadian terms), dwelling indeed not merely "in time and space," but "far diffus'd." The poet's terms here remind us of Whitehead. This vision he obtained in part from a sense of history, but it was not limited by history, that is, not limited by history viewed as a subject for conventional study.

The emphasis on space and time is notable in Wordsworth as in Whitehead; man lives peculiarly not only in space but in time, because of his subjectivity — because of his subjective relations to them, though Wordsworth is not assimilating space and time as do some thinkers of the twentieth century. Both conceptions are merely necessary parts of the self, and they must be taken together, if we are to understand more fully man's depth of nature. But for the present it is time which received the poet's attention — time in its relation to accidents —

> extrinsic transitory accidents,
> Of record or tradition . . . (779 —)

Wordsworth's feeling of what had been accomplished or done in London in the past, and his experience of "the Shapes" which were presented to his eyes, commingled and acted as "vital functions" within what Plato or Whitehead would call "the Psyche." Thus "impregnations" operated upon the young man, and became interrelated with his remembrances of his early life in the open spaces of Westmorland with its "dashing lakes" and with its "pointed crags," that somehow, with other forms, had the effect of music upon "the passing wind." That is, a solid thing like the rock of the mountain becomes a part of effects wrought by a far less tangible force such as the air that surrounds it. How, in spite of "guilt" and "vice" which he observed about him, did such things as he is describing bring a sense of kinship with his fellow creatures, an "elevating" of the status of man in his mind? His view of life — his religion, indeed — was attained in a measure through hours of solitude, but in his thought he was no isolated human being —

> A Solitary, who with vain conceits
> Had heen inspired, and walk'd about in dreams. (808 —)

No small part of a new joyful emotion came to him through the contribution of books, though the living reality of London helped him also. London, he says in Book Eight, made the use of books more meaningful for him. In this way the city was related even to his experience in the wilder regions of the Lake District. He was interested in what a human being may become, and he recognized that this required a world-outlook which included imagination, or a sense of how things could be as if something that does not usually meet the eye were inwardly the case. The person needs at times to be thought of in terms of the ideal — as if certain far from ordinary matters were possible. It is only through such an element of projection — or of faith and trust in life — that certain things included in the dreams we have can later become in some unsuspected way forms having reality. In this reality there are oppositions, subjective feelings in which our spirits are, according to Wordsworth, at times "overcast" or "in eclipse," but the purity of the vision one has had still remains undestroyed — and "unencroach'd upon"; it seems according to The Prelude

> brighter far
> For this deep shade in counterview, that gloom
> Of opposition . . . (814 —)

It is the unity of the world of nature and man, if we include both man's psyche and his understanding of nature, that is being borne in upon Wordsworth in this section of *The Prelude*, a single spirit. If "strongly breath'd upon," with such a "sensation" as this, "whencesoe'er it comes" the person's "soul" rejoices "as in her highest joy"; it is in this "chiefly" that the soul has "feeling" of the source from which "she" comes. Man's life on earth involves in effect a passage "through all Nature," Wordsworth says, but, as in Whitehead's philosophy, it does not terminate with mere passage. The city, which we (and Wordsworth) have called a receptacle, exemplifies this. It is commonly known that the city is often a subject for attack in the period of the romantic movement, and Wordsworth of course contributes to this justifiable criticism of the city, justified especially in view of the social conditions of the time. But the point here is Wordsworth's recognition of the vitally functioning factor, the metaphysical, in the city (he is recapitulating here) not only as it contributes to our philosophical and civilized life, but also as it ministers in countless instances to individual needs. The poet gives full tribute to the city,

> that vast Abiding-place
> Of human Creatures, turn where'er we may,
> Profusely sown with individual sights
> Of courage, and integrity, and truth,
> And tenderness . . . (836 —)

The good in the city, as elsewhere, is merely "set off by foil" — the language is Wordsworth's — by the foil of obstructions, oppositions, and evils to which we have earlier referred. All of the good in the city and in the cosmos, Wordsworth had come to appreciate more fully by slow "gradations" as he was moving toward love of man, though it was to take a drastic experience in the midst of a great social upheaval, the French Revolution, to bring him to a closer, an even more dynamic knowledge of humanity and of himself. This problem of further self-knowledge and knowledge of society, as modified by the impingement upon Wordsworth of the French Revolution, will be discussed in the next chapter.

Footnotes

1. *The Concept of Nature*, Second Impression (Ann Arbor: University of Michigan Press, 1959). p. 2.
2. *Ibid.*, p. 3. He also refers to "thinking 'heterogeneously' about nature."
3. *Ibid.*, p. 13. This book has been very highly praised by J. E. McTaggert and A. E. Taylor.
4. *Ibid.*, p. 14.
5. *Ibid.*, p. 14.
6. *Ibid.*, p. 26. See also p. 30.
7. *Ibid.*, p. 27.
8. *Ibid.*, p. 43.
9. *Ibid.*, p. 47.
10. *Ibid.*, p. 47. The quotation has reference to Schelling. See also N. O. Lossky, *The Intuitive Basis of Knowledge*, trans. Duddington (London: Macmillan and Co., 1919).
11. *Ibid.*, p. 70.
12. *Science and the Modern World*, p. 97. He adds to this words having a religious bearing.
13. *The Concept of Nature*, p. 13.
14. *Ibid.*, p. 123.
15. *Ibid.*, p. 126.
16. *Ibid.*, p. 143.
17. *Ibid.*, p. 144.
18. *Ibid.*, p. 163.
19. *Process and Reality*, p. 268.
20. *Adventures of Ideas*, p. 271.
21. *Ibid.*, p. 84.
22. *Ibid.*, p. 86.
23. *Ibid.*, p. 189.
24. *Ibid.*, p. 354.
25. *Ibid.*, p. 355. Citations for all quotations in the paragraph are from this page.
26. *Process and Reality*, p. 271.
27. *Adventures of Ideas*, p. 56.
28. *Ibid.*, p. 142.
29. *Ibid.*, p. 215.
30. *Adventures of Ideas*, p. 102.
31. *Ibid.*, p. 353.
32. *Ibid.*, p. 371.
33. *Ibid.*, p. 373.

34. *Ibid.*, p. 251.

35. In this context the term "means the notion of release from essential dependence on other members of the community in respect to modes of activity"; see *Adventures of Ideas*, p. 54.

36. *Ibid.*, p. 213. The idea expressed in this quotation Whitehead regards as "one of the greatest intellectual discoveries in the history of religion."

37. *Science and the Modern World*, p. 77. See, also, "misplaced concreteness" in this page in Whitehead as well as references to this "error" on p. 85, where he emphasizes by capitalization "The Fallacy of Misplaced Concreteness."

38. *Ibid.*, p. 227. Concerning cognition in this passage, Whitehead also refers to his book *The Principles of Natural Knowledge*.

39. *Ibid.*, p. 228. See also on this page the "transcendent entities," to which Whitehead refers; they "have been termed 'universals.' " He continues: "I prefer to use the term 'eternal objects' . . . Eternal objects are . . . in their nature, abstract." See also *Process and Reality*, p. 70.

40. *Adventures of Ideas*, pp. 347-348.

41. *Ibid.*, p. 349.

42. *Modes of Thought*, p. 114.

43. *Ibid.*, pp. 207-208.

44. *Ibid.*, p. 59. See also the fine remarks about "the dogmatic fallacy" which "infests the world" in *The Function of Reason* (Princeton: Princeton University Press, 1929), p. 70 and following.

45. *Ibid.*, p. 2. See also in the same work, *Modes of Thought*, references to presuppositions, p. 7, and similar references, pp. 29 and 53.

46. *Ibid.*, p. 79.

47. *Ibid.*, p. 165.

48. *Ibid.*, p. 21.

Chapter IX

Wordsworth's Residence in France: Revolutionary Freedom

At an early point in the previous chapter we said that the human being, particularly in growing from childhood into young maturity, is not merely a physical or biological being. Sociality is important for such a person at this stage of youth. Still, the physical is a momentous factor. As Whitehead says, we "cannot escape habits of mind which cling closely to habits of body."[1] Because of the youth's biological development, resistance to the social sometimes takes place. Erik Erikson has pointed out that "the configurations of outer suppression are related to those of inner repression."[2] Something happens to the inner person if unfortunate outer action is imposed upon

147

the individual. And Erikson gives the example of making a child "stand in a corner or stay in some enclosure"; in his view, "the logic, not to speak of the benefit of such arrangement is certainly doubtful — but not so our satisfaction in having done to the transgressors what they had coming to them."

The hostility of the punisher is here implied and that attitude may give rise to a corresponding feeling of hostility in the recipient of the punishment. We had been thinking of Wordsworth and the matter of biological development as against social adjustments involving the growth of human love. Hostility is likely to be prominent in the youth during adolescence and later. But the youth can seek the woods — or nature — in moments of loneliness and bitterness. So it was with Wordsworth. In our previous chapter the poet was portrayed as giving a backward look in which he referred to his early love of nature in its relation to his developing love of humankind: that is, he was facing the question of whether mature love of human beings grows out of one's love of nature. Concern about natural beauty could lead, in the end, to concern with regard to one's fellows. It seemed to him that there was a connection between the two. He was thinking steadily of the problem of nature in its relation to humanity. The relationship between them had also an implied importance for Wordsworth in his experiences in France.

A growing affection for humanity was in process of development within him. The ground for the connection between warmth of feeling toward nature and friendliness toward persons might seem to be that love and appreciation of nature in its immediate aspects provides a beginning for a love of the whole external universe and of the divine. Man, externally viewed, is an essential part of the totality of visible things. In this sense it would be strange if our love of nature would not, in time, enable us to awaken to a love of our human fellows. Perhaps we grow to love persons coterminously with our love of nature. It may even be that for some people affection for humanity in general antedates any warmth of disposition whatever toward external nature. But the poet had been trying to tell what, to his best remembrance, occurred in his own experience. He was also, however, concerned with what may happen to others with respect to nature.

Wordsworth was leading the reader to the problem of the relation of humanity to the totality of visible things. He may not have been fully aware of this. But it *seemed* to him evident that a profound perception of fellow human beings comes later than a perception of the outer world exclusive of man: that a concern for fellow creatures in any real sense certainly comes late. Possibly he was in part influenced by the sense-data theory of Locke and others which tends to stress, as the earliest influence upon the person, that which is external and seemingly immediate in things as specific entities. The poet, however — especially by the time of *The Prelude* — moved in general away from such doctrines as these which have usually been thought of as emanating from Locke. At the opening of the ninth book of *The Prelude* Wordsworth, for the moment, makes use of retrospect in order to see more clearly the thing that he is trying to examine: that is, a person can sometimes see better what immediately lies ahead by relating it to the past. In his poem the poet is again and again reading his own history backward and forward. This we have seen is a method of approach by which, according to Whitehead, all history should be read. Whitehead thinks in this way of history in whatever period, whether ancient or modern, whether Eastern, Western, or Middle-Eastern, but he could have included personal history as well. He thinks very actively of universal history at whatever point he can perceive something of penetrating importance. And reversals of direction here can be illuminating.

We have said that Wordsworth held that a general concern for one's fellow human beings comes late. The word *concern* in this context has a meaning that fits in with a meaning which

Whitehead gives it. For the philosopher it is perception with an "affective tone,"[3] a kind of loving feeling; in his view it is best recognized as " 'concern' in the Quaker sense." It involves interrelation. Thus it would not be understood with this connotation in a statement to the effect that Russia and Austria were concerned with the fate of Switzerland when it was a question whether Russia or France should gain complete and ruthless control of the small country. That is, there is in this statement no interrelation of friendly feeling (or interaction) between Russia and Switzerland or between Austria and Switzerland. Such was actually the state of aggrandizing affairs, as it happened, about the time of the writing of The Prelude. Wordsworth, on the other hand, cared about Switzerland. This is a good illustration of his warm feeling for other persons and nations. The example we have given here has a connection — an aspect of contrast — with the poet's state of mind at the time that he was writing the ninth book of The Prelude and later, for he was not merely sympathetic but strongly in sympathy with the liberal Swiss people. Near the close of the previous book (referred to in our last chapter) the poet had indicated something of his earlier concern for his fellow men, involving his past interaction with them and their interaction with him.

In The Prelude Wordsworth, then, is repeatedly reading his own history retrogressively and progressively so far as it has relation to time. Such a reading in some respects can be involved in philosophy. He uses the figure of a river as following a sort of path — a river which actually is "sway'd by fear to tread an onward road" because the path is moving toward what seems a "devouring sea"; hence, the river moves backward. The passage concerning the river provides a transition to further events in the ongoing flow of Wordsworth's life. The stream of the self is submitting in a kind of Proustian fashion "to old remembrances"; it is a river which "will measure back his course, far back," fearing, it would seem, what is to come. It has a "fear" that, in proceeding forward, something will be encountered which will give rise to pain.

The direct comparison of a human being to a river having "old remembrances" is an unusual one. Wordsworth is the river, and in this capacity he has a fear of traversing the "onward road"; and it is he personally who dreads moving forward because there is something ahead having the potentiality of consuming, or devouring him. The thing that lies ahead may perhaps be thought of as eternity, or death. The destiny of man is part of this. Wordsworth worked on the beginning of the "Immortality Ode" a year or two prior to his labors on the 1805 *Prelude*, and he completed the "Immortality Ode" in 1806. It may be, however, that the potentially "devouring" thing lying ahead, which might be capable of destruction to his personality, was the remembrance of his leaving behind him the French girl, Annette Vallon. This was on his mind, in remembrance, during the period in which he was writing *The Prelude*. He could well have felt remorse or guilt with regard to an act which had, on the face of it, the quality of injustice. Had he treated her with a full sense of equity and equality? This question could have had a vital connection with the book of *The Prelude* he was now attempting to write. The matter will become clearer toward the end of the present chapter. In any event Wordsworth, at the beginning of this part of *The Prelude*, is a river which tends to "measure back" its "course" a great distance — indeed, to "the very regions" which he had covered at the point of what he calls "his first outset," the days of his childhood.

This reversal of the river and of *The Prelude's* movement, if it is connected with Wordsworth's remembrances of Annette Vallon, or of the horrors of the French Revolution, coming to him at the same moment that he is thinking of what he here calls the "devouring" sea, may represent something acutely important related to his psychological state. Possibly we are speculating unduly about his ambivalent feelings, but conscious ambiguity plays a very important part in the work of poets, as does unconscious or undesigned ambiguity. Wordsworth may well have been thinking of Annette and her tragedy also when he wrote the "Immortality Ode" — where there are references to the sea which has the potentiality of carrying us away. His most complete consciousness in *The Prelude* at this stage was probably focussed on the idea of eternity, related as it may be to attendant material concerning thoughts with regard to guillotine executions. Such emotions could well be in the periphery of his consciousness as part of his immediate theme about his remembrance of his residence in France. The matter of eternity would seem to be the most obvious factor. He has made, then, a "retrograde" movement repeatedly. The backward movement, which he nevertheless refers to with unconscious or possibly with an artful ambiguity as a "pursuit," has had the effect of detaining him. At the moment he feels an "impulse" toward more "precipitate" progress, though he knows that the thing that lies ahead is soon to prove

> ungenial, hard
> To treat of, and forbidding in itself. (16 —)

But first he touches upon his reminiscenses of his further experiences in London where, late in 1791, he led an obscure existence. At that time he was, he says, not seeking the association of men having distinction through "literature, or elegance, or rank"; rather, he sought a chance to observe the common ruck of men, seeing "from a distance" their manifold activities. Reality was around him and any erroneous "preconceptions" or fantasies that he might have had about his fellow human beings or the world were brought close to earth. These things held an awakening force within his imagination and his deeper self. After a year he says — in actuality it was somewhat less than a year — he found himself drawn abroad.

Why was he attracted to France? He had been in that country before. Now he might well have in mind a memory, referred to incidentally in the middle of Book Six of *The Prelude*, the memory of a "great federal day," July 14, still the most memorable day of the year for the French, since it marks the fall of the Bastille. At that time he had witnessed the brightness of countenance "worn," as he says, at the advent of "joy of tens of millions." This he had referred to, along with his loneliness, in the earlier book entitled "Cambridge and the Alps." His reflection about the subject of revolution is, however, incidental at that point. The Alps were then chiefly in his mind. The earlier experience — in 1790 when he was twenty years old — revealed something of his youthful social enthusiasm, but it was centered mostly on his enjoyment of natural scenery. Now he was being led back to France at a time of very great national events, in November of 1791, though, as he says he had initially chosen for his

abode
A City on the Borders of the Loire. (38—)

With regard to his decision to go abroad he explains that his purpose was to learn to speak the French language familiarly, but it seems likely that it was more than this which was causing the country to act as a great magnet upon him. His planned destination was Orleans (he does not name the city), which is in north-central France. But before going to Orleans he "sojourn'd a few days" in Paris where he loitered, visiting "each spot of old and recent fame" — most particularly the latter "from the field of Mars" toward "the suburbs of St. Anthony"; thence he went "from Mount Martyr southward" until he reached the famous church of "Genevieve."

The "field of Mars," (the Champ-de-Mars) to which Wordsworth refers in this passage, probably appealed to his imagination because it had indeed attained "recent fame," though the poet does not amplify this in *The Prelude*. We can, however, amplify it here to good purpose. King Louis XVI in 1789 had agreed to the withdrawal of the troops he had stationed at the field of Mars, but only after "a brief insurrection" had "torn Paris" apart (we use Gottschalk's words); the King's troops had been moved "so hastily that they had left their baggage behind," and the citizens' "National Guard of Paris had taken possession" of the baggage "as a prize of war. . ."[4] Lafayette had been in charge of things, and he "decided that in this case private property" — the baggage — "should be restored but that the Guard might retain military equipment."

Although at this time the King had received a setback, and Paris had been torn "asunder," as the historian had said, there were heavier matters than this concerning the Champ-de-Mars in the imaginations of the French and almost certainly in the mind of Wordsworth. There was, for example, the celebration which took place there exactly one year after the fall of the Bastille. At the moment of that ceremony (approximately a year and a half earlier than the time of which Wordsworth was writing) Jean Paul Marat made a furious tirade against what he called the "damnable" enemies who were a threat not only to the advance of the Revolution but to the maintenance of its position.

This celebration of the fall of the Bastille was also a source of relatively "recent fame"; in other words, it was live current history. But then, almost a year after that, there was the flight of the king from Paris — on June 21, 1791 — with the subsequent talk of the proclamation of a republic free of all kings, and the voicing of the intent of unseating King Louis XVI "by all constitutional means," as Brissot put it. The signing of the proclamation was to be done at the Champ-de-Mars on July 16. The words by Brissot which we have just quoted were, however, unacceptable to the Cordelier group who feared that double-talk was concealed in the language. Hence on July 17 a "new text was drawn up on the Champ-de-Mars, upon the Altar of the Fatherland."[5] The quotation just given with the altar image — taken from George LaFebvre — will serve to reveal how the French regarded this almost sacred spot.

The ambiguity in Brissot's words "by all constitutional means" lay in the fact that while they seem to stress democracy, they could be construed as an authorization *maintaining* a king and a constitution, after replacing Louis by another person. The words "constitutional means" would thus not apply to a true republic in Wordsworth's sense and could lose their force, though to the casual eye they might seem satisfactory. In other words the establishment of a truly free country in a radical sense — the main purpose of the meeting — would not be accomplished. Many of the French revolutionists were exceedingly sensitive to the idea of a very complete freedom.

The connotations concerning the "recent fame" of the Champ-de-Mars were to all Frenchmen manifold. What has this to do with philosophy? It has very much to do with a democratic philosophy of equality. Wordsworth, in marking "each spot" carrying its own "fame," mentions in the passage last quoted "the suburbs of St. Anthony"; these "suburbs" were eastward in Paris at the other extreme from the Champ-de-Mars. The regions of St. Anthony represented the place of "abode" of the lower classes, a place of almost perpetual disruption. As Wordsworth continues in Book Nine he refers in effect to walking from "Mont Martyr southward," the "Mont" suggesting, perhaps unconsciously, a variety of associations of martyrdom. Included in these associations would rather naturally be the sufferings of those who were participants in the revolution.

Then there is reference also in this part of *The Prelude* to the building famous to Paris, the church of "Genevieve." In indicating "objects" associated with various regions, Wordsworth is moving first westward, then eastward, then northward, and finally to the south of the city center. His references to other "spots" in Paris include the noisy hall of the "National Synod" (the National Assembly) as well as the separate disruptive and "clamorous" place where the large group of Jacobins met. The

155

poet personally saw the society, as he says, tossing "like a Ship at anchor, rock'd by storms"; these and other things he reflected on in his walks about the city. He wandered through the arched halls of the huge "Palace"; he traversed, further-more, the regions of "Tavern" and "Gaming-house," the haunts of "worst and best" — of "all who had a purpose, or had not," and beyond such persons Wordsworth, with his observer's eye, noted a variety of figures, among them

> hissing Factionists with ardent eyes,
> In knots, or pairs, or single, ant-like swarms
> Of Builders and Subverters, every face
> That hope or aspiration could put on,
> Joy, anger, and vexation . . . (57 —)

Of the "hissing Factionists with ardent eyes," Marat, whom we have mentioned, might well serve as an example. Anyone who has seen his picture will remember how his characteristic gleaming eyes have been represented. He it was whose divisive tendencies were such that only "one or two comparatively obscure deputies," along with Robespierre, "held any place in his regard."[6] He it was, furthermore, who wished to form multifarious "clubs" — the purpose of which would be "to take decisive action in suppressing public enemies" and for "general welfare."[7] Among these clubs was a "Society of the Avengers of the Law"; the formation of such organizations he was ad-vocating from June 1790 to March of 1791, a period overlap-ping by several months Wordsworth's stay in France. It is not difficult to imagine how "public enemies" would be suppressed by Marat.

More could be said with regard to the associations that might arise as Wordsworth views the various "spots" in Paris that he mentions. We should add reference, certainly, to the people who were fired upon and killed in the Champ-de-Mars. Enraged by this and eager for action, Marat wrote that he would like at once to gather round him "two thousand deter-

156

mined men!"[8] He would like, further, to "go at their head to tear out the heart of the infernal Mottier [Lafayette] in the midst of his battalion of slaves." He wished to go to "burn the monarch and his henchmen in his palace." From these words of Marat, the patriot — as he was often called — we can form some conception of the "knots" or "swarms" of men Words-worth had in mind as "factionists," some of them ready in their own conception to be "Builders," others aiming to be actively "Subverters" of the things that they abhorred.

The terms "Builders" and "Subverters" are Wordsworth's. He refers here specifically, then, to subversion. He knows what it means. But to what extent was he himself a radical? This is a question which comes to mind repeatedly in reading certain passages in his work. As he tells of the spots he first visited, the poet is something of an impartial observer of the difficulties of the French people at this fateful stage. Certain "incumben-cies," or feelings mainly of duty in this world of shifting values, led him to visit the Bastille and to mark the floating dust (doubtless an emblem also) in the air around him, as he sat

> in the open sun,
> And from the rubbish gather'd up a stone
> And pocketed the relick in the guise
> Of an enthusiast . . . (64 —)

Although Wordsworth was without doubt an "enthusiast," or radical of sorts, his sane humility appears now in *The Prelude*, as it had earlier been manifested. He admits having affected more emotion concerning the Bastille than he actually felt. He did have the fall of the Bastille in mind as a matter of importance, but found that he could not feel about it as he thought he should. He speaks of the "various objects" which he saw, and says that they would show the "temper" of his mind "as then it was"; his reflection upon "objects" in this manner and upon his relation to them as a means of revealing the state of his personality may well command interest in connection

157

with his notion of psychology. Objects and their relation to the inner self are important in his reflection.

But it is revealing that the "object" which he now honestly feels was most important in its relation to him was the "rueful" countenance of the "Magdalene" in a painting by Charles le Brun. This was to be seen in a Carmelite convent. It is of special interest in view of Wordsworth's sympathetic remark about a convent that we shall note near the end of the present chapter. Pathos, we shall find, is a factor there, as it is when he observes the Magdalene. Very possibly the poet's presentation of pathos through his description of the "ever-flowing tears" in le Brun's painting is connected with a sense of guilt at his thought of Annette Vallon. We had indicated earlier in this chapter that there may be a connection between Wordsworth's feeling about the eternal sea in the "Immortality Ode" and the "devouring sea" referred to in *The Prelude*. The labyrinthine beginning — the hesitations and backward movements — of the ninth book in *The Prelude* reflect something of his own inner disturbance. A factor that could well have caused this personal disturbance, we have said, was the remembrance of his departure from Annette Vallon when he had been called home to England.

In the very year that he was working on early passages of *The Prelude* (in 1799), recalling the important experiences of his life, he had also been at work on his "Lucy Poems," one of which contains markedly haunting lines. This poem is entitled "A Slumber Did My Spirit Seal." The slumber that sealed his spirit was a kind of numbness which came over him. This part of the poem could well have had a connection with the psychological state of despondency he was in for a period of time after he left Annette late in 1792, or early in 1793, shortly before she gave birth to his child, Caroline. He did not see her again for some ten years — that is, until 1802. The name Annette may be read, incidentally, either in the French fashion, without accent on either syllable, or it may be read with an accent on the first syllable. In either reading it could be fitted very well into the "Lucy" poem rhythm. Authors of poetry often choose consciously or unconsciously the name for a character in a poem because of its possible rhythmical connection with the name of a real person.

If there is any relationship between Annette Vallon and the heroine of the "Lucy Poems" (and no one knows certainly who Lucy really was) we would need to give an interpretation in which Lucy, as Annette, was dead to the poet when the state of stupefaction or numbing "slumber" overcame him. It *sealed* his spirit. This is the conception in the poem. Far off in France, in this view, she was as a part of the surface of the world revolving in dead purposelessness, as in the short poem, "A Slumber Did My Spirit Seal"; she it was who was

> Rolled round in earth's diurnal course
> With rocks and stones and trees.

But to return to the part of *The Prelude* we were discussing: that concerning the Magdalene of le Brun. Shortly after Wordsworth refers to this "Beauty exquisitely wrought" he tells of his travel to the city of Orleans, about seventy miles south of Paris. It was in this region that he first became acquainted with Annette. His mind then was far from revolutionary events — he "scarcely felt" the shock of the "concussions," but rather lived, for a time, like a plant under glass "in a Green-house." He compares his life at this stage to a kind of parlor existence. He lacked the total knowledge that would have been necessary to a full awareness of what was going on in the French Revolution, though he says he had read "the master Pamphlets of the day" and had been

> help'd out by Talk
> And public News . . . (98 —)

Here it can be seen that Wordsworth realized the insufficiency of superficial views or even ordinary book knowledge of the complex of events involved in the French Revolution. What he learned from dialogue and current news was supplementary. He is writing, of course, after the fact, and his conception is therefore wider than it was when he was in Paris. He realizes that the theme of the Revolution is a great one. We have not even today an adequate knowledge of it, for much concerning the French upheaval is still controversial. For the purpose of a true understanding of the times it would have been necessary to have available a genuinely intellectual study of the problem and of the source from which, as Wordsworth says, "the main Organs of the public Power" had come, as well as "their transmigrations when and how" they occurred, so that the "events" might take on both "form and body"; but these things were in his mind in a very "disjointed" state and therefore he gave to them at the moment no really penetrating, or "vital interest."

Such an intellectual study of the problem of the Revolution, as Wordsworth envisages it, would have been of great help to him. It is to his credit that he could realize the value that this kind of research would have. But it did not exist and it does not exist even to this day. Returning to the poet's account we observe that for the moment "outward violence" had subsided, and in the city where he had gone, Orleans, he "loiter'd," and "frequented" at night the "card tables" and certain gatherings of the members of the leisured classes. These people lived under "privilege of birth," talking little concerning "the good and evil of the time"; indeed, they deliberately avoided such considerations, perhaps because some deep psychological factors connected with aristocratic pretensions submerged the problem. This life of passive existence, however, wearied Wordsworth. He withdrew from it, therefore, and became an admitted "patriot," giving his full heart to "the People," for, he says, his "love was theirs."

To all intents, then, Wordsworth at this time was, from the point of view of developments which were taking place, not only in France but in America also, a man of the people in the

Jeffersonian sense. Many examples could be given showing that problems concerning the status of the people were prominent elsewhere in the world at the time that Wordsworth was at work on *The Prelude* prior to 1805. We have to consider, then, the question: just who, for the poet, were "the people" and what could be hoped concerning them? In our last quotation from *The Prelude* he had reflected on the origin of "the main Organs of the public Power" and "transmigrations" or processes of development. Shortly after this passage he refers to "the People" and the fact that his "love was theirs." He was thinking of them in a context: that of France from late 1791 to the beginning of 1793. At this stage, when he was there roughly through the year 1792, a "second French Revolution" was under way, following upon the 1789 upheaval. In that 1792 period the regime of Louis XVI was brought to an end.

The "Convention which assembled on September 20, 1791," as Ernest John Knapton says, "was a wholly republican body. The decree of the preceding legislature which authorized it" had removed "the distinction between active and passive citizens, so that in theory all Frenchmen of twenty-one and over were entitled to vote."[9] This was the theory, though more time had to pass before "the people" used the franchise significantly. Nevertheless, the urban *sans-culottes* — actually, "small shopkeepers, workshop masters and wage earners"[10] — had begun to rise in importance during that year. Thus the "little people" (*menu peuple*) increasingly formed a part — but not the whole — of the government, along with the influence of the big bourgeoisie. The Revolution, radical in some respects, was not altogether so. All of the kinds of people we have mentioned, supplemented by some sympathetic aristocrats remaining in France, and the part of the clergy that accepted the Revolution, constituted a people-concept, or a people-at-large. And we may well assume that this concept was basically acceptable to Wordsworth in his effort to bring all human beings together, so far as this was possible.

In *The Prelude*, however, we see a marked contrast between

those who were aristocratically minded and the people generally considered. The poet had been brought into contact with a group of military officers at Blois, some thirty miles to the southeast of Orleans. All of them, by their own pretexts, were men of traditionally good families representing, as they thought, "the Chivalry of France." To a man — with only one exception — they were eager, Wordsworth says, to negate everything that had been brought to realization by the French Revolution. To any other purpose they would not have lifted a hand. The one exception was a man in the prime of life, somewhat worn-looking, the poet says, because he was distressed by the problems of the time. These had affected both his body and mind. The latter point is given emphasis by double reference; it was seen in a result wrought upon him daily, "when public news was read," affecting both his voice and the coloring of his face. At such times

> his sword was haunted by his touch
> Continually, like an uneasy place
> In his own body. (161 —)

This man was Michel Beaupuy. By double-reference, then — to body and mind — we see what was happening to him psychologically and physically. He became Wordsworth's close friend, and he had considerable effect in reinforcing the poet's social-change philosophy. It was a time of agitation for everyone, bringing, from the houses one passed by, the noise of disturbed voices. All common life was affected. The picture of history which had formerly filled the poet's mind had inspired faith in life and in the efforts and accomplishments of humanity. Now, in seeing the reality of history, he felt that his reading had cheated him to such an extent that his mind had been filled with vain beliefs and ideals which were empty. He had possessed a faith worthy only of a callow youth. In his imagination the country of France seemed covered with locusts: a figure he uses for the journalists of the day,

> Carra, Gorsas, add

A hundred other names, forgotten now,
Nor to be heard of more, yet were they Powers,
Like earthquakes, shocks repeated day by day,
And felt through every nook of town and field. (178 —)

We sense in oblique reference the tragedy in the lives of the
two journalists whose names are given in The Prelude, as well
as of others who were soon to be "forgotten," not "to be heard
of more": Gorsas was to fall under the guillotine. But at the
moment these men seemed to be "Powers"; indeed "shocks"
were given by them, which were felt everywhere throughout
the land. Carra and Gorsas were sympathetic to the Girondists
(Brissot's organization), a revolutionary group to which
Wordsworth felt drawn more and more as time passed. At the
moment, however, Wordsworth is thinking critically of the
aristocratic party and most especially of certain nobles who
had emigrated from France in order to form an opposition to
the revolution of their native land. Was there a "right" behind
their action? These leaders were stationed on "the borders of
the Rhine," and were already "mustered" for conflict. The officers whom Wordsworth knew (with the one exception of
Beaupuy) were prepared, in "undisguised intent," to travel to
the Rhine and join these opponents of the French Revolution.
Their whole desire was focused upon this intention. These
"Defenders of the Crown," as Wordsworth puts it, talked freely
of their purpose and indeed wished to bring him "over to their
cause."

How could these officers be this frank to a stranger who had
come among them? The poet's initial humility with regard to
the complex problems of the time was perhaps a factor, for he
was "untaught," he says, with regard to the issues at stake. He
had not devoted the time to reading and thinking about social
and political world problems that he feels would be necessary
in forming a judgment about a country which was aiming to be
not only a national but an international force in bringing
about social upheaval. It is to Wordsworth's credit that he
shows a critical sense of his need for preliminary preparation

upon "polity" and "law" as well as philosophy, in thinking about problems which he and Beaupuy discussed. Concerning such matters, and others, people make "nice distinctions"; if these conflicting ideas are on "every tongue" they are obviously variable, and the contradictory variables should be considered.

One must distinguish, the poet realizes, between civil "rights" — presumably he means nonreligious rights which have been already enacted by law and in regard to which man has had the advantage of experiential or operational understanding — and natural or theoretical "rights," the rights that should fundamentally underlie the enactments with which mankind is in process of experimenting in the circumstances of living. He uses the expression "natural rights and civil," and he sees that we have to consider in relation to them the "acts" which are done by various countries which have strong self-interests, that is, interests that change from time to time.

How complicated all this is we can recognize if we consider in our own country Jefferson's people-concept. After Jefferson received an overwhelming mandate, in being elected president, Adams "made innumerable 'midnight appointments' of Federalists"[11] just before leaving office. Doubtless Adams felt that he had a "natural," God-given right to do for the people what he regarded as inescapably the thing that needed to be done, what indeed was best for them, whether they wanted it done or not. But certainly for Jefferson the appointments needed to be based on his own people-oriented point of view since he had been given the mandate through the people's vote. Wordsworth may not have looked across to America at this time. But he had a knowledge of events which were comparable to these that were going on in the world. His position may be very well seen when he says:

> Yet in the regal Sceptre, and the pomp
> Of Orders and Degrees, I nothing found

Then, or had ever, even in crudest youth,
That dazzled me; but rather what my soul
Mourn'd for, or loath'd . . . (211—)

The important point for us today is that absolute government, or government in the interests of an alleged elite, cannot
show a record of excellence in the past. The achievement of
democracy, in contrast, is written in Western history. The
record as to this is transparent. And for Wordsworth, too, the
record of the past with its abuses is very clear. For in the future
he feels there is much to come from what he calls "mountain
liberty." The symbol of the "mountain" is of interest. One can
escape from tyranny at times by going to the mountain. What
is this liberty? He has in mind very definitely an ideal, including in it a sense of the worth of human life. He holds as requisite to this ideal "the government of equal rights," and he
adds reference to human "individual worth." What is meant
by this will have to be more fully developed. The need for the
advances which were being made in France seemed to him obvious: a revolution that had come about "late," rather than
"soon." The weakness of any royalist position seemed patent;
there was a need which required to be filled, and his opposition to the counter-revolutionary forces led to a new sense of
"zeal" arising from within himself, which, he says,

burst
Forth like a Polar Summer . . . (259—)

Meanwhile, the flower of French youth meeting the call of
war impressed Wordsworth greatly: as he writes, tears dim his
eyes at the memories that flood in upon him. It was the devotion of self to a great cause that impresses him, even though
such devotion has existed from time immemorial in many
places. A "terrestrial hope" felt with "a martyr's confidence"
manifested itself in France. The events of the day still remain
with him including images such as those of marching strangers
"seen but once" and a single face, that of a stranger too (being

165

"belov'd as such") etched forever upon his memory. These spectacles "uplifted" his heart because of their connection with a "cause" that no lover of "equity" could oppose.

Beaupuy, whom Wordsworth earlier referred to as the exceptional officer among those he knew in France, was a "Patriot" (we have seen earlier Wordsworth's use of this term to suggest a devotion to the Revolution) in contrast to the other officers who were prepared to bolt from France at any moment and join the army of Royalist émigrés who, as we have said, were being mustered in the Rhineland. Viewed from the standpoint of Wordsworth's philosophy, Beaupuy represents many of the qualities of the ideal human being. He had identified himself with the people at the most pitiful level of society and had suffered, as a result, the "loathing" of the other officers of the garrison. Wordsworth is struck by the humility and graciousness of this man's disposition. Though in action Beaupuy could be most spirited, his nature breathed a "sweetness" or meekness (the idea in this expression is repeated several times) — a meekness which appeared even in the face of an injury. By birth holding a position among "the most noble," he was sincerely united in heart to the most poor and humble. Indeed

> Man he lov'd
> As Man; and to the mean and the obscure
> And all the homely in their homely works
> Transferr'd a courtesy which had no air
> Of condescension . . . (311—)

If we are to understand Wordsworth's view of what underlies the "natural rights" concept, to which he referred, we may see the basis for it in the social ethics of Beaupuy. And here we can also compare the view of the poet to that of Whitehead who, in a chapter entitled "The Human Soul," refers to "the essential rights of human beings, arising from their sheer humanity"; this seems to him "a striking example in the history of ideas."[12]

His concern about important concepts regarding these values is somewhat comparable to that of the psychologist Erik Erikson who refers to human justice and psychohistory, as we shall see. Terms about the democratic ideal which Whitehead uses elsewhere have, he says, a relation to "the early nineteenth century" and to the "triumph" of the historical religious and classical "strain of thought."[13] This he points out in a chapter headed "The Humanitarian Ideal." In the page that follows, his basic idea concerning the developing doctrines is emphasized in the statement that "On the whole, their influence has been democratic. They have swept away mysterious claims of privileged orders of men, based on mystical intuitions originated by religion or philosophy."

Whitehead also makes reference to the importance of Stoic legal influence, which he had mentioned earlier. These factors were even in the later ages a power still — "a resurrection of this Stoic legal movement, but devoid of its intellectual grandeur." A few sentences later he re-emphasizes the importance of "Platonic philosophic theories" and religious contributions, both of which have had significance in relation to the "emotion of respect and friendliness between man and man — the notion of brotherhood. These emotions," he says, "are the basis of all social groups." Fundamentally, as Whitehead insists in the next following page, we are considering all along "the ideal figure of man, as man," as well as its relation to "a supreme worth."[14] He refers to the fact that, in the reform movement he is for the moment discussing, "Jesuits had gone to Patagonia" with social purpose, John Woolman, the Quaker, "had denounced slavery," and this had not been all in regard to the revolt "against social oppression": such figures in Whitehead's view represented endeavors purposing human advance. These endeavors were based on consideration and feeling for "men as men" which was "produced by the joint influence of philosophy and religion."

We can see what underlies Whitehead's view most significantly when on the very next page he criticizes Bentham and Comte and their notion that "they had found a clear foundation for morals, religion, and legislation, to the exclusion of all ultimate cosmological principles." For "their pet doctrines" may be thought of as being definitely "liable to sceptical attack"; they are by no means invulnerable. "They have gained nothing in the way of certainty by dropping Plato and Religion." What is needed is "a reconstructed justification for the doctrine of regard to man, as man." Whitehead's repeated use of words like these — his emphasis upon the humanely human — parallels that of Wordsworth. He is thinking of something like a Platonic idea, which is often scoffed at, but which can nevertheless be very important. To both Wordsworth and Whitehead, such a Platonic idea contains a truth of a kind, though it is not an absolute. Both men are tentative seekers. It will not do simply to have competition: as Whitehead says, "mere 'survival value' is not sufficient" because there may at times be "conditions that stamp out" the very individuals that we greatly need.

Whitehead is reflecting profoundly about the spirit of human beings taken as a whole; he would not accept a philosophy based upon a class doctrine: a stress upon the member of the upper class or a member of the lower class, if such a term can be used. The very title of his chapter suggests a broadly human ideal. His conception of the human being is that of a person who has within himself something drawn from the wider society possessing civilization. The individual, too, is an essential creative part (not a mere cog) within it. We have spoken of Erik Erikson's thought about psychohistory and its relation to America and justice. He speaks of "how the most unlettered individual, on the mere basis of how he grew up to be what he now becomes, has a deep investment"; such a person has a kind of spiritual investment in that, somehow, "all citizens stand free, and all stand equally high, while all stand together against those who think they are more equal than others and who manipulate facts, fictionalize reality, and corrupt interaction."[15] America has a heritage of significance in this theme. Erikson is part of a tradition having a relation to that of Wordsworth and Whitehead.

What is requisite in our developing history Whitehead makes even more emphatic after considering the complexity of the much needed essential dignity of the self. He tries to strike to the heart of the matter by re-emphasizing the growth of "an increased sense of the dignity of man, as man."[16] Thus there are many references in which the philosopher uses this expression having a bearing on the dignity of self. It might almost seem that he had deliberately drawn it from Wordsworth, or had been unconsciously influenced by the poet when we find the exact expression used, as it was, concerning Beaupuy, in our last quotation from *The Prelude*. This parallel between Wordsworth and Whitehead would not prove that the poem exerted an influence upon the philosopher in this respect. Our essential purpose, all along, is to indicate relationships between the two figures. But the thoughts of Whitehead and of such writers as Erikson serve, at any rate, as a useful gloss to the ideas of Wordsworth.

But we must return to Beaupuy. He was the kind of man who to some people might have appeared vain, Wordsworth says, but actually he was the very opposite of one who is characterized by self-centered pride. There was a calmness, a radiance in him that came from the love he bestowed on others. From a good deal of association with this officer, Wordsworth had an opportunity to carry on a dialogue concerning various "prejudices" of long standing and such evils as "chartered rights" which were really privileges enjoyed by people who had special advantages through family status. The need for social "change" was prominent in the discussion. In the world at large a sense of justice to all appeared only in a "Few" — in those who had been nurtured in it by family habit in which a sense of "honour" had undergone growth and de-

169

velopment. Included in the discussion was the widespread and gross evil of "ignorance in the labouring multitude."

Beaupuy was an example of the "upright Man and tolerant" — one who in his thinking "balanced" or carefully related the complex factors involving the functional importance of new rights which could be enacted. He contributed to Wordsworth's philosophy in that a sense of what might be accomplished became clearer to the poet through the discussion they carried on together. Wordsworth was able to see revolutionary theory in better balanced proportion when he was with Beaupuy than at certain later stages. When finally he was closer in thought to the vortex of the struggle, he could no longer reflect, he says, in the spirit of Dion and Plato.

A person in the whirlwind center of a movement — being necessarily dominated by the problems of the time and the more immediate ends — finds it difficult to judge rightly and equitably. Does Wordsworth mean that violence was acceptable to him in the later period? He feels the sense of a fault within himself, but he shifts ground as to this. The main fault lay certainly, Wordworth says, in "those who were against us," but he returns in thought to 1792 (from reflections on his attitudes in the 1793 and 1794 period); the warm remembrances of the dialogues that he and his friend carried on still hold him. They thought of the oppressor as one who, often without knowing it, is himself a sufferer of "miseries"; in a situation in which the one who is the "meanest" acquires many advantages through low devices or maneuvers, the person who imagines he is in the saddle suffers himself, even in basic dignity. He thus, Wordsworth says, unwittingly avoids the chastening power of truth, and he reaches the point of being unable to recognize evil with any clarity. This is, of course, critical thought comparable to that of Plato.

But like Plato, Wordsworth is constructive in his attitudes. The nature of the human being is not fundamentally fallen or corrupt. Probably Wordsworth would agree with Whitehead's view that in modern times (in the nineteenth century for Wordsworth and in the twentieth century for the philosopher) the notion of an "absolute despot"[17] over all creation has stood in the way of theological wisdom. Wordsworth's view, like Whitehead's on this, is explicit. For the philosopher the "true enemy was the doctrine of dogmatic finality,"[18] which flourished, as he suggests, in all areas, religious, scientific, or social. Man, for Wordsworth also, is a somewhat blindly developing being, given to a history of dogmatisms, but he has many capabilities at least pointing toward truths — on the one hand those of negative action leading to the breaking of shackles (liberty in its revolutionary sense) and on the other hand the capacity to construct positively a

> social life,
> Through knowledge spreading and imperishable
> As just in regulation, and as pure
> As individual in the wise and good. (366—)

For Wordsworth, then, social regulation can help in the promotion of justice, but justice may also be fostered in nonregulatory action in which the individual initiates things for himself. These were among the topics which Wordsworth and Beaupuy discussed. They were stimulated not only by abstract ideas and actual events in France, but by ideas in the imaginative literary creations of the past. History, Wordsworth feels, moves to some extent in a regular line, but it has also spurts here and there. He was struck, for example, by the value of sects of various kinds. Finally, for him there was the immediate example of risen France, and the "generous love" offered by men even in the lower levels of society, men who were prepared to give their lives "in the midst of fiercest strife," as indeed Beaupuy himself did. Wordsworth compares discussions concerning liberty such as he and Beaupuy had to those of Dion and Plato or to those he had enjoyed with Coleridge beside various streams in England. The thought about the

171

dialogues and relationships of Plato and Dion, along with their problems with Dionysius of Syracuse, is touched upon also by Whitehead. He thinks of Dionysius as comparable to a more modern figure, say in the time of the Renaissance, though he also thinks of figures in "the nineteenth century" when "humanitarian principles" had more greatly advanced and the "basic" features "derived from Platonism and Christianity"[19] were under skeptical questioning and developing into a variety of forms.

Such interchanges as those between the poet and his friend Beaupuy included the subject of labor, or "toil"; that is, Wordsworth emphasizes here and elsewhere that in developing any worthwhile philosophy work is involved. Labor occurs even in a dialogue. But along with labor in a dialogue there is also joy. Shared discourses have a kind of fascination; they can, indeed, be "sweet" even when they are maintained almost at the very moment when "trial" lies ahead, a trial possibly involving a cataclysm. A person so committed finds it necessary, also, to test his conclusions — to put into the form of action his deepest belief, indeed to

> give it outwardly a shape
> And that of benediction to the world . . . (407 —)

Is it true that it is "sweet" to discuss the problems of human beings "by an authority" which is sanctioned (or glorified) by "danger" — by the confrontation of supreme sacrifice? Why, perhaps, might this be so? Wordsworth does not completely answer this question, but a possible answer may be given in connection with the feelings that one has at such a time, including the feeling of a great hope mingled with desire. In such an instance one may be constrained to carry on a struggle which is dignified by the considered thought which precedes it and one may indeed be a deliverer. Such a "conversation under Attic shades" was carried on by Dion and Plato, and they were "ripen'd" by it so that the "Deliverer's glorious task" could be attempted.

Often hope or desire related to doing or action may take the form of unthinking procedures and conflict. This is evil. There is, however, a kind of "philosophic war," Wordsworth says, and if conflict occurs (after sufficient thinking) one may be a deliverer. Can this be connected with the problem of violence we touched on earlier? Such a deliverer is exemplified, however imperfectly, in Dion, who had received the benefit of dialogue with Plato and who with the help of his fellow philosophers, Eudemus and Timonides, directed his force against Dionysius the ruler of Syracuse:

> Surrounded by Adventurers in Arms
> When those two Vessels with their daring Freight
> For the Sicilian Tyrant's overthrow
> Sail'd from Zacynthus . . . (418 —)

For Wordsworth, these men had at least attempted to work out a philosophy which they thought could be rooted in reality — it could become operational. They were, as is commonly said today, trying to be *engaged*. It was a case of war in which three philosophers, perhaps more, were leading participants. So, likewise, Beaupuy with a similar ambition directed not merely his thought but his life toward a cause. As to Wordsworth's relations with Beaupuy, the poet says that he and his friend carried on "many a long discourse" at a time when Beaupuy was "accoutered for the worst." It was in the vicinity of the Loire, a river edging the Vendee, where French "civil slaughter" was shortly to take place. The two friends walked the wide forests under the highly overarching trees "footing many a mile" of ground overspread with "woven roots" and very smooth moss which Wordsworth, in a strange figure, likens to the surface of a sea. The solemnity of the region had an effect upon him, and often he was led by fancifulness to recall what this greatly forested part of France was like in chivalric days when "Knights" jousted. Here we get *some* sense of his youth, his immaturity. On the other hand, he would have us see truthfully the fact of his youthful fantasizing.

We all live in part on the basis of "fictions" we create, along with whatever sense of reality we may achieve. The fictive patterns in our minds have a place in relation to the dreams we hope to see brought to realization, but they can also be unproductive, fruitless — or perhaps serve only as a stimulus to imaginative functioning. So it was with Wordsworth. But he is constantly making an effort to see the reality in a situation in order to provide a corrective to the aberrant wanderings of his consciousness.

Did the man Beaupuy become something of a fictive illusion within the poet's mind? Did Wordsworth idealize him beyond reality? Perhaps so. But testimony seems to show that the real man was very much as Wordsworth portrayed him, and he has surely provided an ideal to readers since Wordsworth's day. The poet does not forget reality; this appears certainly on one occasion when he and his "revered Companion" came upon a green meadow where a convent had been "dismantled," as was evident, "by violence" of the revolution. Wordsworth tells us that he himself had a real enthusiasm for the movement of social change that was going on in addition to a fervor "wrought up" to a degree within himself artificially. But despite this and the "heart-bracing colloquies" he had carried on with his friend, he "could not but bewail" the devastation of the roofless convent.

To what degree must one be prepared for violence as a necessary price of social transformation? We have asked this question before, but it persists in the mind perhaps because it has been presented to us markedly in our own time. Wordsworth recognizes it, and he acknowledges, as does Whitehead,[20] that violence, like compulsion, has a necessary — sometimes terrible — place in the history of the world. But one must have regrets, Wordsworth says, for an evil so "harsh" as that which rendered desolate the convent in the meadow that he and Beaupuy had turned to in their wanderings on the shores of the Loire. One must repeatedly retrace the steps of

one's philosophy and have second critical thoughts, as Wordsworth did, when he said he missed the "Bell," the "Taper" and
especially "the Cross" to which the "Traveller" had formerly
raised his eyes.

In contrast to this, such images as the "home of ancient
Kings" or an aristocrat's "rural Castle" — from which a
"Lady" had sent and received messages through the use of
"cressets and love-beacons" — caught his attention. They excited his imagination sometimes to "virtuous wrath and noble
scorn" but also gave him, in a degree, a sense of contradictory
sympathetic feeling. He realizes at the time of writing that a
certain measure of what he calls "civic prejudice," or secular
bias, ruled him, but he points out that this hardness was also
mitigated by other tendencies, particularly by the force of
chivalry. He was not blind to positive values in the chivalric
ideal, so important to the development of human thought and
culture.

Nevertheless it is to the "patriot" element, the people's
cause, that he returns, for it still laid daily hold upon him, ac-
companied with a feeling of the need in his philosophy to give
a stress to love in the full sense of charity. He abhors the in-
justices committed by those who, while enjoying "immunities"
themselves, exact a heavy toll upon others. We could amplify
this by examples concerning those who, even after the Revolution of 1789, enjoyed an extremely favored position. With his
doctrine of love Wordsworth couples "hope" having a kind of
religious character.

We have touched heretofore upon his philosophy of "hope,"
a word to which he has given double, sometimes triple
reference. Whitehead may be mentioned here in that for him
democracy exemplifies "articulated beliefs issuing from aspirations, and issuing into aspirations."[21] Aspirations are hopes.
But activity is also implied here and most characteristically in
the philosopher's thought. The democratic vision, he suggests
in the next page, belongs to "an age of hope." He combines

175

with this conception the importance of power, a subject to which he returns in a later chapter on force and persuasion where he brings out the importance of "expansive force."[22] Still it is persuasion, not force, to which he pays his greatest respect. Democracy, then, belongs to an age of hope and persuasion. Hope and love, for Wordsworth and Whitehead, play an important part in a world view. To Wordsworth, "where hope is there love will be"; that is, hope for a generous social change is connected with love. Such a love possesses a dynamism within it for Wordsworth and Whitehead: an urge toward social union.

What we have been saying is centered also in Beaupuy. As we read The Prelude it might seem that Wordsworth had met his friend as if in a dream. But it has been authenticated that Beaupuy was such a man as Wordsworth has described him to be. Badly wounded on the banks of the very Loire which is associated in memory with his name and Wordsworth's, he was not actually killed there, as Wordsworth mistakenly says in the continuation of the passage from which we have quoted. He did, however, give his life in battle for his cause some four years later.

The final view we are given of Beaupuy is associated with another human figure unforgettably pictured in The Prelude, that of a girl with a heifer tied to her arm. It is a "cord" which holds the peasant girl. It is as if she is the one tied or in thrall — or is herself an animal as she does her double labor of caring for the beast while working at another task "with her two hands." United, as she is, with this animal, the poet says she "crept along" (he uses another beast-image here), while the creature is "picking" such "sustenance" as it can at the side of the path. This "hunger-bitten Girl" becomes for the poet a symbol of unutterable woebegoneness in her "solitude" and complete alienation. The spectacle filled Beaupuy with "agitation" and he exclaimed that it was against this that he and his fellows of the Revolution were fighting. His manner of expression is such that Wordsworth seems to be included as a fellow participant in the great social movement. Continuing, the poet indicates one fundamental feature of his desire: that the humblest people should enjoy at least the basic necessities of a good life, that they should not be victims of an "exclusion" which maims them. It was his hope that he would one day

> see the People having a strong hand
> In making their own Laws . . . (530 —)

Democracy comes to mind in the lines from Wordsworth which we have just quoted, though there might be some objection to the term, since it was not commonly in use when Wordsworth was writing, except in connection with revolution in Italy.[23] But does democracy, in the sense in which we have been using it, include overt action, street demonstrations, class struggle, violence in which some people may be hurt? Will there be at times under democracy a certain amount of — doubtless regrettable — blood-letting? For one important, though small group in France — the followers of Babeuf in 1796 — democracy meant just this. But quite apart from the term democracy, these conceptions of class struggle were available earlier as applied to the theory of revolution or social change which Wordsworth regarded as very necessary. Did the poet have such ideas? Palmer, whom we have cited, uses the modern conception of democracy, especially for the particular period of 1798 which he refers to in a chapter title as "The High Tide of Revolutionary Democracy."[24]

This high tide was the period in which Wordsworth was writing parts of The Prelude. In it the poet goes on from the passage we have last quoted to provide almost a definitive list of fundamental rights which go beyond the cause of "human welfare" and political equality. The first is the right of freedom of the person, so that no individual could be held in confinement without charge. Second, he calls for a reasonable procedure of "accusation" which is "open" to the view of all.

Wordsworth adds to this, third, that sentencing itself must be "in the hearing of the world" and fourth, that punishment should be also "open," or subject to inspection. To cap the edifice of just government there is presented a fifth conception, freedom from fear, often regarded as a distinctly twentieth-century ideal. Freedom of the press he seems to have taken for granted. It is these things that were close to the heart of Wordsworth and his friend as they felt the effects of

> the ever-varying wind
> Of Record or Report which day by day
> Swept over . . . (546 —)

At the outset of the chapter we referred to Wordsworth's view that one's early love of nature may lead to a love of human beings. This is an affection deeper than the ordinary love for persons which one normally feels in childhood. It is really love of the whole universe philosophically which becomes a factor here. Indirectly this love may perhaps have caused the poet to feel the need of traveling more widely through his own country and abroad, and of having an appreciation of the problems in France and other countries in the midst of revolution. The prospect of writing about his residence in France seemed to him, as we said at the beginning of the chapter, thorny, "ungenial," difficult to deal with, even fear-inspiring, something to be likened to a "devouring sea." But we suggested at the outset that more than the French Revolution contributed to his dread of proceeding with *The Prelude.* He was, in the figure he chose, a river, containing manifold things, and moving toward eternity. This was our suggestion. In moving toward eternity he was advancing not only toward his personal part in destiny, but toward the destiny of humankind itself.

But the devouring thing that lay before him included his conscience, and, we have thought, something very personal: his relation from the point of view of justice to Annette Vallon,

178

whom he had left (we wish to re-emphasize this) when she was about to bear his child. Wordsworth was interested in social problems, but his relation to Annette was also a social problem. Twice in *The Prelude* he tells us that he left France only because of absolute necessity, and we know that at that time his funds were cut off by his family. He did have enough money, however, to linger in Paris for a time before finally going on home. It was the Revolution it seems that markedly held him in the socially disrupted city. Annette was importantly in his mind but the state of society was also a problem for him. Later it turned out that there were many difficulties in the way of his return to France and to Annette, which, it would seem, was in his mind. War between France and England finally broke out.

The struggle between the two countries continued for some nine years when there was a short space of peace. At this moment of peace, Wordsworth and his sister Dorothy traveled to Calais where they were together with Annette and the child for a short time. Direct reference to Annette might well have formed a natural part of the present book of *The Prelude*, though the poet might have wished merely to shadow forth somewhat dimly the essence of his relation to her. What he decided to do was to give his experience with Annette a veiled treatment by incorporating at the end of Book Nine a tale of two lovers who, he suggests, lived in France a little prior to his own visit there. The termination of this story occurs at the time of the earlier phases of the Revolution.

The tale concerns lovers who are separated by class distinctions. Wordsworth says that the story is true, perhaps feeling that the essence of it applied to his experience. The chief figure of the narrative, Vaudracour, had reached an age a little beyond that of a stripling when he "vow'd his love" for Julia, but the youth's plans for marriage were spurned by his father, despite the fact that the girl was pregnant. Vaudracour then offered to give up his "birthright," that of "an eldest Son," so that "sanction" might be granted to his marriage. When this was rejected, and Julia had been committed to a convent, he retired to a forest "lodge," where after the death of the child he neglected himself and sank into the life of an isolate. He had reached a stage in which he shunned "even the light of common day"; though at this point the French Revolution with its new freedom "resounded" in the land, such things did not rouse the youth from his state of torpor and illness. All his life's possibilities were broken beyond recovery.

This story as presented in the 1805 *Prelude* held a place out of proportion to the rest of the work, being too long. It was removed in a later revision, probably so that it could be published separately. The final version of *The Prelude* (published in 1850) contains only brief allusions to the Vaudracour and Julia tragedy. Wordsworth touches upon it as one example of the disintegration in life which is characteristically brought to those living under the conditions of social injustice which were rampant before the French Revolution.

The French Republic itself, which had been projected as an ideal, was by no means a reality at the stage in *The Prelude* which we have now reached. Continuing, we shall see Wordsworth greeting the establishment of the republic along with the downfall of the King. This subject the poet presents in Book Ten. He also records additional themes of social and philosophical importance concerning his further "Residence in France and the French Revolution," as he entitles that part of *The Prelude*. Such matters we shall deal with in the next chapter.

Footnotes

1. *Adventures of Ideas*, p. 58.
2. Erik H. Erikson, *Dimensions of a New Identity* (New York; W. W. Norton and Co., 1974), p. 70.

3. *Adventures of Ideas*, p. 232. There is a disparity of one line between the numbering of the lines in Book Nine of the 1805 *Prelude* (London: Oxford University Press, 1936) and in Book Nine of the *Prelude*, published by Oxford in 1960.

4. Louis Gottschalk and Margaret Maddox, *Lafayette in the French Revolution: Through the October Days* (Chicago: University of Chicago Press, 1969), p. 133.

5. Georges Lefebvre, *The French Revolution from Its Origin to 1793*, trans. Elizabeth Moss Evanson (London, New York, 1962), p. 209.

6. Louis R. Gottschalk, *Jean Paul Marat: A Study in Radicalism* (New York, 1927, reissued 1966), p. 86.

7. *Ibid.*, p. 107.

8. *Ibid.*, p. 78.

9. Ernest J. Knapton, *Revolutionary and Imperial France: 1750-1815* (New York: Scribners, 1972), p. 58.

10. George Rudé, *Revolutionary Europe: 1783-1815* (New York: Harper and Row, 1964), p. 123.

11. Lester J. Cappon, editor, *The Adams-Jefferson Letters: The Complete Correspondence*, 2 vols. (Chapel Hill, 1929), I, p. 244.

12. *Adventures of Ideas*, p. 15.

13. *Ibid.*, p. 45.

14. *Ibid.*, p. 47. It should be emphasized that the title of the chapter is "The Humanitarian Ideal."

15. Erik H. Erikson, *Dimensions of a New Identity: Jefferson Lectures in the Humanities* (New York: W. W. Norton and Co., 1974), p. 95. See p. 12 for reference to psychohistory.

16. *Adventures of Ideas*, p. 105.

17. *Ibid.*, p. 218. The author goes on to say, "The doctrine of Grace has been degraded, and the doctrines of the Atonement are mostly crude." This is not to say, however, that a subtle conception of Grace or of the Atonement would in all cases lack functional value.

18. *Ibid*, p. 208.

19. *Ibid.*, p. 38.

20. *Ibid.*, p. 6. Whitehead refers to "senseless agencies" and "violence"; as to this he alludes to Plato's *Timaeus*. See also Denis Goulet, *The Cruel Choice* (New York: Atheneum, 1971), pp. 328, 344.

21. *Ibid.*, p. 6.

22. *Ibid.*, p. 102.

23. R. R. Palmer, *The Age of Democratic Revolution: The Struggle* (Princeton, 1964), p. 293.

24. *Ibid.*, p. 327.

Chapter X

Wordsworth and Philosophy Residence in France and the Aftermath: The Double Chapter

At the close of the last chapter we touched upon the subject of disorganization of the state in France — with an emphasis upon the problem of social injustice. This disorganization was exemplified in the story of Vaudracour and Julia. Wordsworth in the final version of *The Prelude* omitted this narrative of two lovers, perhaps because it was disproportionately long in relation to other things that he mainly wished to present. His possible reticence concerning a connection that might be made between Annette Vallon and the woman in the story could also have been a factor in his decision. In making this change he did not, however, discard the strong closing emphasis on social

disorganization and human injustice; these problems were undoubtedly exceedingly important to him.

The handling of the broad subject of his revolutionary experience was itself painful for a variety of reasons which we
have earlier tried to clarify. In treating the material he is concerned not only with himself but with a portion of the tragic
moral story of mankind. The side of philosophy touched upon
in his account of the revolution consists largely of social ethics,
though what may seem most dominant is the political aspect of
human affairs, at the time, in France. But political philosophy
is itself, of course, an important part of anyone's philosophy.
Even if one has no political concern, that negative fact is a part
of his world vision or lack of it.

Our next theme to be developed, "Residence in France and
the Aftermath," relates to the unusually long tenth book of the
1805 *Prelude*. In the later edition (of 1850) Wordsworth divid-
ed and modified this material, thus providing for an extra
book in his finally finished work. We have used the subtitle
"The Double Chapter" because the present section of our book
is so extensive. There is a blank space indicated in our text in
this chapter approximately at the midpoint, so that the reader
can readily see the division of the material which Wordsworth
finally chose in 1850. "Residence in France and the Aftermath" will continue the approach followed in the previous
chapter; that is, it deals with the poet's further experience in
witnessing the democratic revolution as a living thing and his
attempt at philosophizing which developed from that experience. Much as we are troubled today by the problem of the
betterment of a woefully inadequate government, so he felt
beset by the growing dynamic thing, the new France, as well as
by the vital new world which he saw in process of forming.

This new world would be molded, he hoped, with an aim at
reaching toward the general public good. Wordsworth's
political confusions, then, have a universal side. Just as we at
times feel the world interconnections of our thought and also a

sense of "aloneness" and social need in our national condition, so also did he. Experience with developing democracy as a potential working thing in any period may have its aftermath of disillusionment. His experience led to such disillusionment as he was preparing to leave France and make his way home. His state of mind had further repercussions later.

There is a striking contrast that appears in *The Prelude* as he describes the "beautiful and silent day" which "overspread the countenance of earth" when he left the region of the Loire on his way back to "the fierce Metropolis," Paris. In this great city he was to remain for a time before going home to England. The contrast between the attractive day and the "fierce" city is emphasized through his reference to the dark "cloud" hanging over the French Revolution. This cloud fills his mind as he thinks of the "victims" who had paid the price of their lives for the revolutionary cause. A very special terror had marked the year 1792, apart from the terrors of the two and a half previous years. There was a rankness of "evil expectations" concerning what for certain people lay ahead. And yet Wordsworth speaks also of the "confidence" he felt as to "the better cause."

A sense of the evil in the cataclysm seems now, however, more fully in his mind than at any time previously. He is ambivalent in his feeling, and, like some activists today, he uses words euphemistically to hide from himself, it seems, certain realities: even perhaps to deceive himself about his great distress of mind. Thus instead of saying "revolution" he refers to the change as a new "transition"; but he still realizes that during his days in France minor revolutions upon revolutions have taken place, and that more lie ahead. Part of his problem is that he is telling how he felt at the end of 1792 and in early 1793, while at the same time he is writing from the standpoint of somewhat later feelings — that is, from the standpoint of a time roughly between 1800 and 1804, about ten years later. He refers to the joy of France as she "assumed" the "body" and the title of a "Republic," but again it is the "lamentable" events

185

which "had gone before this hour" that concern him — events in which masses of human beings began to constitute a veritable machine. Men had resorted to massacres, abandoning their conscious roles as thinking, feeling beings capable of rightness in *judging*. And judging is important in philosophy.

Wordsworth, it seems very clear, is aware of the importance of the concept of "judging," and for Whitehead also it is very significant. Its difficulty conceptually, and in action, is certainly great, though the word seems to us, at first, very elementary. But often it is the use of seemingly simple terms that, as Whitehead several times points out, gives rise to our blunders. Such confusing use of apparently simple terms is one of "two main errors to which philosophic method is liable";[1] that is, the first error, Whitehead says, is the "uncritical trust in the adequacy of language," and, as to this, "Judgment" (capitalized) serves him as an example to which he refers in the following page. It is a common word but its content needs to be reflected on carefully. It is connected with importance. "Importance depends on purpose and on point of view."[2] Other examples of seemingly common but troublesome language could be cited.

As Wordsworth proceeds in *The Prelude* he indicates graphically how man had let *himself* become a mere material object, a "sword," and man was permitting himself to pray to that material object as if it could render succor. The sword, that is, had become an idol. But since, in Wordsworth's figure, man is a sword (which he is *worshipping*) man is praying to *himself*. The human being is making himself God. But mark the figure. It is an unusual one, although it recalls the association of man praying to a sword in the work of Shakespeare. The special freshness of the figure in the *Prelude* instance consists in the fact that the "sword" which man is praying to is a guillotine. Both an idea of religion (praying) and an idea of ethical concern are entwined here, along with a problem of judgment and violence.

Does Wordsworth's philosophy contain a principle of ethical self-identification with these happenings? Would his self-identification with the happenings enable him to take his place among humankind in the terrible events surrounding him? Are the perpetrators alone responsible for the deeds? In other works than *The Prelude* the poet in this period of his career considers guilt, and he deals with the theme of remorse. Is an element of his self-responsibility apparent at any point in *The Prelude?* We shall see that there is such an element. We may also observe that it is present at times by implication. In the *Prelude* passage which we are considering, however, Wordsworth dismisses almost with irony the September massacres and other tragedies of which he had been thinking, and he declares

> but these were past,
> Earth free from them for ever, as was thought,
> Ephemeral monsters, to be seen but once;
> Things that could only shew themselves and die. (34—)

Can such events as the massacres merely appear and then "die," yet be part of Wordsworth's life? In 1792 he apparently supposed so. Notice that he is presenting ironically the account of what he was like at the time of the happenings. In 1792 his mood concerning events was such, also, that it was capable of very swift reversals. It was a time of horrors. But it was also a time in which he was "enflam'd with hope" as he returned to the metropolis to range once more its many regions, including "the Palace" which had recently been attacked with "cannon" by "a numerous host." He crossed a square lately strewn with the "dead and dying" — the Carrousel. As he considered these sights and others, he felt bewildered. Indeed, he was like a person who scrutinizes a book in a foreign language, the whole contents of which he cannot read.

The philosophic comprehension of *events* always involves a difficult challenge. And the sense Wordsworth has of the greatness of this difficulty may be seen in the picture which he gives of his night-time hours. In his room he "felt most deeply" the strange "world" he was surrounded by. He strangely, also, *enjoyed* the height from which he had to look down, perhaps because it gave him a better, a more unified, sense of his new intellectual universe and of all that was about him. There, aloft, his "taper" lit, he "kept watch," at "intervals" reading perhaps for relief. Nevertheless he felt the pressure as he thought of the possibly more tragic events that were to come. These things of the future seemed so close to him that he had a veritably tangible sense concerning them. They became "substantial" to him.

We have spoken of the Carrousel, and perhaps Wordsworth recalled the earlier maneuvers of horses there, for which it was famous. However this may be, he now quotes a passage, including an image concerning the horse and its management although he is probably thinking of this image mainly in its relation to the controllability of man. He passes from the horse-image to the image of a breeze (analogous also to man), which blows now this way now that, then reversing itself and returning. The breeze is like a man wheeling and treading once more "in his own steps" — or as we see the picture in Wordsworth's mind again, man in the world acts like a *tide* which comes and retreats, as day follows day. It is nevertheless not only to mankind but to himself that he refers in all this; it was thus that the revolution worked upon him. And thus he "wrought" upon himself, in the dreams of his night-time hours, until there came to him a voice bidding him sleep no more. He would have us add to this, other "comments" which came out of a calmer state. From them he gathered far less than "full security" — an ironical understatement, for his room was

> a place of fear
> Unfit for the repose which night requires,
> Defenceless as a wood where tigers roam. (80 —)

The tiger image is suggestive, and may be anticipatory of Wordsworth's thought about certain leaders in France. It fits most particularly the poet's view of Robespierre, who, though his reputation has received some rehabilitation in recent years, is still a very controversial figure. Close upon the tiger image — in the next breath virtually — Wordsworth tells of venders hawking about the metropolis the words "Denunciation" of Robespierre's "crimes"; this news was in the streets shortly after Louvet had risen dramatically in an assembly to throw down his famous challenge. That is, Robespierre had previously dared anyone to confront him with the accusation of sedition, and Louvet alone had the temerity to break the appalling silence of the room, crying out, "Moi!" This utterance, the historian Sydenham tells us, Louvet had followed with "a long philippic,"[3] but as Wordsworth says, Louvet was "left alone" by his "irresolute friends," and what he aimed to achieve, the overthrow of Robespierre, was not at that time accomplished.

Who were Louvet's "irresolute friends" and what was their situation? They were Girondists. At this time (1792) France was even more tragically torn asunder than in the earlier stages of the Revolution. The group to which Wordsworth was mainly inclined, and which he might have joined, included Jean Pierre Brissot (1754-1793) and the Girondists. Brissot came from their region in southwestern France. But the Girondists did not have a very clearly defined organization. Innumerable cross-currents of intrigue existed in France, and power was attained by frequent shifting on issues from one alignment to another. Brissot has been often called a moderate. The Girondists, like their opposing group, constituted not a party but a faction. The dangers of belonging to such groups were widely recognized. Wordsworth had given some sense of the radicalism of certain groups in his earlier reference to "hissing Factionists with ardent eyes"; Brissot, the Girondist leader, was however no such hissing factionist. Still, he was eagerly calling for war against Austria and her allies, which led to a problem.

Robespierre, on the other side, had "delivered his first

speech against war" in December of 1792 (shortly before Wordsworth arrived in France), and he continued resolutely, as Lefebvre says, in this effort against war.[4] "With surprising foresight" Robespierre "outlined the potential dangers — popular resistance" to a French army brought to foreign soil, and "inevitable dictatorship . . . " Promoting war on foreign soil — who would wish this? Robespierre regarded it as republican suicide. This position on peace speaks well for Robespierre, but there is a dark side to the picture. On September 1, 1792, well before Wordsworth had left France, Robespierre had condemned Brissot, calling him a "liberticide,"[5] having in mind reference to Brissot's hysterical, faction-fomenting tendencies. As Sydenham says, Robespierre had indicated that the Girondists had "sold France out" to Brunswick, the commander of the enemy; Robespierre "repeated his accusation" on the next day. Brissot and some nine of his fellows would have been arrested shortly thereafter but for the help given them by Danton. "The Brissotins had every justification for believing for the rest of their lives that Robespierre had done his best to have them murdered." It was after this in October that Louvet made his attack in the assembly.

From then on Robespierre was in danger, with the shadow of the guillotine looming over him. He, too, felt that his opponents sought his death. After the *Prelude* passage in which Wordsworth tells of Robespierre and the circumstances of Louvet's speech, the poet goes on to say that these things he refers to not for their terror or for their ultimate significance, but merely as they were "storm" and "sunshine" to his "individual mind"; in other words, it would seem that he is either using additional irony or he is using words that do not express the tragedy of the situation. He is not now trying to evaluate critically the importance of the events in relation to the Revolution. His admiration for the courage of Louvet, however, is evident. Part of Wordsworth's philosophy clearly

190

involves an emphasis on the importance of courage. The poet's uncertainties about taking sides in the Revolution grew out of the complexity of the circumstances in which the various groups found themselves. The pain involved in his situation lay for him in the fact that he saw most clearly that "Liberty, and Life, and Death" were at the moment hanging in the balance for France, lying indeed

> in the arbitrement of those who ruled
> The capital City . . . (110 —)

Though the importance of the provinces in relation to the Revolution should not be minimized, Wordsworth was right in suggesting that the key point which might bring revolutionary success lay in controlling Paris. He was correct also when he went on to single out "indecision"as the great weakness of those who to him appeared to be the "best" — the Girondists. On the other hand he was wrong in the objection he had to what he conceived to be "impiety" in Robespierre. This was a conventionalized notion about Robespierre. His enemies were prone to trump up the charge of atheism against him, but, though he was in disagreement with many dogmas, he stressed "the existence of the Supreme Being," and it was his party which after Wordsworth left France "erected a cloth and plaster statue of Atheism"[6] which Robespierre set on fire. The poet, however, was correct in stressing the tendency of the Robespierrists to follow with almost inhuman resoluteness a "straightforward path" toward a goal. Wordsworth had, in any event, now reached a stage of such great agitation over the state of the Revolution that he says

> I could almost
> Have pray'd that throughout earth upon all souls
> By patient exercise of reason made
> Worthy of liberty, upon every soul
> Matured to live in plainness and in truth
> The gift of tongues might fall, and men arrive

From the four quarters of the winds to do
For France what without help she could not do . . .
(117—)

Wordsworth's reference to the fact that he felt almost like praying for France deserves comment. He is speaking of a desire that a "gift of tongues" might come to many people in many lands and that these people might speak out for the cause of a more constructive revolutionary social change. Here it might seem that, in his greatest moments of emotion concerning the cause, he was longing for magic as a solution to the problems of France. But his *desire* is not an actual wish for something like a genie or for supernatural help. Rather, it is an earnest thought. He is using a kind of hyperbole in order to express the extremity of his feeling and his longings for France. He felt very strongly about her efforts toward freedom. Along with these factors he had an earnest wish to help in the cause. Fear, he feels, could hold a person back from offering one's life, but this he expressly condemns. Courage, as we have said, is one of the great virtues in his creed. Fear he regards as "guilt." He recognizes that social problems are broad, but he sees also that "single persons" sometimes courageously exert extraordinary influence. For "objects" of importance may at any time be within the reach of "humblest eyes," and a person may make the great mistake of mistrust in self. This may occur through a wrong kind of humility. Trust in oneself can indeed be a form of courage.

It is the splendid democrat in Wordsworth that we often hear speaking, the poet as man of the people, with faith in the people and in the kind of life that could lie ahead for mankind. Related to the evil of mistrust of self is failure in "hope" — we must be strongly "faithful" to the spirit, the philosophy within us. The self, however, the ego in the narrow sense, must not be paramount. This ideal with regard to the self can be seen also in the works of Goethe written almost precisely at the same time as Wordsworth's. However, the self and self-realization, stressed by Goethe, often unconsciously give almost complete rein to the narrow ego.

We may wonder at this point how Whitehead would view the problems that Wordsworth was facing. What did Whitehead feel about revolution in general and about the French upheaval in particular? The record is plain. He speaks of great forces in history as waves, remarking that "the seventh wave is revolution — 'And the nations echo round.' "[7] He comments also on America and France, referring to "the last quarter of the eighteenth century" when "the earliest incarnations" of the social-change philosophy were taking active form, but he goes on to give England credit in somewhat later movements for contributing to the force. Revolution for Whitehead, then, is an "incarnation" (we may almost associate religious ideas here), and it is thought of not merely as an incarnation in America and France but as an ongoing world movement. So Wordsworth also viewed it, but it is possible that his endorsement of revolution would be given in less wide-reaching terms. Whitehead, like Wordsworth, thinks of the tremendous influence which the self can carry, and the related problems of self-centeredness or of the "self-assertive" factor, as a reflective writer somewhat alarmedly describes it.[8]

Thought about such conflicting forces as the high importance of the self and the danger of the ego may have had some relationship to Wordsworth's introspective study of the character of the man Robespierre, who at this point was apparently much on the poet's mind. Wordsworth had spoken of the "Spirit" which is within man "unsleeping," not to be quenched or dismayed, and of a "mind whose rest" was centered in "circumspection and simplicity"; in this last we may especially think of Robespierre and his tendency to look forward and about him on either side — as well as behind. In addition to having this tendency to be super-vigilant, Robespierre had created an image of himself (perhaps sincerely) as one of the most simple of men, a quality which can be related to Wordsworth's interest in simplicity. The French leader was also prepared to take, in a crisis, very great chances when they seemed absolutely necessary. Doubtless Wordsworth was not directly thinking of Robespierre, but the analysis of character traits we have referred to in The Prelude could have had a connection with some French figure. Certainly, as we have said, Robespierre was much on the poet's mind. Had Robespierre possessed a character on a somewhat higher level, the chances could have played more completely in his favor. In that case his nature, following Wordsworth's somewhat ideal conception, would have fallen

> rarely in entire discomfiture
> Below its aim, or met with from without
> A treachery that defeated it or foil'd. (156 —)

Here Wordsworth is referring to the chances that are involved in life: he is referring to the fact that one has to consider a kind of calculus in the percentages of possible success in anything that is undertaken. It seems that Robespierre did this, and things worked pretty much in his favor except for the occasion of his last tragic moment. Brissot, his opponent, on the other hand, did not estimate his own chances well; he often blundered, and the percentages worked against him, though it was treachery in the end which foiled his group and finally brought about his defeat. But Brissot and Robespierre are not important here, except as examples. It is the ethical side of Wordsworth's thought that we wish now to bring out. Both of the French figures were egoists to a considerable degree and both may have been somewhat tyrannical. However one may view the two leaders and their tragic struggle there is some comfort in the idea subsequently developed by Wordsworth "that tyrannic power is weak" in the long run, and that it cannot count on "gratitude," "faith," or "love" — nor ultimately upon support from the "evil men" who for a time may seem to

194

co- operate with such power. There can be no such thing, he says, as "trust" under a tyrannic rule.

The character trait of trust united with wisdom is an ideal (along with hope and love) which the poet represents variously in *The Prelude*; the triad of trust, hope, and love celebrated particularly in medieval times (and going back to Paul) was very much alive for him in modified form. Wordsworth's "trust" or "faith" is wider, however, than that represented by the Pauline outlook. Whitehead has this same breadth in common with the poet. He has a faith in the respect that it is an active joy in life and a belief in our human world, and in the equitableness of the universe in which we carry on our earthly lives, as well as a faith in universes beyond it. Wordsworth's trust appears in the declaration

<blockquote>
that the Godhead which is ours
Can never utterly be charm'd or still'd
That nothing hath a natural right to last
But equity and reason . . . (171 —)
</blockquote>

What can we say of such a nondogmatic faith? What can we say of a natural religion? Can we believe there are things that have "a natural right to last"; what, further, can we in the modern world believe, concerning nature or, rather, the "natural" as it applies to "right" in the *Prelude* passage? Is there any viability for such ideas in the twentieth century? To this we shall return. But can Wordsworth's reference to the "Godhead which is ours" have any bearing on the concept of the humanity of God which has appeared at times in our own century? In one twentieth-century approach, that of Barth, this humanity is "God's relation to and turning toward man."[9] The phrase quoted is understandable in a possible liberal sense. The author, Barth, admits that about forty years before this, he would "indeed have been somewhat embarrassed" if at that time he had been asked "to speak on the humanity of God";[10] he and his friends of that time would "have suspected evil implications in this topic."

But Barth's earlier view had also been the result of a "change of direction" he had made (as against the thought of certain predecessors); he is able to recognize that his change at that time was not "the last word." Modification in views have to occur. He almost immediately adds that what he has also to say now "cannot be the last word." He seems impressed with the value in changes. This is not to imply that he is a radical. He does object, as we rather soon see, to his earlier view of God as "this 'wholly other' in isolation, abstracted and absolutized"; such a view should not be "set over against man, this miserable wretch,"[11] for the human being, in Barth's new conception should not be thought of as a "wretch" incapable of valuable social action. The author is by no means a liberal in the sense that Wordsworth is, but like the poet and like Whitehead he sees a danger in absolutism, whether in religion or philosophy.

Wordsworth does not take a basically authoritarian or conservative approach to the idea of the "Godhead which is ours"; he believes in creativity or development in thought. He would have us emphasize within ourselves the idea that everything other than "equity and reason" will meet "foes irreconcilable" and fall into ultimate disaster. He would apply his religious doctrine to his philosophy of political and social change. The liberal political conviction to which Wordsworth gives expression has not been annulled, he says, by "ten shameful years"; that is, in the years from early 1793, when he left France, until 1803, his approximate time at the moment of writing. Had there been in the Revolution "one paramount mind" operant in a key place, he believed things could have been much different in the ten tragic years, quite apart from "what the People were" because of the lack of historical development and because of their "ignorance"; such a paramount mind would have provided the essential thing needed, or

> clear'd a passage for just government
> And left a solid birthright for the State . . . (186—)

It is to this problem that a thoughtful contemporary

philosopher, Charles Frankel, addresses himself in various volumes — among them his work *The Case for Modern Man*. In it he points out that Americans not only have had a glorious dream, but have from their heritage of the soil rightly "been suspicious of attempts to find unchanging conditions in nature or fixed goals for man."[12] When we consider Wordsworth's expression "what the People were" and add to this his words "because of ignorance" we may think of a conception of nature and the laws of nature which could lead to an erasing of both trust and hope. Trust and hope were very dear to Wordsworth. Some thinkers in our own day have lost their faith in man, have even a love for anxiety, Frankel says. They regard faith as naive. But Wordsworth would aim to establish "solid" social conditions leading to improvement in the state of affairs of humanity. Conditions modify persons. In essence he believes, as does Whitehead — we use the philosopher's words here — "Progress consists in modifying" nature as we see it at a given time in the life of man: even "modifying the laws of nature so that the Republic on Earth may conform to that Society to be discerned ideally by the divination of Wisdom."[13]

The statement we have given suggests that even natural law, whatever we may think of it, is an evolving thing which man is in process of creating. Our thought about nature may become troublesomely labyrinthine, but as Whitehead says elsewhere, "The status of life in Nature is the standing problem . . ."[14] And again, to quote a different but also vital passage from him: "It is a false dichotomy to think of Nature *and* Man. Mankind is the factor *in* Nature which exhibits in its most intense form the plasticity of nature. Plasticity is the introduction of novel law."[15] This statement suggests the importance of creative social thought, as does the last passage which we quoted from *The Prelude*, concerning the need for a new, more "solid" construction of values for society. But what, further, are the things that have "a natural right to last," in Wordsworth's phrase? They are, clearly, *things that make*

197

sense in the long run. They are neither given to man, nor God-given, without work. They are not things that are necessarily in the cards.

So important, in Wordsworth's view, was the need for the establishment of this "solid" social construction (or social condition) that but for the absence of money on which to live he would probably have acted with the Girondists and perhaps have lost his life. As he says he might have given the "poor mistaken and bewilder'd offering" — himself — which would then, he believes, have been of no use to anyone. There is a fine humility in the remark Wordsworth makes about himself. It is combined with a certain self-respect also — the latter factor being seen in his desire to be a person who is dedicated to an ideal. Very evidently he would not have been, for that moment, a paramount mind, or anything approaching it. To his credit, however, had he followed Brissot he would have been working with one who stood staunchly in defense of Black freedom, a cause in which Wordsworth, too, most firmly believed. With regard to Black slavery he says "this most rotten branch of human shame," he hoped, would be destroyed at the same time that general human freedom would become a reality. Like Brissot, when put to the practical test of events, however, he would have failed with the Girondists, for their cause did fail.

The kind of fluctuations to which the Girondists felt compelled may be seen in the change of Jean Pierre Brissot from his early days, as a "prominent Jacobin" in the "left wing"[16] of the 1791 parliament, to the time later when he feared the growing Jacobin strength. We can sympathize humanly with Brissot's wavering in the case of the execution of the king. He dreaded this bloodshed. The Girondists at first held that the "determination of the king's fate had to be ratified by the people."[17] This was clearly impossible. It was almost certainly a Girondist maneuver. In the end Brissot voted for the execution,[18] which took place on January 21, 1793, some days after

Wordsworth had left Paris for home. War against France was declared by England on February 11, 1793, twenty-one days after the guillotining of the king. This attack upon France, the putting forth of "the strength of Britain" along with that of the "confederated Host," appalled Wordsworth. It made him, like many a youth of our own day, extremely "subversive"; indeed, it turned his feelings strongly against his own country. Not only was he, in his "single self," affected but he found

> in the minds of all ingenuous Youth,
> Change and subversion from that hour. (233—)

This for him was indeed personal revolution. It was a violent change in direction, not a revolving round the circle of his development such as we associate with the root meaning of "revolution." Never before had he undergone such a radical change in his "moral nature": it was a "stride" carrying him into "another region." He had been steadily aware, he says, of his country's unfriendliness to liberalism. He knew of its indifference to "regenerated France," and he felt in his *mind* "that this day" — that is, the day on which the British declared war — would certainly come. But the real fact of knowing when the state of war became actual was quite another thing. A further tension came to the poet in the experiential realization that he was capable of behavior very far from his ethical ideals. He was capable, that is, of feeling malice, and almost of acting upon it, of rejoicing even, or exulting, when his countrymen "by thousands were o'erthrown"; this brought him, he says, conflicting "sensations without name," including a revengefulness on which he voraciously "fed" his spirit.

Can we say that an *attitude* such as his with regard to England's declaration of war can become an action? From the point of view of ethics, was Wordsworth now, in the stage at which he had arrived, deserving of condemnation? He had contemplated the importance of the concept of judgment, earlier. In the present instance, might we not most naturally ask: Is there a sanction within the self which should condemn such vengeful feeling? There is little doubt that Wordsworth felt this to be so: that his action (he could call it that) was reprehensible. Especially was this so when he found himself seated in an English church, feeding silently on a feeling of vengeance against his countrymen. His own expressions make it clear that he felt alienated, "like an uninvited Guest," in company with his fellow British human beings. What does one do when one has feelings of alienation of this kind? It is a common device to blame greatly some person or some thing apart from oneself. And this the poet does when he cries

> Oh! much have they to account for, who could tear
> By violence at one decisive rent
> From the best Youth of England, their dear pride,
> Their joy, in England . . . (276 —)

Wordsworth had been made subversive and vengeful, he had said. Now he had lost his "patriotic love," through being goaded as it were into subversion. Still feeling in this mood, in the summer of 1793 when he was on the Isle of Wight, he observed bitterly the "Fleet of Britain" pursuing its "unworthy service"; for a month he associated its common presence with the "monitory" evening sound of the "sunset cannon." The mournful, even dismal mood, along with his impulse toward vengeance, was contrary to his normal nature. His ethics, taking a condemnatory position toward revengefulness of spirit, nevertheless included the view that such an emotion was understandable and could be forgiven. He points out, in the tone of the subversive youth of today, that the older generation, or the establishment — the political leadership — was even more blameworthy than was he in his behavior. It is no exaggeration to say this is how he felt even some ten years after the event he describes. Perhaps he is in the main right in what he says. He distinguishes the time in which these events occurred as being such that rejection of things one had believed in — rejection of patriotism toward England, for instance — would seem "conversion to a higher creed"; in this period his is an ethics of circumstance, using the term in no bad sense.

Ethically, Wordsworth is condemning England in very strong terms and from a wide perspective. He is thinking "in sorrow for mankind and pain of heart." His pity is for France, because, in the direction she has taken, she represents, for him, the general development of mankind toward that which is good. In a word, France stands for the cause of a new and developing democracy. The subject of democracy came up for consideration in our previous chapter, but there are additional matters about a democratic philosophy that need to be mentioned. Wordsworth favors revolutionary democracy, both politically and socially. But more: he is an international revolutionist in that he has seen that the many recent movements toward democracy have been crushed in virtually all countries except for America and France.

Even the new accomplished governments represented achievements which were something far less than the ideal. For him democracy is a thing of process, involving an establishment through a variety of enactments of a created, man-achieved government. His view is no mere dream. Subsequent developments make this clear. Wordsworth had seen realistically the two sides of the struggle in France: first, Robespierre and his group on the one hand, and second, Robespierre's opponents, including Brissot, on the other. It is little wonder that the poet felt disturbed. News of distressful events was reaching England now, he explains, in successive blows. We can therefore feel his situation after his return to his native land almost as if we were there.

His sympathy for the Girondists was based, as we have said, on his belief that they represented the better cause. And it is true that they were known as idealists. But what kind of idealists? We can gather something of the disorganized mental state that the leader Brissot was capable of showing if we note his remark near the end of 1792: "We cannot be calm until Europe, all Europe, is in flames."[19] This sounds much like the statement of a madcap incendiary of our own times. Brissot was an idealist but so was Robespierre. The potential violence of the two forces — the Girondists and the Robespierrists — was for practical purposes almost equally balanced. The year 1793 marked the organizing in France of what was meant to be a temporary government with extraordinary powers. These powers were granted because of the extenuating circumstances of war. Committees of public safety were formed which were little controlled and often acted ruthlessly. From week to week conditions much like anarchy prevailed. This was sporadic. As Wordsworth says

> Tyrants, strong before
> In devilish pleas were ten times stronger now,
> And thus beset with Foes on every side
> The goaded Land waxed mad . . . (310—)

It is all too easy to say that nations sometimes go insane. The remark seems, of course, nonsense. To one who has experienced a serious revolution at first hand, however, the statement probably has a kind of fitness. Briefly to indicate a few events: in June of 1793 Brissot and the Girondists fell; on July 13, Marat, while in his bath, was assassinated by Charlotte Corday, an educated girl who was under a misapprehension as to the value of her action; in October 1793 Queen Marie Antoinette was guillotined. In November Madame Roland, the friend of the Girondists, met the same fate with words on her lips concerning violence done in the name of liberty, to which Wordsworth alludes. In April of 1794 Danton was executed. The events we have mentioned represent only a minuscule token of what occurred, for "the crimes of few," as Wordsworth says, expanded into the "madness of the many," the acts themselves seeming "sanctified like airs from heaven" to their fanatical perpetrators.

In a manner of speaking, Wordsworth was right that the nation had "waxed mad"; the philosopher Charles Frankel, to whom we have earlier referred, speaks of "ferocities of society" in the twentieth century and makes the considered statement that "ideas can make men mad."[20] There are multiple, and controversial, reasons for the actions indicated in summary in the previous paragraph, and for the anarchy that led to them. These reasons, however, cannot be explored here. From an ethical point of view Wordsworth shows understanding of mitigating circumstances in the situation: he shows *caritas* (charity) toward the "goaded" nation, and indeed much charity is necessary in viewing with comprehension human beings who seem driven to the violence of revolution. But perhaps he generalizes too sweepingly when he attributes the main events that occurred to the tendency of human beings to bow down before the mere "understanding" — the faculty connected, as we have seen, with a philosophy founded upon the fallacy of "simple location" (Whitehead's words) or the conviction that life can be understood in terms of the analysis of isolated material particles.

Whitehead deplores the effect of this fallacy, as he calls it. What he attacks under the term of "simple location" is materialism, the chief origins of which, as he points out, may be found in Democritus and Lucretius. If the particles, isolated in simple location, are once set in motion it is held by the materialist that one can explain the whole story of the world, from the ethics of an isolated person to the problems of nature. Such a position was held by some French revolutionists. The view has been attributed to Robespierre most mistakenly. Wordsworth was aware that there were grave faults on both sides if one thinks of the Revolution broadly. Doubtless he was correct in feeling that the thing chiefly lacking among most of the participants was insight, comprehensive wisdom. Certainly he was astute in condemning, as he did, in effect, the tendency of letting one's means become ends, that is, bartering

short-lived pangs
For a paradise of ages . . . (321—)

But could the "pangs" be so minimized and was a "paradise of ages" likely to follow from them? Surely the events were gruesome indeed, with "never heads enough" to fall, the victims including women, the old, and even those who were not of mature age. Put bluntly, we may say: Are even *children* to be brought under the guillotine? The question is paralleled in Euripides in ancient Greece when, in effect, he asked, "What! Are you afraid of a child, that you would *kill* him — and that even after you have brought his whole city to destruction and ashes?" The distress of mind of Euripides can well be thought of as a counterpart to that of Wordsworth during the cataclysmic days in 1792. People in the French Revolution were forgetting their goal: liberty with justice. They were forgetting, Wordsworth says, "such a sound" as the *sign* behind the concept of liberty. They were losing remembrance of it, as corresponding to the notion of "Liberty upon earth" — we quote the poet's words concerning the crisis in which the loss was "this blessed name." It is here that he appropriately mentions Madame Roland and her sense of the ironical character of that stage in the Revolution. To this irony she gave utterance at the very moment of her death.

Even such a person as a peasant who had never had any initial hope was brought to agony in this time. But the people who felt the pain most keenly, the poet says, were those who continued to have "trust in man." The philosophy of Wordsworth and that of Whitehead call, as we have seen, for hope. But in such a time as the poet had reached, a philosophy calling for hope would only bring added pain. So Wordsworth expresses his feeling, thinking of Coleridge here.

Most melancholy at that time, O Friend!
Were my day-thoughts, my dreams were miserable;
Through months, through years, long after the last beat

Of those atrocities (I speak bare truth
As if to thee alone in private talk)
I scarcely had one night of quiet sleep . . . (369—)

In this period Wordsworth suffered "ghastly visions" which filled him with "despair" — visions indeed of "implements of death" filling his imagination. Here we think, naturally, of guillotines. In his dreams he mad "long orations" pleading to "unjust Tribunals" with broken voice, with "brain confounded" — with a sense of "treachery and desertion" even in himself. What does this later point mean? Wordsworth explains: in speaking of the "self" he refers to it as the "holiest" thing he knows; that is, the "holiest" thing is his "own soul." His point of view here represents a natural religion. It includes a sense of moral culpability in the self, or "treachery and desertion" to one's own being; perhaps he is thinking here of the possible danger to self of giving up any belief in his cause.

This giving up of belief in a cause of major and active liberal reform is what Karl Barth in our own century also thinks of in various works. Social causes at first loomed very large in his thought. In one of the contexts in which he reflects on such problems, he wonders whether, in his development, an "encounter with socialism"[21] itself perhaps led him in the end to take an opposite direction: led him, in a word, to turn away from his earlier emphasis upon social reform. In his turning away from such a social and economic emphasis within his religion he was moving toward a view of God not as man-centered but as "wholly other"; in making this change toward the "wholly other," he wonders whether, in addition, he was influenced greatly by the sense of twentieth-century war horrors.

Once again, he could ask: did Kierkegaard, Dostoevski, or some other thinker in the public eye cause him to make the change which in the end brought him toward an emphasis on the power and majesty of God? "Or," he also asks, "was it something more fundamental"[22]; could there be a matter far more basic than a man-centered morality and religion? Could there, indeed, be something more important than man's "secret divinity?" These are Barth's words. The idea of such a notion as that of the secretly divine within man seems to Barth out of the question. The solution which he in the end offers cannot for the present be developed here.

But Barth's problems serve as a useful counterpoint to the problems that beset Wordsworth. The poet's encounter with revolution and social change led him finally to a sense of deep moral culpability with regard to the answers a person could find. Along with his general grief about the revolution he had a feeling that profoundly within his own personal soul it was he who was guilty. Could this perhaps have been the familiar concept that we are all guilty before the bar of judgment when social evils mount tragically? Perhaps. But we must add that what probably goes with this is the sense that his philosophy — at times, in the period, tainted by materialism — was not large enough in any event to shed meaning on all of the horrors. He could not easily counterbalance the evils of the Revolution with saving factors. There was also the nagging sense of guilt over Annette Vallon, who was bearing his child at the very moment that he was witnessing some of the latest tragic events in Paris.

At that time, then, he felt deserted in the most precious part of himself, that is, in his "own soul." Still, it was not possible for Wordsworth to forget those "bright spots" in human experience, including "fortitude, and energy, and love," where "worst trials" were faced. Nor could he forget his earliest trip to France and his experience in the town of Arras where he walked with a friend through a recently constructed rainbow "Arch" dedicated to "Liberty" and the Revolution. This remembrance was in Wordsworth's mind now, and it made him think of Robespierre. Arras was the town of Robespierre, and the poet's anger rises to the point of fury as he thinks of the violence of the French massacres.

Perhaps he mistakenly attributes to Robespierre certain acts of Chaumette: for example, the act of sacrilege, or notoriety, in the Notre Dame cathedral service of November, 1793, when a Parisian actress was crowned in almost a religious sense in the name of Reason. What Wordsworth has most specifically in mind, however, is how the city of Arras acutely suffered under the Terror brought about by the temporary dictatorial government in 1793-1794, and he tells of his indignation, amounting even to irrationality, when he felt he could almost vent his rage against the artificial rainbow arch spanning the street at Arras, and tear it to pieces. The remembrance he could see as "an image" which "mocked" him "under such a strange reverse." Hence his seeming irrationality.

Following the account of this painful recollection, he describes with an excellent effect of contrast a beautiful day when, some seven months after his return to England, he walked "beneath a genial sun" toward a "prospect among gleams of sky," where peaks of mountains seemed made of one "ethereal substance" suggestive of "Seraphs" sitting within the "Empyrean." This scene, forming as we have said a contrast, is used as a background against which Wordsworth develops thoughts on death, as well as concern about lines "from the Elegy of Gray," and a mood of "gentleness and peace." Suddenly after this, however, he tells how he came upon a "variegated crowd" near the sea, and asked, in view of the clustering of people, whether "any news were stirring"; in response to his question he was told that "Robespierre was dead." Rarely indeed, he says, had he been more happy. Having in mind a kind of paean for the occasion, he exults:

> Great was my glee of spirit, great my joy
> In vengeance, and eternal justice, thus
> Made manifest. 'Come now ye golden times,'
> Said I, forth-breathing on those open Sands
> A Hymn of triumph, 'as the morning comes
> Out of the bosom of the night . . .' (540—)

We may feel that it is strange that Wordsworth should continue as he does. He speaks with reference to the magnificent "might" of the guillotine, which is now a "helper"; he glories in what has happened to Robespierre and his group. Their madness, he says, has been "declared" and rendered "visible" in the sequel which has been under development. We may especially wonder at the mood, almost of gloating, in which Wordsworth continued (this was his feeling in 1794), anticipating the coming of "righteousness" and even forming "schemes" whereby "Factions" might be tranquillized and the "renovation" of France become a reality. He goes on his way, still exulting in "uneasy bursts," and it might seem either that his ethics affords place for such moods or that he wished to emphasize his youthful ingenuousness. Perhaps a clue suggestive of this latter interpretation lies in the expression "uneasy bursts," and in the fact that the material that follows seems to provide an association, whether by chance or intent, with boyishness or youth. Possibly it is his aim merely to report the reality of his experience — to tell what he himself was like at the time that he heard of Robespierre's execution.

It was on this note that Wordsworth brought the tenth book to an end when he was forming the new version of *The Prelude* which was finally published in 1850. The terminal point of this portion of the work should rest, one would think, on something the author held to be of special moment, and perhaps the answer to our earlier question lies in the emphasis on ingenuousness, or youthful fluctuations of mood. But in the 1805 version he chose no such ending for the tenth book; rather, he continued the development of his material in Book Ten to a very considerable extent.

We are deliberately emphasizing the fact that the rest of this chapter deals with material which the poet placed in a separate book in a later version of *The Prelude*. But our main concern is with the content of the earlier, the 1805 form of the poem, and what follows is still part of Book Ten in that *Prelude* edition. After the guillotining of Robespierre on the 28th of July, 1794, there was less violence in France by impromptu tribunes and dubious committees of public safety, Wordsworth says, but "everything was wanting" still to give a person confidence in a rational future "in the spirit of past aims." The goals of republicanism and democracy, Wordsworth rightly felt, were in process of deterioration. Actions of the Senate and "public measures of the Government" were of "heartless omen," but the poet retained his faith that "the People" would finally gain power, that the triumph would be

in the end
Great, universal, irresistible. (585 –)

For Wordsworth, "faith" as here exemplified was an important principle, but at this time he was proceeding in his thought on the basis, as he says, of "passionate intuition"; the "Republic," he felt sure, would not ultimately be overthrown. It was not that he wanted to speak like an oracle on this; his whole tone is the opposite of self-complacency. However, he meant to suggest clearly that it seemed to him that what we would call democracy had the strong possibility of a long and significant history lying ahead. It is true that he did not fully realize the difficulties of establishing a sound society once conditions of "unambitious peace" were established. The later history of France fully illustrates these difficulties. It would seem that by "unambitious peace" he has in mind the abandonment of the goal of world social-change, extending beyond France. Writing from a vantage point of some ten years later than the events, he realizes that the liberal re-establishment of France would require time and much "fortitude." In the distress he had felt, he had, he says, been putting together in his mind quantitative entities and had failed to make adequate qualitative distinctions. He did not dream that a "fall of be-

209

ing" (or a loss of deeper reality) could occur after "a great ascent" in social reformation had begun.

The poet has recounted certain of his errors — some of them in the very processes of thinking — and he now explains that he had held the conviction that youth maintains under "all conditions of society" a more "direct and intimate" interrelation with the natural order than older persons (what he has in mind is ordinary human experiential perception), and he holds that youth had, in addition, a sense of "Reason too" which often surpasses that of their elders. The special period and the circumstances to which Wordsworth refers are important — that is, the period of his own youth about which he is speaking and the power he feels he had at that time. This force in his nature was being directed in such a way, in 1793 and 1794, that "custom" and the laws of society were held in abeyance. Conclusions he arrived at, he says, were the "warmest" of "judgments"; they were such as to "shake the authority of canons" based on "ordinary practice."

What are the conclusions that "shake the authority of canons" based on customary rules of behavior? They are clearly far from conventionalism. Wordsworth was in a circumstance such as Goethe, in the same period, often experienced, and he is similar to Goethe here in that he felt so self-driven that he could not help seeing things in the light of what he felt was necessary for the right moral development of his personality. Those who opposed the advance of the French Revolution with its social change were to Wordsworth like men clinging to insane delusions. He had become convinced of the democratic cause broadly through "experience," but he tended now to go beyond the basic conclusions he had reached; he took credit to himself "where less was due" to him. The fault here lay, he says (once more in self-exculpatory terms), not in himself but in the acts of "Britain" which were turning *all* judgments out of their "right course," and perhaps he was not altogether rationalizing. Indeed, he was thinking of things comparable to the

British effort to condemn to death Hardy, "the organizer of political movement among the working classes,"[23] for in the poet's terms, Britain

> at that time
> Thirsted to make the guardian Crook of Law
> A tool of Murder . . . (646—)

In a kind of Proustian fashion again Wordsworth now turns to the earlier stage of his own history so far as it is connected with the French Revolution. At first he had considered "human nature from the golden side," that is from the side seen in youth. He did realize something of what is best "in individual Man" — for example, in the wisdom which can exist behind "passion" or the strength that can be present in "household love," as well as the benevolent element at times showing itself in small communities where the virtues of decentralization manifest themselves. He knew also what can be truly excellent in large societies especially when it is brought forth, as it sometimes is, on "great occasions," but he did not at first know the complexity of these things sufficiently well. What this amounts to is that in 1794 or thereabouts he did not realize the nature and the activity of a higher reason, the force within the self to which we have previously referred. Nevertheless he was dedicated to the problems of nations and their management — their actuality and what countries ideally might strive toward. He knew that the solutions of the problems largely

> depended on their Laws
> And on the Constitution of the State. (688—)

Recalling at this point his earliest revolutionary enthusiasm and emphasizing the importance of love, he gives the famous passage concerning the "bliss" that he felt "in that dawn" in human advancement when "to be young was very heaven"; he felt an enchantment in those days, but he also realizes now that, as we have said in an earlier context, he was close to the tendencies in which one seeks a solution for problems by means of magic. In his youth he was prone to try to encompass all the problems of mankind over "the whole earth"; perhaps we overstate the case because he says it was the "promise" that he was contemplating. He recognized that solutions of difficulties must be attained

> in the very world which is the world
> Of all of us, the place in which, in the end,
> We find our happiness, or not at all. (726 –)

In so far as Wordsworth had erred in this period he was "erring on the better part," being inclined toward generosity of spirit. He stresses the view that human beings have frailties which involve misconceptions that they have been exposed to through the inevitable effects of the things that surround them. What amounts to a kind of brainwashing occurs. Circumstances, or the time in which one lives, may give sanctions, or "rights," to error. He adds, however, that extremes may be necessary in a time of revolution. In such a circumstance one should not worry greatly "if the wind" blow somewhat keenly upon "an eminence" which gives so "large" a prospect "into futurity"; he was

> In brief, a child of nature, as at first,
> Diffusing only those affections wider
> That from the cradle had grown up . . . (753 –)

Is Wordsworth, then, a Rousseauistic child of nature? Does he mean that "nature" cannot make a mistake with its child? By no means. He is indicating his own limitations in a certain period of his life. He is telling what he was like when England declared "open war" against the French revolutionary cause. At this point he began to lose the "love" that had been characteristic of him, and to become "corrupted" or perverted. His sentiments were modified so abruptly that he became virtually the opposite of what he had been. He was led to "false conclusions of the intellect" which were "gross in their degree" — and "in their kind" exceedingly dangerous. Godwin's *Political Justice* had lately been published and for a time it considerably affected Wordsworth. It was Godwin who had said (quoting Home's *Douglas*) that men, under injustice, can be readily made to do deeds to which fiends might tempt them.

Wordsworth had contemplated man in action under the extremes of philosophical belief.[24] Rational murder, though not treated in *The Prelude,* is one of the themes dealt with in his poetry of 1795. In a moment we shall have to give a picture of William Godwin's thinking which is somewhat distorted because of certain omissions that will necessarily be made, but for the present we may say that whether through Godwin or some other influence the poet now became ashamed of things which he had formerly honored, or viewed with pride. His "loves" were affected in a manner that might at first have meant only loss of judgment, but they now worked their way into his very "sensations" in most fundamental aspects.

The poet goes on to explain that "wild theories were afloat" along with wild actions. To these he had at first paid small attention. Now they began to take possession of him. What were these wild attitudes? In the discussion of democracy and France, toward the end of the previous chapter, mention was made of one important, though small organization of theorists, the Babeuf group, which might serve now as an illustration of wildness of thought. This group stressed overt action, class struggle, and violence. The theories of these men were associated with anarchy. Apart from their organization, such ideas (except for anarchy) were not uncommon in France at various earlier stages. Wordsworth may have been attracted by some of these ideas in one way or another, for he had a collection of Revolutionary pamphlets, books, and related matter in his library. These materials were sold after his death. Ideas

213

that were in the air, or radical material that he read, may have affected him from 1793 to 1796 or later, combining with thoughts that he tried subsequently to analyze when struggling with the writing of *The Prelude*. Theories of violence and other kinds of radicalism during the Revolution were common in the thought of the time.

But to resume our examination of Wordsworth's problem about the "wild theories" that began to exert an influence upon him, he had formerly held that the hordes of deprived people in France would, as the result of the Revolution, suffer oppression "no more." This view he could no longer hold as he had held it in "faith" and "hope," and he therefore sought "evidence" (through a kind of physical or material analysis) which he then imagined "could not be impeached"; what he aimed at was a kind of materialistic absolutism. This he thought would promptly give satisfactory results. Ideas related to those of Babeuf (and anticipating Marx to some extent) would fit in here, but conceptions of Godwin, combined with other revolutionary concepts, were definitely within his mind.

A form of materialistic absolutism may be seen in Godwin's emphasis upon sensation as primary to all thought and upon a calculating approach which (to give an extreme instance) would lead one to leave one's mother in a burning building in order to rescue, by preference, a stranger who was more intelligent. He it was, who, like Babeuf to some extent, recommended the use of reasoning without any trace of feeling as well as a necessitarianism which gives to the egoistic self a confidence that one could arrive at conclusions no one of which need ever be false. Human beings could arrive at such an infallibility. If there could be a person who lacked such rational characteristics, it was Godwin's thought that he should be properly regarded as a monstrosity, one of earth's abortive productions. In view of this approach it is understandable that Godwin (again like Babeuf) felt contempt for many persons. The poet was considerably influenced by Godwin at this stage.

214

And a philosophy involving contempt for human beings was far indeed from his fundamental quest. Still, he was greatly affected by such conceptions during this period. In *The Prelude* he does not mention Godwin directly, perhaps because of the difficulty of representing him with justice, in view of his many merits, which the poet may have felt would need to be indicated as against the gross faults.

Wordsworth's main theme now is his own philosophy in relation to France. He goes on therefore almost at once to explain that it clearly brought about the doom of liberty to Frenchmen when they changed from "self-sacrifice" for an *ideal* to a desire for conquest. Nevertheless, Wordsworth continued to hold his tenets strongly — even stubbornly. He does not use this last word stubbornly, but it does apply to the context. As to the tenets he followed, he "strained them" beyond wise judgment, forcing them to fit situations that were extreme. Thus he soon came to be ruled by "opinions" rather than by wisely established conceptions. The problem of judgment again arises here. From these "opinions" he accepted consequences until a quite new pattern became the very life of his mind. Wordsworth is thinking here of how a young, perhaps somewhat ill person — and he had become psychologically ill after his return from France — can fail in pursuing sequential thought. He had tried reasoning without any trace of feeling and it had failed. Would an absolute reverse of this process bring better results? The reversal seems absurd, but he decided that he would try

the Philosophy
That promised to abstract the hopes of man
Out of his feelings . . . (807 —)

The approach involved having one's "hopes," thus abstracted, firmly established "in a purer element" — so it was imagined. The prospect on this basis, Wordsworth says, offered a very decided temptation. Here he seems to be harking back for the moment in certain ways to Rousseau, one of Robespierre's chief masters. The region Wordsworth was turning to, he says, was extremely attractive (especially for a wayward person, one would think), in that it offered an easy manner in which to accept "passions" without ever hearing "the sound of their own names," and hence to proceed toward no clearly discerned destination. Wordsworth declares that in judging youth, which is especially vulnerable to "extremes" (the excess which the Greeks warned against), he would urge the importance of charity. A tendency to imagine that one is relying upon emotion exclusively may indeed change quickly to an ingenuous supposition that one is relying altogether on "human Reason's naked self"; the two tendencies that appear to be at opposite poles can be almost interchangeable if one is psychologically ill.

Here was the conflict within Wordsworth over the theories of Godwin and other presumed revolutionary leaders. One would judge this from the way that the poet juxtaposes emotion and reason in *The Prelude*. It is to be noted that this "Reason" is distinguished by its adjective "human," being therefore different from the "Reason" which according to the poet can partake of the divine. This latter, involving the divine, is a faculty to which, in his theory, mankind can also aspire. And it can at times be attained. The "naked self" of "human Reason," however, is the intellectual faculty without a tempering of the imagination. Here ego in the narrow sense tends to predominate, being flattered by an imagined highly rational "self-knowledge" — or knowledge which is self-authorized. Along with this, Wordsworth adds further emphasis to his thought through using the term "self-rule" — not in any Greek sense of restraint and control, but in respect to "the freedom of the individual mind" which "magisterially" chooses only one criterion. This criterion is "the light of circumstances,"and the danger in its use is that it may proceed on the basis of *various* "circumstances," as individual whim might wish. We cannot be adequately guided, the poet says, by such a light

flash'd
Upon an independent intellect. (829 –)

Is Wordsworth inveighing against the independent mind in favor of authority? Clearly not. He is criticizing the results attained when a particular kind of light is flashed upon the self-guided *intellect,* as he has tried to make clear. If we are to be fair to him we must notice the central tendency, the continuing thread, in his story. This appears when he declares that, with all his present criticism of himself, "never once" did he change in his feeling about the worth of "human kind," nor did he cease to be concerned most deeply about the "welfare" of human beings. What he is criticizing is not the liberty of the movement toward democracy, in thought or deed, but the tendency of the individual to spread his "wings" as lord and master. He associates such action, as it takes place in "undisturb'd delight," with conceptions, or "thoughts," that are gross and inadequate. A "delight" of the individual which is perpetually undisturbed would be self-oriented. It would amount to the authoritarianism of the self, or of the ego in the narrow sense.

A word should be said here about the ego conception. We are referring to it, as we have done sometimes earlier, not as what Erik Erikson calls a "balancing function in mental life which keeps things in perspective and in readiness for action."[25] We are not referring to a mediating force "between the higher and the lower selves." Rather, as Erikson also says on the next page, "one must grant that the popular use of the term *ego* which ascribes to it a certain egotism and grandiosity, has its point." It is this danger that we have in view. Earlier Wordsworth had been sacrificing "exactness" and the "comprehensive mind" and accepting minuscule views. These minuscule views were based upon something akin to free fantasy rather than "experience" and its "limits"; the wise use of limits is necessary to evidence and judgment.

What he then needed was a spirit of inquiry leading tentatively toward possible confirmations. He is not saying that ancient institutions are right and that we should return to the past for a base. He has pity for the man who "had not eyes wherewith to see" that a revolution had taken place which could not be turned back, that a "veil" of tradition no longer covered things so that one necessarily was *blinded*. His mind had been released, "let loose"; indeed it even had been "goaded." England had destroyed his patriotic love, to use the expression he employed earlier, in relating his feelings. The debasing animal-image of being goaded expresses well what had happened to him. It helps us to understand his effort to justify his feelings and what he calls errors. Why, then, is Wordsworth apologizing for himself? For this is what he seems again to be doing. Why does he feel a compulsion to explain his own psychology? It is a question that has arisen before.

Wordsworth has had a kind of tendency toward joy in his nature. He has always been essentially a "happy man": two things — joy and happiness — along with a certain boldness to face things that are unpleasant or painful, enabled him to take "the knife in hand" and cut within society's "living body" to its most vital life. The choice of scientific or surgical imagery is important because it fits in with the material emphasis in his thought at this time. He with his "knife" tries to reach the "heart" of society. There may come a time, he feels, when he will be able to tell his close friend more adequately what the surgical exploration of society revealed concerning "truth," as well as "errors" to which people are prone because of the influence of "present objects," or too restrictive views. We have to look beyond the immediate, present situation of things. What Wordsworth would like to tell Coleridge more fully seems to be something which is radically fundamental. There is evidently a material not readily apparent which he feels is deeply rooted in reality and which he would like to clarify even for himself. The truth with regard to this he would aim to impart. He speaks with modesty when he says

Time may come
When some dramatic Story may afford
Shapes livelier to convey to thee, my Friend,
What then I learn'd, or think I learn'd . . . (879 —)

Wordsworth apparently thinks he learned in the French
social revolutions certain foundational or root things concerning the problems of the world. What were they? This we may
well ask. The exaggerated emphasis upon one's own nation, or
one's own nationalism, is among these root things. This — the
evil of what we might call *nationism* in relation to new
democratic developments — was notable earlier than the 1796
period about which Wordsworth was now writing, and it has
been a continuing problem throughout the modern world. Nations are ruled entirely by their *interests* it is often argued. Nationalism has burgeoned in the twentieth century side by side
with republicanism, as is evident and as Wordsworth could see
in his day in Poland, Italy, France, and elsewhere. One great
burden on Wordsworth's mind was certainly connected with
England's drive toward nationalism in opposition to English
democratic trends and even to the rights of people in other
countries.

Also involved in the growth of nationalism was the problem
of the expanding population of the world, along with the
phenomenon of mass metropolitan living and mass action, including all the local and wider tensions that come with group
living and the incidence of violence. Wordsworth had reflected
upon crowded living in his London days. He painfully watched
mass violence when he was in Paris. The ongoing stages of
revolution brought mass action more acutely to a head. This
and nationism, or expediency, he might have wished to discuss
with Coleridge in order to clarify what he had tried to learn
concerning the world and society and the conflicts that were
occurring under the developing democratic tendencies. There
were in addition the deeply-rooted difficulties of accepting the

role of the revolutionist as such, which Babeuf was concerned with, as we have seen. We might well have cited also the case of Babeuf's friend and associate — some had said his fellow conspirator — Philippe Buonarotti. These men were consciously, unabashedly disruptive in their theories of social action, as Wordsworth himself was during the Revolution.

The poet had not hesitated to use the word "subversion" in reference to himself. Babeuf and his friend aimed to bring about the overthrowal of the Directory, or the government, in France. They were concerned, as the poet was, with the social problems of poverty, and of the patriciate, as well as the lack of education among the multitude, and the immediate necessity of a vigorous program of fundamental reforms. The conditions were a national disgrace. For Buonarotti such matters had subtle religious and moral connections which he felt needed study and careful consideration. In this, Wordsworth's thought paralleled Buonarotti's. So far as the poet aimed at "subversion" he purposed similar results to those that Buonarotti tried to promote. He knew some of the problems of one who assumed the role of revolutionist. Certainly from his observation of the methods of Robespierre and Brissot, if not those of Babeuf and his fellow theorists, he was aware of the incipient threat of action by a dictator or by a committee of smaller dictatorial forces.

Social authoritarianism was perhaps the greatest problem. The remembrance of Robespierre and Brissot was in the poet's mind in 1794 and later, while the last books of *The Prelude* were being written. The goals and actions of these figures, along with those of Napoleon who receives mention in the tenth book, were before his consciousness. They and the thought of their consequences represented a part of what he learned concerning social change. All of the problems involving mass action, violence, and the role of the revolutionist and of the ruler he might well have wished to comment on. But for the moment in *The Prelude* he concentrated mainly on his mental state in his time of trial and confusion.

Wordsworth believed he had been guilty of making errors in reasoning and judgment and that his "heart" had been "confounded" in the process. As a result he had been guilty of "misguiding" others, just as he had let himself become "misguided." The sense of guilt he expresses with regard to letting oneself fall into errors of action and even of thinking is characteristic of him. The latter — thinking about thought — is part of his philosophy as it is part of Whitehead's. The poet's moral concern reaches even into his reflection about the nature of thought. It is a person's responsibility to clear up such matters. His ethical emphasis is a part of his sense of self. Was his moral preoccupation tied in, perhaps, with the melancholy which was markedly present in him, as he says, in the earlier passage in which he likens himself to a probing surgeon? In discussing that part of *The Prelude* we did not mention the characteristic of melancholy, but it is pertinent here to the subject of the poet's sense of guilt. Feelings of guilt may be largely an outgrowth of a sense of responsibility in the very conduct of thought.

In his general ethics he clearly feels that one should be a responsible person. Doubtless this too could be connected with his thinking about Annette Vallon. He could have projected his guilt about her in part to a feeling of guilt over his actions and attitudes with reference to revolutionary violence. Shortly after the last context of *The Prelude* to which we have referred, however, he says that he had been scrutinizing "all passions, notions, shapes of faith" bringing them as if they were "culprits" before the bar. He was doing this "suspiciously," requiring that every aspect of the mind establish its status or "honours"; at times he accepted his own findings and at times he was radically skeptical. He wondered, for example, how one should evaluate the tendency toward "impulse"; again, when is our "motive" justified or unjustified?

What basis is there for "moral obligation," and what is the meaning of "sanction" — these last were problems not only for Wordsworth; our own time has found them more than puzzling, and it is no wonder that the poet was brought by them to a state of perplexity. He was "demanding *proof*," he emphasizes, and he was irrevocably "seeking it" in each particular problem. In the end he lost all sense of "conviction"; having made an impossible demand upon himself, he had been so struck by the dichotomies or the "contrarieties" of things that he apparently could find no middle ground, at least approaching something satisfactory to his method of inquiry.

The upshot was that he felt complete "despair" with regard to "moral questions," and turned for relief to mathematical exercises of the mind. Here we may recall the reference in Chapter Three to Newton. What might be included in the exercises of the mind that the poet turned to; what geometrical or other exercises in mathematics did Wordsworth perform? Is this question beyond the possibility of speculation? For the present we shall not attempt to deal with it, but will observe that only in this field did an adequate handling of "evidence" appear to him possible. Here again, in an interim period, the poet was thinking about thinking. Was Wordsworth turning in his desperation, to mathematics with a mere desire for mental gymnastics in the field — seeking such relief from his tensions as he could find? It would appear that his situation was somewhat comparable to that of Descartes who, in trying to solve his problems, maneuvered himself into the area of intellectualistic constructions or high-level abstractions remote from every-day reality.

For Wordsworth the questions of everyday life had seemed paramount — the basic field within which he wished to work. Now he had reached a state of extreme depression of spirits toward the end of 1795. The mental tension he was under could not be easily overcome. The poet had been trying to integrate himself, and the difficulty of *attaining* knowledge (which is his concern along with a sound psychological integration of the self) is coupled with the difficulty of the ethical life which he had been dwelling upon all along. Since ethics as related to social justice has been a main theme of our chapter we may recall again Wordsworth's problem concerning Annette and the child Caroline. The period of his most profound depression of spirits occurred some three years after he left Annette. Now in the time of the poet's present composition of *The Prelude* — roughly ten years after the separation — is he still dwelling on his responsibility to her, which had remained unsettled in the interim? Does this, along with his expressed concern for the Revolution and England's opposition to it (as well as his concern about the recent war for conquest implemented by France), combine to cause the distress under which he suffered? Is Annette a factor in his decided concern with regard to ethics?

It is difficult not to feel that this relationship weighed heavily on his mind; it was important to his thought, especially in view of the visit he finally paid to Annette precisely in the midst of his work on the 1805 *Prelude*. Wordsworth had given stress to "impulse" in the point of view he had been developing; this, along with an emphasis upon emotion and feelings generally, had, according to his theory, ruled him and many other human beings in the period. It is an interpretation of life which he presents, an interpretation concerning our passion-driven actions and the importance of "individual" (or particular) items of behavior. This interpretation may be set in contrast with an ethical theory based on the general category or rule: the problem which Kant had made pre-eminent. Such conceptions were then very much in the air. If Kant (who died in 1804) had not worked on them, they would have been dwelt on attentively by others. Certain of the ideas now expressed by Wordsworth may represent his thinking after the fact of his illness which amounted in the view of some critics almost to a nervous breakdown.

What could help him in such an extremity? A mode of thinking certainly, but of what kind? There was an element of personalism developing perhaps somewhat unconsciously in his

223

philosophy. This may be noticed in the number and the depth of the portraits of persons that one finds in his poems from approximately this stage on in his life. At first the figures were drawn according to superficial and familiar lines; this broad portrayal gradually changes until he is producing a kind of art of portraiture which is singularly his own. We are focussing on Book Ten of *The Prelude*, however, and the personalism appears there in two particular instances. The first is seen in his references to "most precious" Coleridge, whom he had met in the period of stress we have discussed and who gave him "living help" — indeed a regulating service of a highly individual sort. Coleridge had also helped Wordsworth in the process of thinking.

The second instance related to the personalistic element in Wordsworth's philosophy occurs in his portrait of his sister, referred to as "beloved," who had been separated from him during long periods of time. In her he almost literally found himself in renewal, and through her he at any rate saw himself more clearly. Today in a form of personalism it is common for one to say, "I don't know who I am," and, because of this lack, to seek a better knowledge of oneself. This current psychological (and philosophical) tendency seems a very distinctly modern feature. But we find Goethe in the early nineteenth century using almost identical words with reference to the self-search he so often undertook, and surely Wordsworth from 1795 through 1796 was engaged in a similar quest of the self. He was aiming to find himself.

But to return to his portrayal of his sister Dorothy. She it was mainly who rescued him from his "clouded" state, who he says preserved him particularly as one who was to become in a true sense a poet. She helped him to seek "his office upon earth, and nowhere else"; all of these things, along with "Nature's Self" and the assistance of general human love, brought about his sense of identity and recovery. A seeming regression may be of service to the ego and may provide an assistance in the creative process. Such an experience caused Wordsworth to return, though he was of adult years, to the childhood he had experienced, and it renewed for him

> knowledge full of peace,
> Enlarged, and never more to be disturb'd,
> Which through the steps of our degeneracy,
> All degradation of this age, hath still
> Upheld me . . . (926—)

Wordsworth thought his period was a burdensome one. What is "knowledge full of peace" and what does Wordsworth mean by "degeneracy"; is there anything personal in this passage? When he speaks of "our" degeneracy he seems perhaps to include himself in the indictment. But what, perhaps, is the "degradation" of the age? We had thought that to the poet the time in which he lived was glorious. Clearly he still feels that this is true. It is a time of glory and a time of "degradation" as well. An example of degradation, or sinking to a new low, had just occurred (December 2, 1804) in the crowning of "an Emperor" (Napoleon) at Notre Dame Cathedral. Contrasted with this falseness — this hypocrisy as Wordsworth deemed it — is the "sun" of the Revolution which formerly had risen "in splendour" and contained within it something alive and organic. It is no exaggeration to say that the event of Napoleon's crowning is not merely theatrical to Wordsworth, but completely disgusting. The living day has put off all its "glory," and the sun has been made to set, not in reality, but as if by the machinery of "an opera phantom." For Wordsworth this, after all the shame, is the final indignity to a mind which has lived

> beneath
> The breath of great events, its hopes no less
> Than universal . . . (944—)

Religion is in the background here, in the boundlessness of

the hopes included in the poet's thought. Likewise it is included in the world-embracing "love" that he shortly speaks of; but the distinctly personal note that is a prominent feature of *The Prelude* is not lost here. Except for this the poem with its strongly introspective quality might seem like a mere work of lonely egoism. The deeply personal quality reappears in the theme of friendship. How many friends should a person or can a person have? The answer is not easy. Wordsworth is a friend to all human beings. This is part of his philosophy of universal love in so far as it can be expressed, through effort, in an imperfect world.

The point here is that one cannot be quiescent but must give *direction* to a philosophy. But in addition to trying to be a friend to all humankind, Wordsworth shows most intimate and personal feelings. There is a warmth of special personal friendship which almost glows in *The Prelude*, particularly, but not alone, when he speaks of his sister or of his ill friend Coleridge. The epistolary element in the poem, from time to time, brings this out. Having written on periods of "honour" and of "shame" he now more personally addresses his friend, who, having traveled from England, was at the moment (in 1804) in Sicily, in the "city of Timoleon," founded by the ancient hero who established many city-states as small democracies on the island. For Wordsworth, Timoleon speaks as a "great voice" which is "heard from out the tombs" of Syracuse. The people of this land, the poet feels, should above all others have been awakened to republican reforms through the memory of the great deeds accomplished in this ancient country. Some of these deeds were connected with Dion whom we referred to in the last chapter.

The Dion reference, along with an allusion to France, is tied closely to the situation then current in Sicily where an extreme social disaster had recently occurred. But Syracuse, as the poet feels, is not the world. Here as a contrast to the theme of hope is an example of reversed hope. Syracuse in its disaster is without even one "memorial hope," or indeed a hope deferred which could enliven the heart "in such entire decay." It seems that in Wordsworth's insight a sense of tragic catharsis nevertheless appears, based not, as in the conventional theory, upon pity or terror, but upon the ordinarily hated emotion of wrath. We gather that wrath or "indignation works where hope is not," and in a dynamic way Coleridge, as Wordsworth thinks *wrathfully* of these injuries to democracy, will be healthfully refreshed.

Coleridge is part of the truly "great Society," not only the society of those who have nobly lived but that of "the noble Dead"; in this spirit Wordsworth addresses his friend with words of consolation for his illness and with the hope that "Time" as well as "Nature" shall "spread" before him in great store "thoughts" that are imperishable. It is Wordsworth's hope that the actual place, Syracuse, will in some fashion become sensitive spiritually to Coleridge's presence. Through Coleridge's benefit to Syracuse and its profiting perhaps in a seemingly minor way from his being there, both will be helped. Thus Wordsworth would have Syracuse serve as a benefit to his friend. What he is conceiving is related to the actions and reactions of persons one upon another through personalism. He hopes that something "sanative" there may assist his friend to health.

For Wordsworth at this moment (it was 1804, we have said, when Coleridge was in Sicily) small vestige of hope for Europe remained. England seemed the "last spot of earth" in which "Freedom" might find "sanctuary"; in the present "heavy time of change for all mankind," future developments for social evolution presented many difficulties. Still, thinking of Coleridge, Wordsworth mentions his friend's intellectual and spiritual ripeness for religious philosophy and poetry (and "all divine enjoyment"); freedom may be mentioned here, for religion is a personal thing in Wordsworth's philosophy and can develop properly only in an independent, nondogmatic, creative mind. Wordsworth closes Book Ten on the note of his feeling for Sicily, "that honour'd isle," and for such of her renowned sons as the philosopher Empedocles and "Archimedes, deep and tranquil Soul."

The philosopher-physicist-mathematician Archimedes was one of the greatest figures in the ancient world. And Wordsworth's phrase concerning him is very suitable. Whitehead also admired Archimedes. He speaks of this famous Greek as not merely a "lucid" thinker, but as being — along with Aristotle — "at the very top"[26]; here he is thinking not only of "bold" reasoning but of the imaginative reach of thought. Whether Wordsworth appreciated the significance in history of Archimedes and Empedocles in equal degree to that of Whitehead's appreciation may be doubted, but he is not insensitive to their significance and the remembrance of these and other citizens of old Syracuse is a "comfort" to him. He thinks also of Coleridge in relation to these figures. As one might address a friend somewhat playfully, he refers to legends with regard to "miracles" of poetry; miracles in ancient Sicily were of assistance to poets and to the cause of poetry. The springs of Sicily should deservedly, Wordsworth thinks, be associated with Coleridge and with the powers of the poetical muses. Coleridge is conceived as a "visitant" who salutes or congratulates ancient Arethuse or, as Wordsworth says, some other fountain, with joy and thankfulness.

Of what importance to philosophy is the material we have given in this and the previous chapter? France, with its revolution, is of interest in itself, but perhaps the fascination is just political and sociological. What importance, further, should be attached to "chivalry" (related to Beaupuy) and such vague concepts as "love," "faith." and "nature" and some others which have been touched upon? Are they really important in a philosophical consideration of Wordsworth? Such questions one might still ask. Various problems of this kind might well have been raised in these pages. In answer we could have begun the chapter with a consideration of "caritas" (or "love") in its importance to philosophy, particularly at certain historical stages, for example the medieval. But the reader might well question further the importance of even this in relation to Wordsworth and modern times. Could not the matter of love and much else be dismissed? And what of the substance concerning Wordsworth's personal life as it has been depicted? Isn't philosophy mainly a matter of abstract things rather than events?

Addressing ourselves to this final point we could make reference to a modern philosopher who was nonplussed on completing the reading of a work on a certain writer's philosophy. His remark was: "This book has been exceedingly abstract. I should like to have more, much more, given to me concerning the *life* of the man who is being projected; I should like to know how his philosophy came into existence through such events, or how perhaps it may have been even a mere rationalization of such circumstances. The life should be included even though the man being considered is well known." The comment was made by an acute thinker, and it represents one modern point of view with regard to the discipline on which he had spent his life. This philosopher's basic emphasis is to some extent the point of contact that we have partly used, and that which was used by Wordsworth himself for the purpose of revealing not only his growth but his thought.

In our next chapter we shall be moving into the area of the destruction or the impairment of the imagination that can occur under devastating circumstances. We shall observe how the imagination can be related to such a broad outlook as philosophy may give — indeed, how it is related constructively or sanatively to the sense of self in the sense of self-analysis. If we think of the ideal of self-realization, prominent in the early part of our century, we shall see that Wordsworth is not merely centered in the self. The self was not a central goal for Wordsworth. His vital social emphasis, embodied in a self as related to others, is closely connected with Whitehead and with other creatively challenging figures of the twentieth century.

Footnotes

1. *Adventures of Ideas*, p. 293. The other error is "the strained attitude of introspection" which we employ in striving for an understanding of the nature of our knowledge.

2. *Ibid.*, p. 295. Note also on p. 293 the statement that "Language is imperfect both in its words and in its forms." Kant's book on judgment could be recalled here.

3. M. J. Sydenham, *The French Revolution* (New York: Putnam's Sons, 1965), p. 132.

4. Lefebvre, p. 218. See also our Chapter IX.

5. Sydenham, p. 120.

6. Knapton, pp. 70 and 71.

7. *Adventures of Ideas*, p. 23.

8. Arthur Koestler, *The Ghost in the Machine* (New York: Macmillan, 1967 — American edition 1968), p. 225.

9. Karl Barth, *The Humanity of God*, Second Printing (Richmond, Virginia: John Knox Press, 1960), p. 37.

10. *Ibid.*, p. 38.

11. *Ibid.*, p. 45.

12. Frankel, *The Case for Modern Man* (New York: Harper and Brothers, 1956), p. 10; see also *The Democratic Prospect* (New York: Harper and Row, 1962) where this problem of judging, to which we have referred, comes up, p. 15; also, *The Love of Anxiety* (New York: Harper and Row, 1965) contains many ideas that could be related profitably to Wordsworth's, for example, Frankel's criticism of the "tendency to employ moral and social ideals that are . . . left unexamined . . ." (p. x).

13. *Adventures of Ideas*, p. 53.

14. *Nature and Life* (New York: Greenwood Press, 1968 — originally, University of Chicago Press 1934), p. 23.

15. *Adventures of Ideas*, p. 99.

16. Sydenham, note, p. 65.

17. Lefebvre, p. 271.

18. Sydenham, p. 140.

19. Lefebvre, p. 274.

20. Frankel, *The Democratic Prospect* (New York: Harper and Row, 1962), p. 3.

21. *The Humanity of God*, p. 40.

22. *Ibid.*, p. 41.

23. *The Prelude: Text of 1805*, ed. by Ernest De Selincourt (Oxford: Oxford University Press, 1936, 1964), Notes, p. 306.

24. Compare Wordsworth's *The Borderers* and Home's *Douglas*.

25. Erikson, *Dimensions of a New Identity*, p. 92. See also p. 93.

26. *Science and the Modern World*, p. 11.

Chapter XI

Imagination Impaired and Restored: Relationships to Philosophy

The title of this chapter in part echoes deliberately that of Book Eleven of the 1805 *Prelude*. Near the close of the last chapter we saw that Wordsworth, after his return to England, had reached a troubled stage through which — as he viewed things — his imagination had undergone injury. He had, for one thing, polarized reason and emotion unduly, relying too exclusively first upon the one and then upon the other. The restoration of the faculty which he regards as of utmost importance is the theme of Book Eleven. That faculty is the imagination. Since the subject of Book Eleven in *The Prelude* is in part the imagination, then, it necessarily takes us into the philosophy of beauty. Here we have to think very widely of the aesthetic, or of the beautiful. We could include in it various general considerations which may be vaguely suggested by such words as sublimity, terror, the grotesque, the arabesque, compassion as connected with aesthetic emotion, and the relation of feelings of unhappiness to tragedy.

Thinking of the arabesque we may remember the poet's keen interest in the *Arabian Nights Entertainments,* also his interest in the subject of "The Ancient Mariner" as well as his initial co-operation with Coleridge in the writing of that work. These facts give one some general sense of what is meant by the arabesque as it is related to aesthetics. We shall not deal with sublimity, terror, and the other factors as definite topics, however, for Wordsworth was aware of such matters more or less tangentially; to demonstrate the kind of interest that he had in them would involve, also, too tortuous a path for our purpose. If at times we seem far from the topic of imagination in considering the poet's thought on a variety of things, we can still be close to it. It must be remembered that in exercising or using the mind greatly, as in science, one moves inevitably into areas of imaginative activity. This could be illustrated also through intuitive examples in the field of mathematics which might be given, but which are not pertinent for the moment.

Wordsworth had reached a stage, we have said, in which he polarized reason and emotion. For a certain length of time in 1794 he attempted to be most coldly reasonable, and then, following such a period of coldness (and being dissatisfied with its effects upon him), he turned exclusively to the emotions hoping that this radically changed approach toward man would guide him more satisfactorily. The two polarized tendencies alternated within his psyche until he reached a stage in which he felt uncertain as to what he was, or, perhaps, even who he was. The question of the essential nature of man, then, would be natural to raise in philosophizing about a person in such a situation; that is, what is the general nature of man viewed as a being compounded strangely of reason and emotion? Since Wordsworth is troubled, and wondering about himself personally, there is secondly the question: what is the nature of the individual person? This latter is the main problem in the poet's autobiographical work in that he is seeking to know himself through examining his experience.

Returning now to the substance of Wordsworth's eleventh book of the 1805 *Prelude*, the reader as we have suggested may at times wonder why the word "imagination" appears in the title, for there are many ideas that Wordsworth now presents which might seem unrelated to the subject he has put before himself. The connection of these things will gradually become evident. At the outset of Book Eleven he recapitulates the fact that he has been dealing with the "unhappiness and guilt" of man and the "dismal sights" of life that one may encounter. Thus he has in mind his remembrances of the French Revolution. He explains that he had suffered from disturbances of "opinion" which were confusing to him. The word "opinion" is well chosen for his purpose in that it is not necessarily equated with *knowledge* — which presumably man may somehow attain. He had then, he says, through conflicting opinions, been brought to "utter loss of hope," as well as to the destruction of "things to hope for."

Here we see that the idea of the nature of man which we have earlier referred to makes its appearance. The human being is a creature with a need of hope, in contrast to the agony of total despair. Such a state of depression might especially come to one who had seen men guillotined and who had felt troubled by what he regarded as even more terrible things. The need of hope as contrasted with despair belongs also to our own century, as does our question concerning man the individual and his human dignity, or utter lack of it. Reason and emotion play a part in this, and both function in close connection with the imagination and the stress the poet places on "things to hope for." Proceeding, he emphasizes even more strongly than in previous books of *The Prelude* the importance of hope in his philosophy. As we shall see, Whitehead also stresses hope fundamentally. Indeed he does so in various volumes, often by implication but on other occasions with very particular emphasis. His three best known books are part of an aim to see ideas and to note how they are "promoting" (and thus hoping for) the slow movement of mankind towards civilization. These books are *Science and the Modern World, Process and Reality,* and *Adventures of Ideas.*

In Whitehead's hope regarding the advancing of civilization, there is patently present a sense of adventure. Humanity indeed thus, through hope, faces adventure. But for the philosopher the writing even of a particular book is itself also an adventure of hope. He would stress particularly "the importance of Adventure for the promotion and preservation of civilizations."[1] The concept of adventure is in his very title. The idea of *promotion,* moreover, appears twice in the page from which we have quoted. A person does not aim to promote something if he is without the element of anticipated results as part of his thought. Whitehead speaks of the volumes which we have just referred to as works which "supplement each other's omissions or compressions." In all this there is an adventure.

Wordsworth likewise has written in *The Prelude* a work which is not only an adventure on his own part but, as in the case of Whitehead, a record of aspects of the adventure of mankind; he, like Whitehead, has in view the idea of advancing mankind in its movement toward an increased civilization. The poet, as he proceeds, is re-emphasizing a basic theme of his total work; he explains that he did not *begin* his song (*The Prelude*) with a mind focussed on the destruction of hope and of "things to hope for." And it will not be "with these" — these things — that his song will end. He goes on to give a highly appreciative portrayal of nature, with "the motions of delight," and the "breezes and soft airs" that breathe and find their way into the soul of man — indeed, into all its recesses.

These phrases might well be questioned as sentimental, and yet in Whitehead also we find an appreciation of nature that is closely parallel to Wordsworth's here. Whitehead has a sense of the religion of nature.

The philosopher speaks of the fact that in Wordsworth there is found, in many passages, a great appreciation of "the haunting presences of nature."[2] The poet recognizes in nature more than meets the eye. It is not the "dry" things, often thought to be found in philosophy, as Whitehead says, which Wordsworth gives in such portrayals. The poet may not deal much with analytical abstraction in these contexts. "But it would be hardly possible to express more clearly a feeling for nature, as exhibiting entwined prehensive unities, each suffused with modal presences of others . . ."

In these words, Whitehead is covering certain key ideas which are fundamental to his own philosophy, as we have indicated in previous chapters. But the ideas importantly parallel material in Wordsworth. There is more to say, however, concerning the poet's philosophy and its relation to certain key ideas for him in these respects. Let Whitehead first speak again for himself. "Wordsworth, to the height of genius, expresses the concrete facts of our apprehension, facts which are distorted in the scientific analysis. Is it not possible that the standardized concepts of science are only valid within narrow limitations, perhaps too narrow for science itself?"[3] His next volume, *Process and Reality*, makes evident that this is so.

It is clear that Wordsworth, in his own works, apprehends the fact that we need a sense of nature other than that radical abstraction from it that is so often limitedly characteristic of science. This point Whitehead has just stressed. Knowledge, scientific or otherwise, requires an interpretation of the aspect of experience that one is attempting to deal with. Hence simplification is necessary. We need something more than the reductive process, however, the naked formula, the cutting off of the properties of nature which science finds momentarily useful. The artistic approach can become basic philosophically in a different way from that of science. It requires, for example, something beyond the formula or formulas of mathematics.

It is not science itself, however, that we wish to attack here. And in Whitehead, too, it is only the "standardized concepts of science" held by many scientists, that he subjects to close questioning. This he does, not only in the volume from which we have just quoted but frequently in his other books. It is true that in one *aspect* of science we murder to dissect, but in saying this we are not implying that science should cease its dissection. It is to say, only, that dissection is not all that there is to a more complete science. And here we have a final important word about Wordsworth, since, in a *Prelude* passage shortly after the one to which we have last alluded, we find him saying

> in nature still
> Glorying, I found a counterpoise . . .
> Which, when the spirit of evil was at height
> Maintain'd for me a secret happiness . . . (31 —)

Observe here the counterbalancing of the loss of hope, mentioned earlier, by its opposite: a "secret" sense within the individual. Joy is in the background. But we must go on to Whitehead's remarks which follow his references to Wordsworth's expression of the "unities" in nature as *prehensive* unities. What meaning can we pour into this italicized word and into Whitehead's reference to "modal presences," which he says are also to be found in the poet? Then there is Wordsworth's expression "the spirit of evil" which was touched upon in the quotation at the close of the last paragraph. This evil should receive comment.

Taking these potentially troublesome terms one by one, we may note that Whitehead refers to a "prehension" as a *feeling*. Here he thinks of F. H. Bradley. Whitehead analyzes feeling first into the subjective: that is "into the 'subjective form'

236

which is Bradley's 'living emotion' "; he also analyzes it further "into the 'subject' which is Bradley's 'me' "[4] conception. The word "prehensive" has reference, then, to the "me" — the living, individual being and its strong emotional feelings. Wordsworth, we see, stresses this living self. As Whitehead expresses the matter, relatedly, he himself is stretching, he says, "subjective form" beyond the mere meaning of the term emotion. "For example, consciousness, if it be present, is an element in the subjective form." It is an important element, and it could point toward a philosophic idealism such as Royce developed.

Whitehead admired Royce, but this is not the place to point out the differences between the thought of the two men in their philosophies. We mention Royce because certain analogies between Royce and Whitehead are helpful to the understanding of philosophy. Consciousness is especially important in both of these men. The reader if he goes along with Whitehead, will at any rate see that "consciousness" in the passages from Wordsworth is "an element in the subjective" — an element in the "feeling" (or "prehension," to use Whitehead's preferred word); the philosopher departs somewhat from Bradley,[5] as he says, but Whitehead's "component of feeling 'which is not an object before me' is the subjective form."[6] It is useful to add that in the volume Science and the Modern World Whitehead speaks of things that are "together in space, and in time, even if they are not contemporaneous."[7] He adds, furthermore, that he "will call these characters the 'separative' and the 'prehensive' characters," respectively.

We would think, then, of togetherness when we think of space, and we would think similarly of a kind of unification when we think of time. But we would also, more conventionally, think of the separativeness of things in space as well as in time. The word prehensive as used by Whitehead is not generally regarded by readers as a simple expression, but perhaps it will be made somewhat more clear as we see it in

237

connection with Wordsworth. The philosopher himself connects it with the poet as we have observed. As applied to Wordsworth, the expression would suggest that the poet's presentation of nature (to which Whitehead referred in the earlier quotation we gave) includes something akin to Bradley's "subjective form" which contains "living emotion," or it *is* living emotion. It involves the "me" conception.

Wordsworth, that is, refers, at times, to an interacting *presence* that is virtually a *joy;* thus we can relate the presence to the problem of the individual which we mentioned at the beginning of this chapter, where we showed the poet attempting to find himself (after suffering distress) and we noted his inability to do so at the point in which he had strongly polarized reason and emotion. This was the stage that Wordsworth had reached in the previous book of *The Prelude* when, as he said, he gave up moral questions utterly. In his state of despair he turned to the contemplation of mathematics — *anything,* seemingly, for the sake of relief from the kind of concentration he had undergone.

How, perhaps, could mathematics help a person who had polarized reason and emotion? Is there any possibility of reconciling these two forces, for example, through geometry? Is this too fanciful? The point to be remembered is that Wordsworth did not at first reconcile them, but, rather, tried to proceed on the basis of reason or (somewhat later) on a foundation of emotion exclusively.

Mathematics, at least initially, might appear to be altogether a matter of reason. So, for Wordsworth it probably did at first appear to be. What geometrical or other exercises in this connection could he perform? This we asked near the midpoint of the last half of the preceding chapter, and we did not answer the question. We suggested only that an answer to it was not beyond the possibility of useful speculation. We shall refer to the possibility now. In doing so we shall speculate for a moment, considering certain aspects of a number which is simple enough to enable us to see clearly its multiples and certain of its other relations.

Contemplating number, as such, Wordsworth might, for example, have observed that the number ten raised to the second power (that is squared), and then raised to the next subsequent power, gives rise to a sense of rapid increase. Ten raised to the third power gives one thousand; proceeding progressively upward we are moving toward infinity as a limit. This the poet could have perceived. Reversing his movement he could have moved downward until he reached ten to the power of zero, and shortly thereafter to ten to the minus-one power, this latter being set to one-tenth. Thus he might have continued further downward, fractionally, now toward the infinitesimal as a limit.

We have presented these ideas largely in words rather than in figures — or in a tabulation — because a poet considering such matters might naturally think of them in a verbal manner. That is, a poet would tend to use the everyday means of communication with which he would be most familiar. Perhaps we should avoid concreteness and move with Whitehead in "complete abstraction from any particular instance,"[8] in the realm of mathematics. Such a view of mathematics is, however, not necessary. Such a view is far from being obvious, as Whitehead says. So far is it from being obvious that even today "it is habitually thought that the certainty of mathematics is a reason for the certainty of our knowledge of the physical universe." If people today still tend in general to think so tangibly of geometry and other forms of mathematics — as seems likely — Wordsworth, in his day, could be excused for seeing ideas at times rather physically.

Whitehead, in the page preceding that from which we have just quoted, speaks of "the pursuit of mathematics" as "a refuge from the goading urgency" of accidental pains we may suffer or, to use his more abstract expression, "of contingent happenings."[9] If the philosopher had been influenced by the thought of Wordsworth in this connection (and he may have been) he would have seen that this was exactly what the poet was doing. For Whitehead, however, the reputed "certainty" (and Wordsworth was seeking certainty) could arise or be generated by mathematics only from "its complete abstract generality."[10] But one can surely think concretely of multiples of ten and then, swiftly, see the general idea behind them. In the conception of such multiples as related to an approach to infinity Wordsworth might also have seen a kind of rhythm or curve ascending in its upward movement toward the zenith.

The imagination is awakened here and in many other matters which arise in mathematics broadly; for example, one could try to see spatially or geometrically the problems we have just referred to, and could try to relate them to the seeming infinity of the universe, or to eternity and immortality. Apart from writing passages in *The Prelude* which may be connected with such ideas, Wordsworth was working on his "Immortality Ode" in 1803, and after setting the partly-finished poem aside for a time, took up the problem again in 1804 and 1805. Questions relating to destiny, infinity, and immortality are difficult, but they are little more so than the subject of consciousness, thought of with reference to the "prehensive," or that of grasping emotionally the world that surrounds us in its relation to the subjective "me" which for the moment may seem lost in the ambient world or, a moment later, to contain it.

Perhaps Wordsworth began centering his thought on mathematics by thinking about thinking (which some people consider philosophy itself to be); this was a subject in regard to which, as we have said, he was interested. But it was natural, surely, to go beyond this, and also beyond any tendency toward mental gymnastics as a mere relief to disturbed feelings. We can see, through reflection, not only the great importance of mathematics to the developing thought of the nineteenth century and indeed to the culture of our world today, but also its basic possible relation to Wordsworth. We can see, in addition, its connection with the imagination or the extensive projections of the imagination.

We had said that we would take, one by one, three troublesome expressions in Whitehead and make certain observations upon them. We can connect them with the imagination. The first (which we have earlier commented upon to an extent) was the word "prehensive." The next potentially troublesome expression requiring a number of remarks is the word "modal," a term which Whitehead uses in application to the prehensive. In Whitehead's discussion of the prehensive (to which we have referred) in *Science and The Modern World,* he also speaks of the modal. The word "modal" has what Whitehead calls a "character" beyond the prehensive character which he had been discussing. It has a character concerning the apprehension of nature in both space and time.

The aspect of the modal can be brought out somewhat better through relating it to the work of Wordsworth. That the term has a character concerning the apprehension of nature in space and time may be seen in *The Prelude,* though an exemplification of it might have been given by Whitehead through "Tintern Abbey" or, again, through the "Ode on the Intimations of Immortality." "Everything which is in space," Whitehead says, "receives a definite limitation of some sort, so that in a sense it has just that shape which it does have and no other"; in addition "in some sense it is just in this place and no other. Analogously for time, a thing endures during a certain period, and through no other period."[11] Whitehead goes on to say, "I will call this the *modal* character . . ." That is, it is the modal character whereby a thing is *together* in space and in time. He would avoid an extreme absolute idealism or a reality above reality. What is important to him is an emergence into a finite-mode aspect of an entity.

The reader may naturally feel some uncertainty here, but this could perhaps be partially allayed by Whitehead's comment in which he refers to "change and *endurance*" as having a bearing upon time. In *Science and the Modern World* he quotes Wordsworth directly in making an application of his idea[12]; but, further on, in the page following, he refers to "aesthetic values" in our experience of perception, and he says that "these values arise from the culmination, in some sense, of the brooding presence of the whole onto its various parts."[13] Or, as the philosopher elsewhere still more emphatically says, referring to Wordsworth: "His theme is nature *in solido,* that is to say, he dwells on that mysterious presence of surrounding things"[14] which forever keeps us from living in a world of separate, isolated entities. This statement concerning "Nature *in solido*" would in other words involve space, as well as time.

For those who may find Whitehead's remarks about Wordsworth somewhat involved here, we may plead that the ideas he is dealing with are very important. They have a vital place in Whitehead's philosophy and, further, it is evident that he felt convinced that they were manifested prominently in the poet's work. Perhaps Whitehead was himself able to develop his point of view by reading the poet. Help may be given also to the reader in understanding these ideas by referring to parts of Bradley's volume *Appearance and Reality* and by re-examining T. S. Eliot's passages concerning time-present and time-past, as well as those on space, and the "rose garden" of life in childhood. Eliot's views related to time-perception and space, as we move into it through gates leading to expanding experience, were strongly influenced by those of Bradley. If the reader finds the terms on which we have just been commenting troublesome he will not be alone in feeling that this is so. Other words in Whitehead are likely to be more easily handled.

The third term on which we had planned to comment (after dealing with "prehensive" and "modal" in their relation to Wordsworth) was "evil," and here somewhat more familiar ideas may prove helpful. We had seen that in the *Prelude* passage last quoted, the word "evil" gives rise to a problem, and this is especially true in that "spirit" is mentioned. If "the spirit of evil" was animistically abroad, or "at its height," could Wordsworth have meant something akin to the sinister and hostile spirit of Ahriman, familiar in early Greek conceptions as well as in other primitive views, for example in Zoroastrianism? Or would it be better, in using an idea related to a religion of nature, to consider that we may escape evil, when it appears to be at its height around us, through the fact that we have in mind a purpose, and can conceive a purpose? That is, we can perhaps partly accomplish a personal intent or ideal which is related to the very idea of purpose and of something beyond us which perhaps is connected to something greater than ourselves.

The latter view could well grow out of a religion of nature in its realistic or naturalistic aspects, although there is present also an idealistic tone in the conception. Thus in this philosophy we may say that we are working, in whatever limited way we can, toward a larger harmony in the world. The total larger harmony is beyond humanity. The virtue of endurance here forms a part of the world toward which we are striving, as does the virtue of courage, which was dear to Wordsworth. The poet has referred to "the spirit of evil" which he felt was manifest in the world from 1793 to 1795 after his return to England. But at this point he was finding himself sanatively, a term the associations of which the poet himself finds useful. He was attempting to integrate himself throughout the two years after his return from France. But the actual time of the composition of the 1805 *Prelude* represented an additional period of renewal in his health. In writing *The Prelude* he was furthering or creating ideas which were bringing him to a new, a larger view of the world and its disasters. He was learning foresight by the aid of hindsight. The term *evil*, it seems, needs to be understood in relation to its counterpart, which involves working in the direction of a more beneficent harmony having a dynamic relation to life.

And it is through this dynamic or constructive relation of

evil to other things that a human being can live without loss of hope. For Whitehead the problem of hope is connected with a broad vision of life which has overtones related importantly to religion. "The fact of the religious vision, and its history of persistent expansion, is our one ground of optimism."[15] Here his approach is not a conventional matter. Very early in the chapter from which we have quoted he indicates that throughout its development he wishes to keep in abeyance any "particular creeds" of religion. He is thinking of breadth of vision such as one finds in a combination of Judaism and many other religions, in addition to Christianity. Except for a large religious vision "human life is a flash of occasional enjoyments, lighting up a mass of pain and misery, a bagatelle of transient experience." A few sentences later, on the next page, he adds, "Evil is the brute motive force of fragmentary purpose, disregarding the eternal vision."[16] This statement is characteristically Whiteheadian.

Notice the conception of *evil* here. The vision of a beneficent harmony over and above the brute problems requiring a high degree of constructive creativity has a philosophic suitableness to Wordsworth, and yet it really fits a down-to-earth quality in the poet. Here again Whitehead may be of further help, for in *Adventures of Ideas* he has a word to say on the finiteness of experience which has an important connection with Wordsworth's thought. "This finiteness is not the result of evil, or of imperfection. It results from the fact that there are possibilities of harmony which either produce evil in joint realization, or are incapable of such conjunction."[17] For Whitehead the arts help to illustrate the point. In the arts, he tells us, evil appears variously. Evil is there, as well as finiteness. But the finiteness is not the *result* of evil; evil does not bring it about.

The point, however, can be better stated for Whitehead's purpose, and for ours, by relating it to history. With reference to political philosophy, Whitehead declares: "History can only

244

be understood by seeing it as the theatre of diverse groups of idealists respectively urging ideals incompatible for conjoint realization."[18] And he adds, "You cannot form any historical judgment of right and wrong by considering each group separately. The evil lies in the attempted conjunction."

Wordsworth, we see, speaks of the "spirit of evil" which was "at its height," but adds that he was not being overwhelmed. There was a source of comfort to him beyond this evil. So also in Whitehead: evil is not something which we are to be overcome by — it is a part of life which may be fruitfully met (if it is met) by creative thinking. And in *Process and Reality* Whitehead makes clear that creativity may be thought of as "divested of the notion of passive receptivity, either of 'form' or of external relations"; as "the pure notion" of an "activity" which occurs in "the actual world — a world which is never the same twice,"[19] it is connected for Whitehead with the *substance* in Aristotle which cannot be characterized. Creativity "cannot be characterized, because all characters are more special than itself. But Creativity is always found under conditions, and described as conditioned." These lines from the philosopher are very pertinent to the point of view of Wordsworth; original sin (or perhaps "sin" in any sense) is not a theme that either Wordsworth or Whitehead often takes recourse to. Neither is reduced to such a desperation. It is no more appropriate to them than the concept of the hostile spirit, Ahriman, which people have used in many forms to escape their own requirements of responsibility. Hope lies for the human being in creativity: individual creativity and the world's.

Lest the Whitehead passage be misunderstood we might note that for him creativity is "a factor of activity"[20] or an "origin" which gives rise to a situation. It is also called "a 'real potentiality.'" It is connected with the theory of Plato, about which more will be given later. Creativity is opposite to evil. For, with Whitehead, we may say fundamentally "that 'de-

245

struction as a dominant fact in the experience' is the correct definition of evil."[21] Constructiveness is its opposite. Wordsworth had known destructive forces (or "destruction") which he encountered in the French Revolution, but he did not yield to these forces as far as his spirit was concerned. Life for him continually involves "loss or gain"; the one or the other is from moment to moment inevitable, a "sure alternative." Or to put it as he does a few lines later in *The Prelude*, his work, his "business was upon the barren seas" — or, again, his errand was "to sail to other coasts."

What has all this to do with the poet's title in Book Eleven, "Imagination, How Impaired and Restored"; how does the material from Whitehead have a bearing on our theme? We shall see. The poet had turned, in a certain measure, from things connected with a nature which in his earlier life he had valued most. This was nature as separated from humanity, but he had to learn how to come to terms with the actions of persons. He had to expose himself again periodically to his earlier concept of nature at the same time that he had to go on along the way which involved the problems of human beings, a way, whether stony or rough — whatever it might be. This was the dynamic process of life amid its pathways of change. The poet is looking back upon himself as he was some nine years earlier. The vantage point of 1804 enables him to see with increasing clarity the problems he had faced and had gradually overcome. His theme, as it was proposed in the title of Book Eleven, is imagination impaired, which concerns the state he was in during his depression of spirits, with loss of poetical insight; but this theme, as he hopes to make clear, will tell also how his poetic faculty gradually returned to him, came back in its fullness.

In his period of despondency, he tells us, ideas concerning "Sage, Patriot, Lover, Hero" seemed to him more and more open to cynical reflection; "virtues" of such men, the qualities which had formerly seemed to him inspiring, now, in his moments of depression, seemed sullied, or of dubious actual value. The ideal characters (so he had viewed them in the past) now contained "something false and weak": what he was for the present seeking, apparently, was hardness or strength.

Wordsworth found unendurable the thought of being a person unable to face open-eyed "Reason." And it seemed "the poets" portrayed characters having a weak blindness. Such characters could not sensibly be thought of as "purer creatures," since true "nobility" should certainly be characteristically marked by reason. It will be noticed here that Wordsworth, at this in-between stage, was accepting a hasty generalization: "the poets" portray characters who are not markedly endowed with reason; hence, the admonition "Go to the poets" is futile — that is, if one is seeking true wisdom. Where could one go? To the philosophers perhaps. Wordsworth, it is evident, was thinking syllogistically not only in the example given, but in various ways. His summary concerning himself at this stage is

> Thus strangely did I war against myself;
> A bigot to a new Idolatry
> Did like a Monk who hath forsworn the world
> Zealously labour to cut off my heart
> From all the sources of her former strength . . . (74 —)

The poet's conception is that he had unsouled himself, and he goes on to refer specifically to the "syllogistic words" and "the charm of Logic" which, for all men, and especially for him at this stage, was "ever within reach" — easily accessible. He also speaks, in contrast to this, of the "mysteries of passion" which have produced fellow-feeling among human beings. But for the present we will direct our attention to whether reason has the defect that the poet mentioned. Is Wordsworth overstating the case against logic? How would a philosopher such as Whitehead view this? The evidence shows that he is very close to Wordsworth in this respect. And as to the poet's

247

being guilty of overstressing the matter of the criticism of reason, there is an emphatic appreciation of this faculty in the *Prelude* context which we have been considering. The lines on this which Wordsworth has written concern the place of reason in human history, in the past and the present, and he gives full credit to

all that Reason hath perform'd
And shall perform to exalt and to refine . . . (86 —)

Though Wordsworth's theme in Book Eleven concerns the imagination, he makes very clear that in his view reason, even in a narrow sense, has had an exalting, even a refining influence upon humanity. Whitehead, too, speaks of "this great art" (deductive reasoning) but adds in an immediately following sentence that "it has been often disastrously misused."[22] A further citation from the philosopher — this time from his most penetrating work — indicates that "interest in logic, dominating overintellectualized philosophers, has obscured the main function of propositions in the nature of things."[23] Propositions he says on the next page are of importance, chiefly, "for feeling at the physical level of unconsciousness." They are important for action, for the dynamic. Logic, restrictedly viewed, focuses attention on the static material entities.

This defect, which Whitehead sees as its great danger, is also the main point of Wordsworth's concern in the context we have been considering. The special danger of Wordsworth's hasty generalization concerning "the poets" (and their portrayal of presumably "purer creatures") was a matter of logic, and the use of faulty premises. He points out the weakness in this, his period of confusion, the weakness of his thinking in regard to "the poets"; similarly in Whitehead the matter of faulty premises is a major point he makes as to the defects of the Scholastics. The philosopher explains that the Scholastics did deserve high esteem, but only within narrow limits; they deserved esteem because they were "supremely critical."[24] In addition, as he points out on the next page, they were able to recognize the importance of Aristotle's coherency, the tightness of his "system of thought." But shortly after making this point, Whitehead adds that they failed to perceive the value of the empirical side of Aristotle's philosophy. As Whitehead puts it, "Unfortunately they did not reflect that some of his main ideas depended upon his direct acquaintance with experienced fact."[25]

The point for us here concerns unthinking generalization. We see the point also in Wordsworth's statement about the poets and their weakness in human portrayal as he had viewed their work. He was generalizing in his criticism of them. In contrast to the weakness of generalizing which is present in the practices of the Scholastics, as referred to in Wordsworth's comment and as seen in Whitehead, there is the strength of action in another power of the mind. The poet and the philosopher both emphasize this other power. It is a kind of light. Turning now to "reason" in this other sense, in *The Prelude* there is reference to "light" which might guide one better to "power" and life. In this guidance of the "light," Wordsworth is thinking of the importance of being led to the conception of a "God of Love" — and is making allusion to shadowy or vague "recollections" which may recall the "Ode on the Intimations of Immortality" upon which he worked, as we have said, while writing the latter part of the 1805 *Prelude*. These things he connects with "feeling," and they were not utterly lost to him even in his state of deepest depression. Still, there had been temporary interference with the "more noble influence" (the imagination or higher reason) and this had brought about a loss in the "animation" of the self "and its deeper sway." Here the special activity of the self which is referred to is the imagination.

Can anything in all this be related to Whitehead? We shall see. The "animation and the deeper sway" of the more "noble influence" is connected with the "mysteries of passion" which

Wordsworth referred to some forty-five lines earlier when he was considering passion in the sense of emotion to be endured or felt by all men collectively; here we must include, also, the compassion leading to a common brotherhood of man. Wordsworth's theme of the imagination, and the aesthetic, is evident here. This compassion stretches, as an earlier passage makes clear, from all of the years of the past into the complexity of the years that lie ahead. There is an analogy in this to the extensive conception of the past and the future as treated by Whitehead.

It may be helpful, as we consider the word "passion," to recall also that which was endured by Oedipus as the evidence of his crime unfolds or that portrayed with reference to Moses, or indeed with reference to religious sorrow, or even to religious ecstasy. The word "passion" has broad aspects. The important point now, however, is that such passion (seen also in the case of the character Hamlet) is experienced — that is, it is endured. This factor of the *enduring* passion — that is, the passion which is endured — applies equally to Dante in the *Inferno* or to Macbeth after the crime against Duncan — that is, in the overwhelming feeling that encompassed him in the sequel after his first crime.

But our present theme is "reason" with its ambiguity or complexity. Again in *The Prelude* we find the poet circling back to a consideration of the point of his troubled state after his experience during the French Revolution, a period in which he was from time to time dominated by reason. He takes pains deliberately to explain that this dangerous reason to which he had referred is not the "grand" faculty, or that "simple Reason" which is to be identified with the higher power and the immense creativity of the greatest poets. His use of the word "simple" here presents a difficulty, but before speaking further in regard to this factor of real perplexity we shall comment again on the subject of Scholastic approaches to knowledge which seem to have been much on his mind. He had further praise, in effect, for the method of the Scholastics, but he himself was misled by it because of his youthful disproportionate admiration for them.

The poet refers in fact to that "logic and minute analysis" which "of all Idols" is the most attractive to the young and expanding mind. Youth, he believes, tends naturally to play with logic in the process of growing. On the other hand the poet speaks again of the value of such logic. But he feels that he would be naive (merely "a Trifler") if he were to belabor the point. He would then be dwelling upon its "obvious benefits"; these benefits, as he knows, have provided an important contribution to the history of the human mind. Again one could ask: Can the general tenor of our discussion be related directly to Whitehead? This question we can answer.

One could write of the limiting influence of this lower reason, or of what Wordsworth calls "its narrow estimates of things," and in doing so, the poet believes, one would be dealing with a worthy theme. Such criticism is necessary. Indeed, the subject could be presented worthily in "philosophic Verse," he declares, provided it would be treated with sufficient scope. Is he to be taken seriously here? Could such a subject as reason be a "worthy" one for a poet? Perhaps it would be so, we may imagine, if treated with the full scope of Whitehead's entire philosophy, but this would present a difficulty staggering to the imagination.

Reverting again, however, to the "danger" of syllogistic reasoning, Wordsworth mentions the negative side of its approach and its failure in the area of feeling, or what we might call the area of the prehensive, or that of the "event" in Whitehead's deeper sense. This danger in the area of feeling would need to be emphasized in the grand subject for "philosophic verse" which logic offers; it is indeed a detraction that

> cannot but attend
> Upon a Function rather proud to be

251

The enemy of falsehood, than the friend
Of truth, to sit in judgment than to feel. (134—)

There is in actuality a work on reason somewhat like that
which the poet envisages, though not written in the form of the
"philosophic verse" which he would prescribe. It is Whitehead's volume *The Function of Reason.* A part of the title of
this book echoes a capitalized term that Wordsworth uses (the
word "Function") that appears in the passage which we have
just quoted. The basic material which Wordsworth perhaps
had in mind is analyzed and exemplified for us in Whitehead's
careful treatment of the subject of reason. This we shall try to
amplify.

Turning now to what Wordsworth calls the *higher* faculty,
could we say that he blunders in that he uses the word
"Reason" in an exceedingly lofty or intuitive sense, and yet also
uses the term "Reason" (he capitalizes the word in either case)
for a kind of faculty that seems to have no connection with the
creative? Should he have chosen a different word for what he
feels is the glorious, the higher human power? In attempting to
deal with this question it is helpful to examine parallels to the
poet's statement in the expression by Whitehead when he deals
with the same subject. These parallels are notable in the
volume *The Function of Reason.*

Can it be, one might ask, that a book with such a title as this
— emphasizing reason as it does — would contain material
having an imaginative stress? Judging from its title the book
might seem like the last source to which one would go for
analogies to the part of Wordsworth's theme in *The Prelude*
which concerns reason as imaginative creative power. For
Whitehead, however, there are, as in the poet, two sides to the
concept of reason. Reason is involved in an attack which
should be directed by the person upon both the environment
and upon himself.

There is need for the use of the imagination also in directing such an attack. Whitehead makes plain that "Reason" is a two-fold force in the process of living, and his conclusion "amounts to the thesis that Reason is a factor in experience which directs and criticizes the urge towards the attainment of an end realized in imagination but not in fact."[26] This thesis of *imagination*, he submits, needs to be explored, and he makes an exploration of it involving "two contrasted ways of considering Reason." One of these ways he connects with Homer's character who "shares" the thought process of the lower reason "with the foxes."[27]

The other approach is that of Plato. In the higher reason of Plato (as in that of Wordsworth) we have a strong emphasis upon the speculative and the intuitive. For Whitehead the higher reason involves the production of the great religions of the world. This development has occurred through a long historical process and includes the complete transformation of humanity and its conscious life. The practical, the earthly reason, on the other hand has only begun, in very recent years, to make effective contact with the truly theoretic or speculative factor. Great intellectual power was in action during the period of the sway of the lower reason, for example during the thirteenth century. But despite this, what Whitehead calls an "asymptotic" approach was needed. The asymptotic factor would involve a tangential direction of one's thought, steadily and daringly approaching a goal. This is the *process* needed even though the goal is never completely reached.

Whitehead devotes a separate chapter to the development of the concept of the higher or speculative Reason, and he indicates that where it is at work there is an underlying orderliness in which the "mutual relatedness"[28] of its parts gradually provides self-correction. In this action "thought precedes observation."[29] In the next page after this quotation Whitehead further speaks of the Speculative Reason involving "imagination far outrunning the direct observations." As the philosopher conceives the problem "no one had a keener appreciation than Plato of the divergence between the exactness of abstract thought and the vague margin of ambiguity which haunts all observation."[30] This is not to say that all abstract thought in Plato is always excellent. But higher and higher generality can proceed in the hands of Plato largely to cure itself. Whitehead could have cited the history of the intuitive side of mathematics, in which he was greatly interested, as illustrative of this. The intuitive aspect of it was of great importance to him.

We have said earlier in the chapter that Wordsworth, in his time of greatest depression of spirits, turned to mathematics for a kind of relief, and we have explained that what he contemplated at that time was by no means beyond the possibility of speculation. We cited as a conceivable example a problem the poet could have reflected upon, concerning multiples of ten, and the fact that he could have continued in a backward movement. He could have set ten at the power of minus-two (equal to the fraction one-hundredth) and ten at the power of minus-three (equal to one-thousandth), and so further downward to the point approaching a limit looking toward the infinitesimal. Had Wordsworth done so, he would have been making two approaches — one forward and the other backward to the complex of ideas concerning the very large and the exceedingly small. In a way he would have been reading history concerning numerical matters at times forward and at times backward.

The two approaches in regard to mathematics involving reversals are very natural to make. And he might have contemplated more difficult arithmetical concepts of number. Those we have dealt with, and certain others that are more complex, could have been conceived — as we have suggested — geometrically. But it is unnecessary to our point that such a spatial exemplification be described. All this, had Wordsworth's mind moved in such a direction, could have been well within his reach. In fact, even putting the matter in the way we have presented it may seem to some readers almost patronizing in our attitude toward the poet.

But we will nevertheless mention a third approach to the very large and the very small to illustrate further how Wordsworth's thought could have probed with reference to certain possible ideas which might have proved valuable to him. For in moving forward or backward — there are possibilities of intermediate *fractional* powers. We could, for example, have the power of one and a half (with ten as a base) which would equal forty-five, the power of two and a half, as applied to ten, equalling 450, and the power of three and a half (similarly applied to ten) equaling 4500, and so further, indefinitely. As the figures suggest, we have been presenting a kind of curve, or rhythm. Here, in the many fractional possibilities between any two whole numbers, something approaching infinity as a limit would again have been suggested. Such contemplation of the multiples of ten (or some other problem of the sort) would by no means have represented to him a mere idle amusement.

Mathematics could have had an appeal to him as a kind of monism — as a movement toward a quickly *unified* result of audacious width of view. What we have said concerning powers of ten might have been represented far more briefly, in order to emphasize the point of the economy which is fundamentally characteristic of mathematical statement. Thus instead of using ten as a base we could have used a symbol such as the letter alpha (covering all conceivable bases, including quadrillions and more), and the letter beta to represent all conceivable results which could be imagined arising from *raising* any of the bases to any generalized power representable by the Greek letter nu, or, since the choice of letters is entirely arbitrary, the letter N. The whole concept with regard to ten could have been included, thus, in a short formula taking less than a single line. This last approach may seem troublesomely abstract, but it has its place here.

We have mentioned this more extreme (or more concentrated) type of expression because it is an instance of a somewhat higher level of abstraction and because the tendency toward an extreme in reflection characterized Wordsworth at times. It is indeed referred to by him as we shall see. The extreme had its attraction for him and for Whitehead. But the formula to which we have made allusion, though it would have suggested the imaginative capacity for extension of thought which lies in mathematics, would not, because of its concentrated abstraction, have been appealing to the average reader, and it would not have been the way most characteristic of a poet. As to this kind of width of view which we have just mentioned, the answers given to problems may appear to have a kind of precision or certainty in their coverage.

So far as mathematics seems to go, it covers perhaps all cases, and if one continues far enough with the subject it seems, to the enthusiast for it, to include all that could be. And thus in a way it seems to be the reality of realities. Whitehead elsewhere gives expression to the danger of this overenthusiasm in regard to mathematics. It is, in a fashion, the attempt to reach the increasingly simple, the parsimonious expression. We should strive for this, the philosopher believes, but we should also beware of its dangers. The hazard of mathematics for Wordsworth, as he tells us, lay in its tendency to move from the concrete world of experience which meant so much to him.

To return now to the subject which Whitehead treats in *The Function of Reason*, it has been evident that for Wordsworth — as for the philosopher — there were two ways of viewing reason, the first of which, the more narrow Scholastic approach, we have sufficiently dealt with. The second way, which Wordsworth thinks of as the "grand" way, was related as we have seen (in both the poet and Whitehead) to Plato. And mathematics in reference to an approach to infinity has been considered in relation to reason in its "higher" aspects; the conception "higher" is used by both Wordsworth and Whitehead with reference to reason as viewed in this grand way bearing on problems of approaches to infinity. Mathematics is a factor in connection with this in Plato, whose speculativeness has been central for Whitehead in the interweavings of the higher function of reason. We may add further that in Whitehead's view, Plato's idea "of the interweaving of Harmony with mathematical relation has been triumphantly vindicated."[31]

So Whitehead views the story of history, not in one of his volumes only but in various works, and thus in *The Function of Reason* he regards it steadily as a continuing thread. The reign of reason, in both of its senses, he would hope mankind will see increasingly manifested in the future. As he says, we do, fortunately, find evidence of the fruitfulness that it had brought, however hampered it may appear to be in the human condition of our world today. Wordsworth speaks of the higher reason as being "grand," but he also refers to it, we have seen, as being "simple" in a certain sense. Using this latter word he may be contrasting the higher reason with the logic-chopping of the more narrow reason, which may often have many intricacies such as would be suggested by our remembrance of certain matters concerning philosophers of the Middle Ages.

Whitehead, we may say again, relates our experience with the higher "Reason" specifically to the "speculative imagination."[32] In its own swift, at times seemingly intuitive fashion there is something simple about the directness with which the higher imagination, or reason, acts. We have seen this, for example, in striking moments, such as that recorded in the *Prelude* passage when Wordworth was suddenly told (and he italicizes the words), "*Robespierre was dead.*"[33] A great web of life surrounds the moment, along with the fact that the report of a death has come to him in a sudden instant.

It is the higher, the grand reason, united with the imagination, that is performing, we will suggest, in a *Prelude* passage concerning nature, with its reference to "powerful waters" and the changing landscape with its "lights and shades"; this is the sort of scene that Wordsworth had responded to in youth, "all eye" in one instance and "all ear" in another case — but now, at the present writing, Wordsworth realizes the importance of the response of the whole person in which eye and ear are one — always with "the majestic intellect" — creativity — operative, and with it something coming from the outside world to perform an act of correlation with that which is within the total person. The "passion" and the "life" in nature receive mention in *The Prelude* at this point, and he finds himself brought back, in reflection upon his period of depressed spirits, to a tendency he has had toward "presumption."

What is involved in this human frailty? In Wordsworth's case presumption appeared in the form of an overweening preoccupation with the aesthetic (or with art, perhaps, for the sole sake of art) which may cause one to forget to give attention, proportionately, to one's fellow man. Art then becomes virtually identified with undifferentiated pleasure, and no more. One is at such a time "in pleasure pleas'd" Wordsworth says, and he had a tendency to become more and more prone to consider, most negatively, his own very private artistic dislikings. This was a negative tendency that he had developed. A person who so reacts has reached a condition of character which usually includes an emphasis upon what he regards as complicated artistic effects, along with a self-conscious emphasis upon both likings and dislikings. Pride is a factor here.

For Wordsworth, at the stage he had reached sometime in 1795 or 1796, this involved an artistic theory stressing simple mimesis. That is, if one stresses mimesis greatly, one thinks of art as a copy-process. For example, one may copy a scene without, in the action, putting very much of one's inner personal contribution to work. One is then concerned with pseudo-art rather than with art in a deeper respect. In a way, on the other hand, there is always the possibility, as Wordsworth feels of producing work that is "above all art" — that is above artifice. The problem also involves the active perceiving, the prehensive perceiving we may say, in that one can perceive a person (say one's mother or brother) in a way that is far above all copy-art.

Again there is danger, in the problem, of yielding to formal rules. Wordsworth calls them mere "rules of mimic art" which are in one's head. There is the danger of operating upon the basis of them mechanically. One can conceive how this might be done in writing a commercial story in our own day, or a motion picture created on demand for Hollywood. But the poet is mainly interested in explaining what such an attitude does to one's perceptions, and in the case about which he is reporting it *had* begun to affect him so restrictedly, so limitatingly, that the eye, above all other senses, was constantly functioning in a way which might almost be described as a disease.

We can imagine an artist who, with greatly activated eyes, might dart a thousand glances in many different directions, seeing a variety of things in unique ways, whereas in the same space of time his companion, if he had one, might see only six or seven things, and those very simply. With Wordsworth an "infection of the eye" (as he calls it) began to focus, also, on "superficial things" or "meagre novelties," although he says this tendency had never been natural to him in his previous stages of development. To both "colour and proportion" and to states of mind, and to "moods" which might accompany his responses, he paid most studied attention, but to "the moral power," as related to the world under his observation, he gave small heed. Not only this high moral power was lacking, in the person that he had become eight years previously, but also the affective side of life. He puts it in essence thus: he had in viewing a scene become to

> the spirit of the place,
> Less sensible. (163 —)

What does Wordsworth mean by such things as "moral power," "the affections," and "the spirit of the place" in this part of *The Prelude?* The expression "moral power," it is to be noted, does not have reference to a moral-sense psychology having a cut-and-dried character. He is speaking of power, and this implies process. The term "Affections," similarly, is not restrictive or simplistic, and the same may be said of the expression "the spirit of the place"; each place, in the context, refers to the response a person could have to it. This would occur even in the instance of a small scene which he might glance at. Having mentioned "moral power" (along with "affections" and the spirit of the "place") and having criticized the lack of such qualities in himself in the period he is discussing, he adds that his response to scenes involved an unfortunate tendency of constantly wanting to evaluate or to put his private stamp of approval upon them. This habit may in certain instances be an outgrowth of pride or presumption. So it had been with Wordsworth.

Beyond the fault of "sitting thus in judgment," his attention is further directed toward a dichotomy, or what he calls the "two-fold Frame of body and of mind"; this is the morass into which many have fallen, particularly from the seventeenth century on. The morass presents a problem even to our own time. The fault, we could say with Whitehead, was importantly stimulated in men by Descartes. It represents a divisiveness which comes under criticism here in Wordsworth and it receives criticism in Whitehead in various works. We find the philosopher remarking, "In truth, this formulation of the problem in terms of minds and matter is unfortunate."[34] And a moment later he begins a new exceedingly emphatic paragraph with the words: "The effect of this sharp division between nature and life has poisoned all subsequent philosophy." Often it is the stress upon body (in contrast to mind) that he deplores, but we find him also criticizing the neglect of the physical that can occur through an exaggerated stress upon

"Platonic culture" in which, for example, there is a "neglect of technical education as an ingredient in the complete development of ideal human beings."[35] It occurs through "two disastrous antitheses, namely, that between mind and body, and that between thought and action."[36]

Such a statement in its down-to-earth quality parallels a similar side in Wordsworth's thought. Many other supporting passages from Whitehead could be given. But in The Prelude all along Wordsworth is talking mainly of the dangers involved in the limitation of an exclusively sense-oriented approach to life. He emphasizes this by showing how one can be dominated (in such an area) by one of the senses acting virtually alone. Here he begins his presentation of one of the two most widely-famed features of Book Eleven in The Prelude: that which concerns the eye. The second feature — to be discussed later — is in regard to his theory about what he calls spots of time.

With reference to the eye (for example the eye of the painter) the question of the imagination or of the aesthetic arises. In making his point concerning the problem of the eye the poet refers to the visual as a "most despotic" sense — one which exercises virtually "absolute dominion." He would like to discuss this, using a somewhat complicated analysis or employing "abstruser argument," but he contents himself by focussing his attention narrowly on the "tyranny" of the eye. Man he feels was made for liberty, not for any subservience — least of all in respect to the eye.

A general resemblance between Wordsworth and White-head here may again be seen in the philosopher's observation, rather formally put, that so far as perception is concerned (and this had been Wordsworth's subject of comment) a "first error is the assumption of a few definite avenues of communication with the external world, the five sense-organs."[37] Whitehead deplores such an approach because it "leads to the pre- sup-position that the search for the data is to be narrowed to the question, what data are directly provided by the activity of the sense-organs — preferably the eyes." He grants, however, that this approach "has a vague general truth, very important for practical affairs." We should note, as parallel to Wordsworth's comment on the danger of a stress upon the visual, Whitehead's emphasis upon the "eyes." The poet would certainly agree with this point: the evidence is clear. At times he would go even further.

But there is something more than the senses to be considered. This something more needs to be borne steadily in mind, as an example from Whitehead also will make especially evident: "The scientific categories of thought are obtained elsewhere." Such categories are not obtainable from the senses. And there are other categories — in the area of aesthetics, for example — that need to be remembered, according to the stress given by Wordsworth and Whitehead. For the philosopher "the living organ of experience is the living body as a whole." And in the next page he says so far as our relation with the totality of experience is concerned "the body is continuous with the rest of the natural world."[38]

The main problem that we have just been treating is, of course, related to that which was involved when, using Whitehead's phrase, we referred to Wordsworth's theme, in various passages of The Prelude, as being "nature in solido," and here we would give an example. The example may be found in the poet's portrayal of a girl who, being one with her background, is yet a living soul. This portrayal appears in the passage "and yet I knew a Maid," one of the memorable parts of the poem. What do we mean by saying that she was one with the landscape? She was part and parcel of it. She is to be regarded as a portion of nature. The portrayal of this girl (most critics feel she is representative of the poet's sister at an early age) is that of one who had been growing up under "genial circumstance"; the circumstances have been genial in that they have been importantly generative of her. She has been under fruitfully developmental or generational condi-

262

tions in her environment. Speaking of her, he says, to each
scene she responded equally — each new experience stood out
pre-eminently and

> to that she was attuned
> Through her humility and lowliness,
> And through a perfect happiness of soul
> Whose variegated feelings were in this
> Sisters, that they were each some new delight . . . (209 —)

Here the problem of the imagination, in its relation to the
aesthetic, receives continued treatment. The portrayal of the
maid, a brief excerpt of which we have given, is from one of
the especially memorable passages in *The Prelude*. It acts as a
counterpoise to the material concerning the danger of the
more or less exclusively dominating eye, in that we see, exemplified in the character of the girl, a multifaceted sense of
the world. But this multifaceted view is also in a way simple.
Its simplicity appears in its directness. On the other hand, the
wideness of sympathetic understanding includes a balanced
sense of the self — the self of the girl in relation not only to all
humanity but to all nature.

Humanity at all levels and in its many varieties finds place in
this total perception. Wordsworth himself through his power
of vision — we might call it his visionary power — sees beyond
the sex of the individual, blends himself equally with woman
or man. So it is in his portrayal of the girl. In effect he becomes
the girl, whose every thought is piety — a kind of natural piety
such as we may associate with the pietists of the seventeenth
century. It is in this respect an honorific word. And here
something may be said concerning Whitehead's view of
religion which "is wholly wrapped up in the contemplation of
moral and aesthetic values."[39] It is concerned with "the contemplation of the beauty of holiness."

But we must turn to a later passage in Whitehead in which
he emphasizes his view that religion deals with something

beyond mere "pleasing social relations."[40] It is a vision, as he says one page later, a "vision of something which stands beyond, behind, and within the passing flux of immediate things; something which is real, and yet waiting," and which needs to be brought to fulfillment: "the greatest of present facts," and yet "something whose possession is the final good . . . something which is the ultimate ideal, and the hopeless quest."[41] What Whitehead emphasizes here is the aspect of *discovery:* the human being's discovery in life manifested in religion. His is a noncredal religion that may be associated with the natural piety of the maid.

The maid, we are told by Wordsworth, is one whose very "life is blessedness." So, too, the poet, when he was a child, and later also in his young adolescence, loved whatever he saw, nor did he "dream of aught" that might be conceived as superior or "more exquisitely fram'd"; his own neighborhood, however humble it might seem, was magical in its potentialities for perception. He "did not judge" — indeed, he "never thought of judging" but found himself with all that he was experiencing completely filled, and satisfied. In his many wanderings, almost like a vagrant, his experience came to be very much a thing of fulfillment. This perception, or the remembrance of it, helped to save him during his time of profound depression. In *The Prelude* he is relating this perception to the activity of the higher imagination. The habit of viewing nature under the tyranny of the eye, then, no longer held compulsion over him; as he says of himself,

> I shook the habit off
> Entirely for ever, and again
> In Nature's presence stood, as I stand now,
> A sensitive, and a creative soul. (254—)

Thus Wordsworth's imagination which had been impaired finally reached a stage of restoration. Aside from the portrayal of the "maid" there are two justly famed features of the closing portion of *The Prelude* in Book Eleven, each of which illustrates Wordsworth's doctrine concerning what he refers to as "spots of time" possessing "distinct pre-eminence"; coupled also with this is what we might call a kind of psychological energy, in Wordsworth's terms, a "vivifying Virtue," for the individual who experiences these spots of time. This "Virtue" is an energy which can come to us unexpectedly, and it "lifts us up when fallen."

Such spots of time are somewhat analogous to Whitehead's moments in which, as he says, "all men enjoy flashes of insight beyond meanings already stabilized in etymology and grammar."[42] As in the case of Wordsworth, the imaginative or the aesthetic is involved here. The "line and a half of poetry," Whitehead says, or the moment "in which Euripides compresses the main philosophical problems which have tortured European thought from his day to the present"[43] may serve as an example. In Wordsworth's theory there is an emphasis upon the lifting power exerted by the spots of time when we have "fallen." He may have learned of this through his experience of depression. Apart from his state of depression, it is reasonable to suppose that he felt strongly his own various shortcomings, and it was in some degree for this reason that he wished to write *The Prelude* as a poem on the growth of a soul.

We have spoken earlier of the mind-and-body dichotomy which appeared in Descartes and subsequently gave rise to a theory of mind with strong emphasis on sensory experience. Definitely in contrast to such a theory, Wordsworth's view about spots of time would stress the miracle of mind and one can, without undue exaggeration, relate his conception about this to what in our time Maslow has referred to as peak-experiences.[44] For Wordsworth the "moments worthy of all gratitude" are very likely to appear to one in childhood, although they may occur at any time. In Maslow the peak experience represents an internal "*creative moment*." It constitutes itself in such a way that it affords us one of "the highest

265

reaches of human nature,"[45] and yet it comes without effort. It is referred to as "beyond striving" and it appears, thus, to be almost like a miracle. So, also, in Wordsworth the "moments" impress one. It would seem further that, for the poet, as for Maslow, the special moment was regarded as a form of being which is related to love.

This emphasis on love is clearly present in the work of the psychologist Maslow, and we shall see whether a case may be made for its presence in Wordsworth. Wordsworth's memory, he says, is full of the moments of special "Virtue" (or strength), but he chooses for the present purpose in *The Prelude* two examples. The first traces back to a time when he was very young — scarcely old enough to be placed on a horse by a family helper, James. Somehow the child became separated from his companion by a "mischance," so that in fear he dismounted and led his animal until he came down to a spot where a criminal had been hanged "in iron chains."

The man had committed murder, but all that remained of the act, the poet says, was some embossed or "monumental writing": his name, which was placed perhaps on a stone at a spot where the grass "from year to year" was "clear'd away"; what the boy fixed his attention upon now, however, was the letters standing out from the "green sod." After seeing them he turned away, perhaps in horror. He had come down a path to this place, but thereafter, continuing his experience in this spot of time, he rose again to a higher level and came upon a sight that was forever engraved upon his memory. This was a view consisting of "a naked pool that lay beneath the hills," along with a "Beacon" on a summit. Before him was

A Girl who bore a Pitcher on her head
And seem'd with difficult steps to force her way
Against the blowing wind. (306 —)

In a sense it was a very "ordinary sight," but the scene contained "a visionary dreariness" which somehow came to him

266

from within the surroundings, including the "naked pool" (this is doubly emphasized), as well as the "Beacon on the lonely Eminence," the girl with "her garments vex'd and toss'd," and "the strong wind." The girl becomes for him a symbol of mankind, as we may say, struggling forward in the midst of the cosmos, and the child Wordsworth shares with her the struggle. Is it a transient experience of "absolute Being" (Maslow's word) that the poet has imaginatively re-created here? The picture remained with Wordsworth, and even in his days of young love it brought to him surprisingly a "spirit of pleasure," including "youth's golden gleam," along with whatever may be associatively added through the "power" and magical influence of memory.

The point is that the affective aspect of the experience is complex in that one feeling comes and assists another. Feeling, that is, "comes in aid," and psychological strength is involved in this. Life is not a thing of the misplaced location of Whitehead's phrase, or a tendency to locate substances in an ultimate sense as isolated entities. Such a position receives Whitehead's repeated criticism, and it is rejected by implication again and again also by Wordsworth.

The present chapter had dealt in a number of ways with the complex relations of the imagination, or the aesthetic, to other things. We have been thinking about the aesthetic as related to a variety of aspects of life. The process of imagination evidently involves not merely mechanics but an imposing by the human person of something which is inward upon pure contingency (or upon accident) in a world which unifies the seemingly physical with the mental. Yet its humanistic elements may be stressed also, as, for example, in Maslow's being-love which is directed toward the inner reality, or *being*, of a person, rather than toward externals such as blondness or a special sort of brown eyes.

The process of imagination, we have said, involves an imposing of something by man upon pure contingency, or accident. The view of the importance to aesthetics of that which is inward — which we find in Wordsworth — is paralleled in the aesthetics of Kant and Coleridge, and finds its reflection in complex ways in Whitehead. The human individual is not passive. There is something important in the self that had an internal dynamism, for, as Wordsworth says,

> from thyself it is that thou must give,
> Else never can receive. (333 —)

Wordsworth's remembrance of the first of the spots of time — that concerning the criminal and the girl who is straining to make her way against what we have called opposing cosmic elements — unites two forces: moral wrong, in the case of the man, and human effort in the struggle of the girl. The two coalesce for the child Wordsworth, young as he is, and they provide an aesthetic experience involving tragedy. The effect is dramatic. And this experience is of value to him on future occasions. It brings to the boy, even in the time of young love, a "spirit of pleasure," as we have said. This "pleasure," of cosmic character, which Wordsworth has may seem somewhat hard to account for, but it is part of the almost magical process, as we may conclude, by which the imagination performs its task. A word from Whitehead may prove helpful in that he makes clear that "the essence of dramatic tragedy is not unhappiness. It resides in the solemnity of the remorseless working of things."[46] Our enhanced awareness of the nature of tragedy and of the aesthetic may even bring pleasure with it. For understanding — even partial understanding — is one of the great sources of comfort in life. It involves and clears the ground for a sense of moral action, as Wordsworth and Whitehead well realize.

We turn to an additional example of what Wordsworth means by the "spots of time" which we have connected with peak experiences. It appears at the close of Book Eleven and it has reference to a happening in his boyhood, as he tells us, near "Christmas-time," when he had waited alone for the arrival of "two Horses" on which he and his brothers were to ride home. The incident (it was about three years later than the first example of spots of time) again concerns an "eminence" where "two highways ascending" stretched a good half-mile in either direction. There he had waited upon a crag of the "highest summit" where he was "half-shelter'd by a naked wall," for it was a day of bad weather. Close at hand, at his right, "a single sheep" served as a companion, and on his left was a sounding hawthorn. These are, in a way, one with himself. He had been impatient for the coming of the horses, and he does not tell now of their actual arrival. What he gives stress to is the animal near at hand and the "whistling hawthorn" which together served him as "companions" when he waited and watched with straining eyes, peering "intensely" through the mist at the

> prospect of the wood
> And plain beneath. (363 —)

This is all, except that he tells us with abrupt transition how within a few days he and his brothers had the painful ordeal of following their father's body to his grave, a circumstance which he says was chastening. How was it chastening? He recalled the anxious hope with which he had waited in the wild and stormy time on the crag, and he now "bow'd low"; thereafter he often remembered the day of "sleety rain," the animal at his right hand and "the one blasted tree" at his left, along with "the blcak music of the old stone wall" and the sound of "wood and water," as well as the shape of mists advancing where he strained his eyes, looking from left to right in anxiety along the two roads. With this event, which Wordsworth refers to as one of his spots of time, and which we have related to Maslow's peak experiences, Wordsworth closes Book Eleven, except for a salute which he gives to Coleridge.

The parts of The Prelude — including the two examples of

269

the portrayal of extraordinary "spots of time" in one's experience — were gifts to his friend. Do they contain something of the love which Maslow emphasized in his account of peak experiences? It is difficult to doubt that they do. They seem also in the poet's thought somewhat being-oriented or related in a particular sense to reality — "metamotivated," to use the somewhat formidable term of Maslow. It is hard to doubt that Wordsworth's tendency here is parallel to that of the psychologist. For the poet, at any rate, the "spots of time" are important in that they represent something he can share with Coleridge in a kind of special personalism, and perhaps he can also share it deeply with others: his readers. Such sharing represents an important part of the province of the writer. It is his hope, he says, that Coleridge will be invigorated, that he will "not languish," and that, even though he is a pilgrim elsewhere, he will be of spiritual assistance to Wordsworth himself.

Coleridge, indeed, is an inspiration in that he has gone on a quest not only of health but of "highest truth." To conclude, Wordsworth presents himself, too, as one who has been in a process of recovering health and who is now "restored," with the creative faculty of the imagination at least very largely returned to him. He has moved definitely beyond the psychological distress under which he has suffered, and he is "strengthened" anew, carrying with him, as we recognize, the "memory left of what he had escaped," but having established, through his progress, "habits" which are partially religious in their character.

They are religious in the sense that they represent an earnest devoutness and are directed toward sympathy and cosmic insight. These factors do not embrace, of course, all that there is in religion, but they are important to it. Thus Book Eleven of *The Prelude* ends with the poet revealed as a person who has undergone considerable change. The effects of the change, and the factors involving imagination — particularly as they refer to human sympathy — will be developed further in the following "Concluding Consideration."

Footnotes

1. *Adventures of Ideas*, p. vii.
2. *Science and the Modern World*, p. 122.
3. *Ibid*. Note also *Process and Reality*, p. 23, on philosophy and "its close relations with religion and with science, natural and sociological."
4. *Adventures of Ideas*, 297.
5. In this connection, the reader may wish to see F. H. Bradley's *Appearance and Reality*, which greatly influenced T. S. Eliot.
6. *Ibid.*, p. 298. Whitehead indicates in the context various ways in which he agrees with Bradley.
7. *Science and the Modern World*, p. 94.
8. *Ibid.*, p. 32.
9. *Ibid.*, p. 31.
10. *Ibid.*, p. 33.
11. *Ibid.*, p. 94. See additional pertinent comments by Whitehead in the page that follows. Note also his oral comment " 'super-reality is an under-reality. Reality is always emergence into a finite modal entity.' " Single quotation marks indicate the oral character of the evidence. William E. Hocking in *The Philosophy of Alfred North Whitehead*, ed. Paul A. Schilpp, second edition (La Salle, Illinois: Open Court, 1951, 1971) p. 386.
12. *Ibid.*, p. 126.
13. *Ibid.*, p. 127. Whitehead immediately goes on in this passage to say "Thus we gain from the poets the doctrine that a philosophy of nature must concern itself at least with these six notions: change, value, eternal objects, endurance, organism, interfusion."
14. *Ibid.*, p. 121. The sentence in Whitehead's text immediately following this quotation is also extremely helpful to an understanding of Wordsworth at this point.
15. *Ibid.*, p. 275.
16. *Ibid.*, p. 276.
17. *Adventures of Ideas*, p. 356. .
18. *Ibid.*, p. 357-358. Scoundrels as well as idealists of course participate in this.
19. *Process and Reality*, pp. 46 and 47. The passage contains more material on creativity, which for lack of space we cannot include here.
20. *Adventures of Ideas*, p. 230.
21. *Ibid.*, p. 333.
22. *Adventures of Ideas*, p. 107. Elsewhere he says, "The taint of Aristotelian Logic has thrown the whole emphasis of metaphysical thought upon substantives and adjectives, to the neglect of prepositions and conjunctions." *Ibid.*, p. 356.

271

23. *Process and Reality,* p. 283. The place of logic, narrowly considered, has a long history which, for Whitehead, is of great interest.
24. *Adventures of Ideas,* p. 149.
25. *Ibid.,* p. 150. In a later volume John H. Randall, Jr. beautifully develops this same point. See *Aristotle* (New York: Columbia University Press, 1960, 1963), p. 42, "Thus our science too has proceeded from facts . . . to 'reasons why'. . . ."
26. *The Function of Reason* (Princeton, 1929), p. 5. The 1958 paperback edition does *not* follow the pagination of the Princeton edition.
27. *Ibid.,* p. 7. The character referred to is Odysseus. Here one may think of the *Iliad* as well as the *Odyssey.*
28. *Ibid.,* p. 55.
29. *Ibid.,* p. 57. See also pp. 37, 43, and 55 which will be useful for understanding some of the other materials presented in this paragraph.
30. *Ibid.,* p. 67.
31. *Adventures of Ideas,* p. 196.
32. See, for example, *The Function of Reason,* p. 72 and also p. 68.
33. Referred to in Chapter Ten, above. The "simple" aspect of the higher imagination, or reason, may be seen in striking moments in Dante such as his reference to the "will" of God and "our peace," or in the confrontation Dante experiences, when, struck dumb, he hears the three words "I am Beatrice . . ."
34. *Modes of Thought,* Capricorn Books (New York: Macmillan, 1938), p. 204.
35. *The Aims of Education,* p. 77. See also p. 78.
36. *Ibid.,* pp. 77-78.
37. *Adventures of Ideas,* p. 289.
38. *Ibid.,* p. 290.
39. *Science and the Modern World,* p. 265.
40. *Ibid.,* p. 274.
41. Ibid., p. 275.
42. *Adventures of Ideas,* p. 291.
43. *Ibid.* Whitehead refers here to *The Trojan Women,* lines 886-7, concerning compulsion and human intelligence.
44. Abraham Maslow, *Toward a Psychology of Being,* second edition (New York: D. Van Nostrand, 1968), p. 71.
45. *Ibid.,* p. 72.
46. *Science and the Modern World,* p. 15.

A Concluding Consideration

In the preceding chapters we have considered the first eleven books of Wordsworth's 1805 *Prelude* in their relation to the thought of Whitehead. Our main emphasis, however, finds its focus in the impact on the poet of crowds in London (treated in our Chapter VII), the effect upon him of social revolution in France and elsewhere, as well as his problems in a later period of profound depression along with his ultimate regaining of hope — all of these things being taken up in relation to ideas which are to be found in Whitehead's work. Social problems are central here. The philosopher very probably spent a far greater quantity of time on social questions than upon poets and poetry. But Wordsworth was not far behind Whitehead in this concern for the social. Wordsworth spent, according to his own statement, a good many hours pondering society for every one he spent on poetry.

It appears evident that the philosopher gained a very great deal from the poet's major work, as indeed he seems to imply in the remarks he makes about *The Prelude* and its importance. Whitehead did, of course, add much in the way of philosophy to what he gained from poets and poetry. As we have thought of Wordsworth, we have had in mind his vital production or contribution in the period — the ten years ap-

273

proximately — of his greatest power. *The Prelude* is the center of that contribution.

But *The Prelude* is a work which is reflective of time as it is conceived in human experience, and it reaches back and also looks forward, in time, in striking ways. It is not merely representative of a decade in experience. Culturally it reaches for us into a long and dynamic history of social-change philosophy, just as does Whitehead's thought to a larger extent.

We can recall here, also, Wordsworth's "Preface" to his *Lyrical Ballads* of 1800 which was written in a spirit of generous and thoughtful liberalism — social, political, and aesthetic. His critical work of the period in which he wrote *The Prelude* has often been regarded as a landmark: the beginning of the early assertion of one of the important English literary movements at its height. This is a spirit which is notable in the production of other writers of the time as well. Coleridge in some respects is an example of this spirit.

Near the close of Chapter I of our previous book, *About Wordsworth and Whitehead,* we cited Whitehead's quotation from Kant concerning the fact that there are no parts of time "that are not enclosed between limits" — for example, "moments" — and that, similarly, there are no parts of space which are not continuous or enclosed between limits or points; that is, there is in space or in time "*no part that is not itself again a space or a time.*"[1] Here Whitehead sees the ideas of the fluent quality of space and of time, or the interrrelation of them, which appears in Kant, although Kant does at times make statements that are inconsistent with this. The important point for our purposes is the fact that the matter of interrelation was in process of development in the period of Kant, preceding though also overlapping the period of Wordsworth, Kant's birth being antecedent to that of Wordsworth by forty-six years.

Whitehead is interested in Kant here in connection with the

togetherness of even the most minuscule events in the universe. We see things, or understand things, in a compact continuity of spaces and of times — multiple spaces and times. This is an important part of the philosopher's view of relativity: that is, his conception of things as related one to another. We might here have quoted passages from his statement in *Process and Reality* concerning his interest in the extensive continuum as applied to our understanding of the oneness in continuity.[2] What we had been discussing was the interrelation of things, an interrelatedness which is a prominent feature of our present book, in that it forms a part of the thought of Wordsworth as well as of Whitehead.

Preparing the way for this feature of philosophy, we remember the discoveries of Newton which attracted the interest of Wordsworth at an early stage. But there is in Newton (besides a reflection on motion) a static quality against which Whitehead particularly rebels. And in Wordsworth's interrelationism there is a development beyond Newton — beyond the general tendency of Newton toward particularism. Whitehead, in a passage which we quoted near the end of Chapter I, gives emphasis to the importance of Kant in relation to the developing significance of pattern in any given event in the world. It is the active *realization* of pattern with which Whitehead is emphatically concerned. "Endurance," he says, "is the repetition of the pattern in successive events."[3] His remarks about this realization of pattern appears in *Science and the Modern World* near the end of his chapter entitled "Relativity."

But our interest in pattern should never give rise to neglect of "full concrete experience." This quoted expression is Whitehead's, and he uses it in *Science and the Modern World* where he brings out his great admiration of Wordsworth, to which we referred near the middle of Chapter I of the present volume. Any philosophy, he feels, while it refers to full concrete experience, must also take account of the contradictions and fears that are within the self. The self is crucially important. Such contradictions and apprehensions find a place in the thought of the poet and in that of the philosopher. They are resolved by Whitehead, so far as this is possible for him, in the volume *Symbolism, Its Meaning and Effect,* to which we made reference in Chapter I shortly after discussing full concrete experience.

There are many ideas in the first six chapters of our present work, *Aspects of Wordsworth and Whitehead,* which do not receive any treatment in our earlier volume. We have, that is, expanded our treatment of the Wordsworth-Whitehead problem. Among these newer ideas are those related to Wittgenstein and the unfolding of events in the sequences of our living experience. We might think also of William James here[4] and in many other contexts as we consider the poet and Whitehead.

Such an unfolding of living experience occurs in Wordsworth's *Prelude* as we saw in all of our chapters concerning philosophy and certain continuing life problems, including very notably, Chapter VII (on London) and Chapters IX and X (on the French Revolution) as well as in our later discussion of Wordsworth's feeling about "Imagination Impaired and Restored." In thinking of the imagination (and its impairment as well as restoration) the problem of hope arises. And here we need to emphasize particularly Whitehead's concerns with mankind and with the relations of the multitudes of people to general civilization, with all the human retrogressions and advances that occur.

The movement is to some extent cyclical, but that there are many possibilities of advance in its process is clear both in the work of the poet and that of Whitehead. There is an area of freedom for us all, especially as we aid others, personally and in broad ways, to attain their own freedom. But it would be impossible in this respect to summarize the book adequately here. Nevertheless, we should say that the concept of freedom is not left vaguely in the air by Wordsworth; it is presented in five particular aspects, as we develop his thought about varieties of freedom and equality near the end of our Chapter IX. Concerning this, Wordsworth presents an emphatic point on *freedom from fear*. Individuals are not free if they are filled with psychological or physical fears of others or of society.

The later _discussion of "Imagination Impaired and Restored" to which we have referred appears in our Chapter XI, a chapter based on Wordsworth's concern with the widest aspects of the aesthetic (or of beauty): that is, creativity. Dejection of spirits had affected Wordsworth seriously, and we know that such depressive states have very often affected the creativity of artists, writers, and general thinkers throughout time. In his words, he needed "things to hope for." Our very sense of identity requires things pointing toward hopes. In the chapter we indicated also the importance of hoping (in philosophy) as it appears in Whitehead; we there stressed the point that in the philosopher's work of the later period, we see clearly that he is signalling hope, and this is especially true of *Science and the Modern World*, *Process and Reality*, and *Adventures of Ideas*. Similarly, Wordsworth's whole *Prelude* also signals to us again and again the importance of hope. The very title, the embodiment of this theme, gives advance notice of hope. Wordsworth did not himself choose the title *The Prelude*, but it is palpably expressive of the spirit of his aim and achievement.

Thinking of this title, *The Prelude*, one may recall the scene in Shakespeare's drama *The Tempest* (II, lines 215-301) where Ariel is bringing about an awakening of Alonso, King of Naples, who needs to search for his son. Alonso believes that his son may have been drowned. We see how easily things can go awry with Alonso and how he might not find his son Ferdinand, for whose life he has hope. Time is an important factor in the play, as is hope, but, in the case of the scene, hope is in part ironically treated, in that various kinds of hopes can be wrongly directed. Antonio, who had unseated his brother Prospero from a rightful heritage, now has a variety of evilly-directed hopes.

For Antonio, all his projected hopes and plans are a *prologue*, or prelude of what is "to come" — as he explicitly says. Sebastian, through whom Antonio is trying to direct a plot, cries out, "What stuff is this!" But Antonio aims to accomplish his wrongful purpose nevertheless. Except for Ariel's efforts in bringing about an awakening of Alonso, the king, Sebastian's prelude, or "prologue," would have been brought about in its various stages, and this would have led to a sequel of "heaviness" or melancholy — indeed, of horror. But as the play, through Prospero, indicates:

> Let us not burden our remembrances
> With a heaviness that's gone. (V, 1, 198-199)

Shakespeare's *Tempest* could at this point serve, in a variety of ways, as an illumination to Wordsworth's *Prelude*. One can bring about good, or one can bring about evil, through projected plans; the plans are but "prologue," to use Shakespeare's own word, or prelude, to things which time will, in due course, uncover.

But such plans, if they are to be excellent, require, as in Whitehead, multidimensional thinking and premonitory, or warning, *intuitive* effort. What is needed is active *protension* (a sense of vitally appreciated continuance in the workings of time), and a retention of significant factors not only in time but in space. Time and space need to be seen together in a spirit of futurism. This is a matter that Whitehead has constantly in mind and that Wordsworth to some degree almost always senses. There is in Wordsworth a counterbalancing of the loss of hope by a "secret" sense within the individual's own appreciation of self-identity. Whitehead also emphasizes this importance — in his references to prehensions in Words-

278

worth's work. The word "secret," as we consider forces working upon us, is the poet's expression. And here we should think of the very great significance of Plato in his influence upon both Wordsworth and Whitehead.

With this influence we need to connect the combination of the sympathetic and the symbolic, as developed in the middle of our Chapter XI; we need also to connect with our thought about this influence of Plato the value of reason in a very high creative sense. Along with our illuminative reason we must remember the importance of the illuminative "spots of time" in our experience: "spots of time" which are recognized as a dynamic part of life according to the poet and to the philosopher. There is a temptation to say more, in summation, especially in regard to the closing books of the 1805 *Prelude*, which we have left for further treatment in a later volume on Wordsworth and Whitehead. The connection of the last books of *The Prelude* with Whitehead's thought makes increasingly clear, we would suggest, that the debt of the philosopher to the poet is greater, even, than we have thus far disclosed.

But more important than this is the nature of the treatment which we have aimed to present: that of an inquiry. We would not declare that Wordsworth or Whitehead is necessarily "correct" in a given matter. The whole area is available for different judgments. As in all things, then, the field is an open one which anyone who reads may well ponder. Our present book has brought out only selected features of these two thinkers, and it had aimed to reveal their shared nature of philosophy broadly considered — as well as to stress a feeling for the sociology of knowledge in our own time, with its manifold problems.

When we think of Iran, Afghanistan, and the whole Third World as it is related to the Western World and to the Far East, including the People's Republic of China, we can see how important a social understanding of knowledge can be. It

279

seems clear that a premonitory statement could be applied to W. H. Auden's line "We must love one another or die."[5] The statement that might serve as a prelude to the one given in Auden is that we need to take steps toward trying to understand one another lest we perish. To this end we would do well to consider once again the penetrative greatness of Wordsworth and Whitehead.

Footnotes

1. *Science and the Modern World*, p. 184. The emphasis is Whitehead's.
2. *Process and Reality*, p. 183. A special edition of *Process and Reality*, ed. David Ray Griffin and Donald W. Sherburne (New York, Free Press, Macmillan, 1978), p. 120, could be of value here and in many other aspects of the study of Whitehead, although the book is very specialized.
3. *Science and the Modern World*, p. 183.
4. Whitehead's admiration for William James is evident in the "Preface" to "Process and Reality" where he speaks of being "greatly indebted" to him.
5. See 1.88 of his poem entitled "September 1, 1939." Connected with this remark by Auden note also "Auden in Milwaukee," by Stephen Spender, p. 242, as well as p. 247 of "Valediction," in *W. H. Auden, A Tribute*, ed. Stephen Spender (New York: Macmillan, 1975).

Index

This short index at times combines items with the purpose of relating them and it often excludes names frequently referred to in the book.

282